Counseling Series 1

RAISING CHILDREN

"Behold, children are the Lord's inheritance; The fruit of the womb His reward."

(Ps 126:3, Septuagint; 127:3 NKJV)

BISHOP YOUSSEF

Counseling Series I: Raising Children

Copyright © 2021 Coptic Orthodox Diocese of the Southern U.S.A.

All rights reserved.

Designed & Published by:
St. Mary & St. Moses Abbey Press
101 S Vista Dr., Sandia, TX 78383
stmabbeypress.com

Interior design by Dar El Karma El Hakikia Publishing House.
Tel.: +2 - 02-27760267 - +2 - 02-27760268
Mob.: +2 - 012-86822014

All Scripture quotations in the footnotes of this book, unless otherwise indicated, are taken from the New King James Version Copyright 1982 by Thomas Nelson, Inc. Used by permission. All rights reserved.

Library of Congress Control Number: 2019953531

2 3 4 5 6 7 8 9 10

Preface

This book is comprised of several homilies and lectures by His Grace Bishop Youssef, the Bishop of the Coptic Orthodox Diocese of the Southern United States, over a period of twenty-eight years (1989–2017) on the subject of raising children. It is not intended solely for parents, but also for anyone who is called to serve the children of God in any capacity as well as the youth and adolescents themselves.

In some cases, sections from different homilies and lectures were combined in order to minimize repetition as much as possible. However, because an attempt was also made to preserve the meaning and value of each lecture, the reader may notice points that are repeated from chapter to chapter.

Part I addresses childhood; Part II, adolescence, while Part III covers the issue of dealing with difficult cases. Part IV contains questions asked at the end of several of the homilies and lectures and His Grace's answers.

We pray that the Lord may bless your reading of this book, "the eyes of your understanding being enlightened"[1], and guide us all on our search for "the wisdom that is from above"[2].

All biblical references are from NKJV unless otherwise noted.

St. Mary & St. Phoebe Consecrated Sisters
Coptic Orthodox Diocese of the Southern United States

---

1 Eph 1:18.
2 Jas 3:17.

In the Name of the Father,

and of the Son,

and of the Holy Spirit,

one God, Amen.

Table of Contents

	Page
Part I: Childhood	**9**
(A) Becoming Parents	11
(B) The Role of Parents in Raising Children	27
(C) Train Up a Child in the Way He Should Go	57
(D) Spiritual Maturity	91
(E) Spiritual Development of Children	101
(F) How to Raise Responsible and Mature Personalities	121
(G) Submission and Obedience	135
(H) Discipline and Edification	151
(I) Fostering Friendship between Siblings	191
(J) Conflict between Siblings	203
(K) Childhood: Needs and Development (Homily to Servants)	225
Part II: Adolescence	**229**
(A) Adolescence	231
(B) Problems We Encounter with Our Children during Adolescence	255
(C) Sexual Education for Adolescents	277
(D) Adolescence: Needs and Development (Homily to Servants)	283
(E) Adolescence (Homily to Youth)	293
Part III: Dealing with Difficult Cases	**305**
(A) Dealing with Difficult Cases	307
Part IV: Questions and Answers	**323**

Part I

CHILDHOOD

A | BECOMING PARENTS

1. Welcoming a New Child

2. Timing for the Birth of a New Child

3. Challenges and Changes a Couple Faces with the First Child

4. Responsibilities of a Husband and Wife toward Each Other

5. Parental Responsibilities toward Children: Choose, Instruct, and Discipline

6. Parental Roles

7. Parenting Boys versus Parenting Girls

1. Welcoming a New Child

Becoming parents is a great blessing, but it is also a great challenge. Your marriage will change. Both you and your spouse will change. It is considered a transition in the family, and God allows transitions in our lives in order for us to grow. As with any transition, if we manage to go through it smoothly, it will contribute to our growth. However, if we get stuck in the transition and cannot get through it smoothly, then we may suffer, and this may affect our own growth as well as our children and family. Many times, because we do not know how to handle it correctly, the arrival of a new child can be a stressor, and instead of enjoying this blessing and the wonderful opportunity for growth and supporting each other as husband and wife, we start to find that the birth of this child creates distance and disconnectedness between the parents. The fact of the matter is that children take time and attention away from the marriage. We encourage new couples to work together with the arrival of a child and support one another, in order to allow this child to be the bond that keeps the family together and helps them grow together. Parenting does not happen by accident; it is not a passive duty. Parenting requires work from the father and the mother. As much effort and work as you put into parenting, you will reap as much, with joy. Psalm 126 tells us that those who plant with tears will reap with joy.

2. Timing for the Birth of a New Child

There seems to be a new trend that is very common among the young generation, especially in the United States. I see many couples getting married and deciding not to have children because they believe that children will take away from them their joy and fun together. I think this attitude is an attitude of selfishness. God told Adam and Eve to multiply and fill the Earth (Gen 1:28). Earlier, I mentioned that parenting provides an opportunity for growth. This growth comes from going outside of yourself and sacrificing for another, especially sacrificing for a helpless creature like an infant or a child: how to take care of this helpless creature, how to be committed and responsible, how to make decisions for him or her, how to train him or her. There are many areas for growth and many new and wonderful experiences. However, many people, out of selfishness, decide not to have children. The Bible teaches us that children are a gift from God, or more accurately, an inheritance from God (Ps 126:3, Septuagint[3]). When we read the word "inheritance," this means at least two things. First, they are a gift. God gives us this gift to enjoy, to grow, and to thank Him for this gift; but secondly, this also means that these children are not ours. These children belong to God, and He entrusts us with them. They are His and He entrusts us with these gifts in order to raise them according to His way, not according to what pleases us or what we see as right.

Another common trend among young couples is that they delay the birth of their first child for many years after marriage. This is either because they are young when they get married and may still be finishing their studies, and therefore, they are not ready to have a child, or because of various economic reasons. I would like to raise a concern here (I am not saying that this is right or wrong). My concerns with this approach are from a spiritual point of view and also from a medical point of view, which I heard from my professor when I was in medical school. This is why I want to share it especially with young couples.

From the spiritual perspective, suppose a young couple decides to have their first child after five years of marriage. During these five years, they have become accustomed to a certain style of life. The arrival of a new family member, who will require a lot of time and attention, may bring a lot of stress and disconnection between the parents. For example, the mother is now full of emotions and is willing to sacrifice everything and all things for the child. As a result, she may overlook her husband's needs for her affection and love, because she is so focused on their child. Similarly, the father is concerned about how to raise this child, how to educate him, how to handle their finances, and how to raise him spiritually. There are many issues on his mind. Gradually, what is going to happen? They start to be distant from each other and they begin to feel disconnected from each other. That is why many counselors do not recommend postponing the first child for many years after marriage.

From the medical perspective, Dr. Maher El Mehran taught us that there might be some problems with fertility, either with the husband or with the wife. If they decide to use contraceptives for two, three, four, or five years, especially if they are using oral contraceptives, which are like

---

[3] Septuagint is the Greek translation of the Hebrew Old Testament, approximately 300 B.C., LXX.

hormones, this may change the hormonal balance. Consequently, if there is already a problem, the hormonal balance will become worse. As a result, after three or five years, when they decide to have the first baby, the fertility problem may be worse than if they had tackled it from the beginning. Besides, taking care of this issue while you are young is different from dealing with it after five years. Furthermore, taking care of this issue in the first year of your marriage will give you adequate time to handle it and seek treatment, as opposed to waiting or postponing the birth of the new child for several years after your marriage.

Dr. Mehran recommended that it is good for a couple to have their first baby in the first year of marriage to ensure that everything is going right, and then perhaps to wait for one or two years to have a second child. Here, I am mentioning a recommendation. I am not saying it is wrong to postpone the birth of the first child, because I am aware that many couples do so for economic reasons or because they are finishing their education. I am merely bringing up a point to consider, especially for young couples. You need to be concerned about this issue.

3. Challenges and Changes a Couple Faces with the First Child

The big challenge before parents when they have their first child is how to turn "us" into "we." Instead of just being "us," the husband and the wife, now it is "we," father, mother, and child. In turning "us" into "we," we need to understand that there are several changes. The first change is the new member in the family and the second change is your new identity. Before the birth of this child, you are a husband, and you are a wife, but now you are not just only a husband or only a wife; you are a husband and a father, and you are a wife and a mother. You now have a new identity. I remember a man once told me, "After my wife gave birth at the hospital, and I saw the baby for the first time, I went into the waiting room and thought to myself, 'What am I going to do?'" He felt overwhelmed with the arrival of the new child. As I previously mentioned, it is a great responsibility, but it is also a great blessing to have a child in the family.

4. Responsibilities of a Husband and Wife toward One Another

There are some tasks a husband and wife should practice toward each other with the anticipation of the arrival a new child, in order to protect their marriage from disconnectedness. There are also some things to do with their child. The main task of the husband toward his wife is to be involved in her emotions, feelings, and her willingness to sacrifice. This is also a good opportunity and the best way for the husband to grow out of his selfishness of needing all his wife's attention. I remember a husband that told me about two or three months after the birth of his child, "I need my wife back. What she is doing *is* necessary, but from the time she gave birth to our child, I feel that I have lost her. I do not have her anymore." I talked to him about how this is a great opportunity for him to grow out of his selfishness and connect with his wife in caring for their child. The important message to the wife is to share with her husband in planning and taking responsibility for their child. This way, the father will not feel that he is bearing the burden by himself. He is planning for the education of the child, for the finances, how to raise the child—he is dealing with all of these issues.

I understand that nowadays, many working wives are already concerned with planning for the future of their children and are involved with the father in this regard. However, one of the main issues that many young couples discuss is whether the wife should stay at home or go to work. If she is going to stay home, is this indefinitely or temporarily? The answer to this question differs from family to family and from one couple to another, so there is no single answer that fits everyone. The couple should pray together, study this question together, and seek counsel or advice together before making such a decision. The goal needs to be set clearly when making this decision.

The goal is to raise godly children, because as I mentioned earlier, children are an inheritance from God, and God entrusted us to raise these children according to His way and not according to our way. I am saying this because many some couples think that the goal is to provide a good life for their children. Providing a *good* life is great, but it is not everything. Let me give you an example: Many families have decided to emigrate from Egypt to America because they are seeking a better life. When they immigrate here to the United States to provide a good life for their children, both parents workday and night. They entrust their children either to a baby-sitter or a daycare, and thus, they start losing their influence and effect on their children. Somebody else is shaping my children; it is not I. I do not spend enough time with them. In addition, the TV and the media shape the other part of my children. Five, six, eight, ten years after immigration, they find that their children are a different product than what they intended for them to be. This is because they are not their own products; they are the products of the media or the baby-sitter. They start to question whether or not it immigration was the right decision. I do not think they should question the immigration itself, but they should question their planning. They put a high standard of life as the goal, so they have compromised everything else in order to reach this goal, *including* their own children and their godly life. That is why I repeatedly say that it is *much, much* better to live at a lower standard of life and to provide a godly life for your children, than to provide for them a very high standard of life, and end up with the children being unsuccessful in their education, or making wrong life decisions, or being spoiled, or taking drugs, or failing in any of the other challenges they face. The couple has to put the right goal ahead of all else when making the decision of whether the wife should stay home or continue to work. The right goal is to raise godly children. What shall it profit a man if he gains the whole world and loses his own life, or his children?[4]

The responsibility of a husband and wife toward one another is that they treat the birth of a child as a factor that brings them together, rather than separating them. They need each other and they need to support one another. They need to be closer to one another, not to disconnect or distance themselves from one another. They need to plan together, without fighting, and without each one insisting on his or her opinion. They need to think about what is best for the family. That is what I call turning "us" into "we." They have to keep their own time together, especially in the first few years with children when it is quite difficult to find time alone together. With good planning, it is both possible and crucial for the husband and wife to keep time together; they need to have a few hours together just as husband and wife at least every week. This will enrich their relationship together and will be very useful and profitable for their children.

5. Parental Responsibilities toward Children

How does the Holy Bible instruct us to raise our children so that we will have healthy, spiritual, godly boys and girls? First, we will cover some

---

4 Cf. Mt 16:26; Mk 8:36.

guidelines in parenting. Then, we will briefly discuss the differences between parenting boys and parenting girls.

Choose, Instruct, and Discipline

We will cover these three points: Choose, Instruct, and Discipline.

Who is choosing the guidelines and principles for our children? This is a very important question. In our time, where parents are too busy to be involved in the lives of their children and in a society that encourages children to rebel against rules and discipline, we will find, or we have found already, that parental authority is decreasing, while children's disobedience is increasing. There are many influences that affect our children and which have more of an effect on them than we, the parents, do. For example, consider the media. If you think about how the media influences and changes the minds of children, you will be amazed. The language that our children use is the language of the media. It is not the language of the parents; it is not the language of the church. They use the language that they hear in the media. Most of the time, their role models are sports or music stars. This is very clear when I visit homes and go to the children's rooms to bless them by sprinkling holy water.[5] I find that the walls are covered with posters of either singers or famous athletes. With difficulty, I find just a small picture of St. Mary or the Lord Christ on the bed or on something else, which was perhaps placed there by one of the parents.

What does it mean when the children put up all these posters of soccer players and singers? It means these are your children's role models. I am not against soccer or sports; I am not against these things, but I want you to think about when you enter your child's room and all four walls are filled with pictures of soccer players or singers. What does this mean? It means that these are the ones who influence your child. Perhaps one child is very interested in cars, so his room is *filled* with pictures of cars. When you go into your children's rooms, you should not let these things go. You should think about it because there is a message behind this. Who is the one who impacts your child? Who is the role model? Who chooses? The one who influences your child is the one who is choosing the guidelines and principles that your son or your daughter is following.

---

[5] This is a common practice in Coptic Orthodox Church when a priest visits a home. At the conclusion of the visit, the priest prays over a cup of water, and sprinkles a little of this water as a blessing in each room.

When St. Paul talked about the wrath of God revealed against the ungodliness of men in Romans 1:18, you may be surprised to see the word "ungodliness" because it is a difficult word. Romans 1:18 says, "For the wrath of God is revealed from heaven against all ungodliness and unrighteousness of men, who suppress the truth in unrighteousness." St. Paul, then, mentions a list of sins, and in verse 30, he says, "backbiters, haters of God, violent, proud, boasters, inventors of evil things, disobedient to parents" (Rom 1:30). One may ask, "Would God include being 'disobedient to parents' among all these other sins at the mention of which a person would tremble?" Yes, because disobedience to one's parents means there is rebellion against authority, and if they rebel against the authority of the parents, this means they are also rebelling against the authority of God. If they are rebelling against the authority of God, this means that they are ungodly, and that is the worst thing. This will make them commit any sin listed in Romans 1:30.

I do not want to blame our children for their disobedience, but sometimes, it is because the parents were not involved in teaching them, instructing them, and helping them to make good choices in life from their very early days. That is why parents have left the door open to other influences and factors to influence and direct their children. We will discover later, when they grow up a little bit, that these children are not the product of our upbringing. They are the product of the media, school, and friends. So, you have to ask yourself this question: Who is influencing your children? If the answer is not you, then you are in big trouble. Who is shaping their ideas? Who is shaping their lives? Who is directing their minds? Is it you, or somebody else? Is it their friends? There are children who spend hours in chat rooms and talk to friends for hours. Do you think that all of this will not affect your children?

Some parents say, "I do not want to make choices for my son or daughter. I want them to make choices for themselves." When it comes to church, I hear some parents say, "I go to the Orthodox Church, but if my son wants to go to any church, I should give him the freedom to choose. If he wants to choose another church, that is fine with me. I do not want to force him to go to my church. Let him choose and find for himself." I want to tell you something. Would I be too naïve to not think the following: "If I do not influence my child and help him to make the right choices, somebody *else* will influence him?" Do you think this son of yours will make this choice by himself? No. Somebody else will influence him. Thus, in reality, you are taking the backseat and giving leadership of your son to someone else. If you believe that no one is going to influence your child, you are fooling yourself. You are deceiving yourself. If you do not influence your child, there are many, many people out there who are ready to influence him. So, this is the first point I want you to think about—who is influencing your children? Is it you, or is it somebody else?

This leads me to the second point: It is your responsibility to instruct and teach your children. It is a responsibility from God. We read in Deuteronomy 4:9-10, "Only take heed to yourself, and diligently keep yourself, lest you forget the things your eyes have seen, and lest they depart from your heart all the days of your life. And teach them to your children and your grandchildren, especially concerning the day you stood before the Lord your God in Horeb, when the Lord said to me, 'Gather the people to Me, and I will let them hear My words, that they may learn to fear Me all the days they live on the earth, *and that they may teach their children*'" (emphasis added). That is God's expectation. He expects us to teach our children, instruct them, and raise them in His fear. The Psalm says, "Behold, children are a heritage from the Lord" (Ps 127:3). They are not mine. They are His children and He entrusted me with them in order to teach them His ways, His law, and how to fear Him and walk in His commandments. We need to actively teach children. We need to teach them the fear of God, values, virtues, the Holy Scripture, how to love and respect one another, and how to be responsible. As early as you can, start planting in them, in their lives, all these wonderful virtues that you want to see in your children as they are growing up. Do not expect that children will grow and just by accident acquire these wonderful virtues on their own. No. Parenting is an active position. You need to be active in teaching and instructing your children.

Moreover, you have to remember that actions speak louder than words. If you teach your children how to pray and give them a big lecture on prayer, but the children never see you praying, your words will actually be forgotten. All of us may have forgotten the things our parents or Sunday school teachers have told us, but what they *did* is still in our minds. For example, the image of our parents who woke up early and prayed—this is still in our minds. The image of our parents who used to go to church every Sunday, how they entered the church in godly fear, how they worshipped before the altar, and how they stood in prayer—these images are still in our minds. Maybe we forgot what they told us about prayer, but we will never forget the examples in their lives. That is why you need to be consistent between your teaching, your actions, and your behavior. If you begin to give them mixed messages—for instance, you tell them, "It is important to pray" and yet, you do not pray, or "It is important to respect the Lord's Day," but you do not respect the Lord's Day—then, this will make the children confused, and they will not know how to follow the right way.

The third point is to discipline. In the letter of St. Paul to the Hebrews, he explains how to know if you are an authentic son or daughter of God or if you are an illegitimate child. St. Paul says that if God disciplines you, you are an authentic child of God:

> And you have forgotten the exhortation which speaks to you as to sons: "My son, do not despise the chastening of the Lord, nor be discouraged when you are rebuked by Him; for whom the Lord loves He chastens, and scourges every son whom He receives." If you endure chastening, God deals with you as with sons, for what son is there whom a father does not chasten? But if you are without chastening, of which all have become partakers, then you are illegitimate and not sons. Furthermore, we have had human fathers who corrected us, and we paid them respect. Shall we not much more readily be in subjection to the Father of spirits and live? For they indeed for a few days chastened us as seemed best to them, but He for our profit, that we may be partakers of His holiness. Now no chastening seems to be joyful for the present, but painful; nevertheless, afterward it yields the peaceable fruit of righteousness to those who have been trained by it. (Heb 12:5-11)

From this passage, we understand that God is expecting us to discipline and chasten our children. It says, "whom the Lord loves He chastens" (Heb 12:6). Therefore, it is a sign of love that God disciplines me. Again, we can apply this to parenting. You do not love your children if you do not discipline them. Keep in mind your role as parents in the family, that you choose to influence your children, instruct them, and discipline them. [Discipline is discussed in more detail throughout the book.]

Parental Roles: Who should do what? Can we split parenting roles between the husband and the wife?

We are living under the covenant of grace. The covenant of grace is called the age of grace and righteousness. We read in John 1:17, "For the law was given through Moses, but grace and truth came through Jesus Christ." What is the relationship between this verse and parenting? The law tells you that you are a sinner and in order to be righteous, you need to fulfill the law. If you cannot fulfill the law, you will be condemned and the punishment is death. That is the law. The law says: "You are a sinner, so you need to be disciplined." That is why St. Paul said that the law disciplined us unto Christ (Galatians 3). The law disciplined us, but it did not give us grace. In order to be righteous, you needed to keep all the law. If you broke one commandment, then you transgressed all of the law. That is why everybody failed. Nobody was righteous because no one was able to fulfill all the righteousness of the law. That is the Old Testament.

The law was given through Moses, but God started a New Covenant with us that is based on grace and truth. Grace and truth came through Jesus Christ. You cannot acquire your righteousness simply by following the law, but you need the grace of God in order to be righteous and justified, as the Holy Bible says, "justified freely by His grace" (Rom 3:24). In the New Covenant, without doing anything, you become righteous by accepting the Lord Christ and being baptized. We take a small child, who did not do anything yet, and baptize him. As soon as we baptize him, he comes out from the waters of baptism a new creature. Then, we dress him in white, as a symbol of the new life that he received from baptism and as a symbol of putting on the Lord Jesus Christ. Here, the righteousness that this child has taken, the new life—he has taken it based *solely* on the grace of God, because he did not do anything for it. Thus, the new covenant starts with grace, that you are righteous, unlike the Old Covenant that started with you as a sinner and required you to follow all the law to be righteous. However, in the New Covenant, there is also truth ("grace and truth came through Jesus Christ"), and you need to follow this truth—what is right, in order to keep the righteousness. Therefore, righteousness in the New Testament—in the New Covenant comes from grace and truth.

In the same way, let us apply this to parenting. In order to have righteous and godly children, you need to provide an atmosphere of grace and an atmosphere of truth, in which they know what is right and wrong, and what is true and false. It is not enough to provide just an atmosphere of grace and love only but without truth; neither is it right to provide an atmosphere of truth without any grace. You need to provide both the grace and the truth, and in doing so, we cannot split roles. We cannot say that the mother will provide the love, emotions, and grace, and the father will provide the truth and discipline and will set the rules and control. Rather, both of the parents together should provide grace and truth.

If people only provide grace without any truth, this is what we call, "permissive" parenting. They give permission for everything and do not discipline their children. Sometimes, we think that when we leave the kids to do everything they want and never say "no," this means that we love them. No. This produces irresponsible, spoiled children. The Holy Scripture tells us that if you do not accept discipline, you are illegitimate children. Let me give you an example to explain this. You are walking down the street and find two children fighting and causing a problem. One of them is your son. Which one will you discipline? You will discipline your son. Maybe to the second child, the most you would say is, "Beloved, why are you doing this?" However, you would discipline your son, because you are involved with him. However, many parents take the backseat and are lax in their children's lives. Children in this situation are *looking* for a mentor outside the family because their parents are not teaching them the truth or training them to follow it.

On the other hand, if there is no grace and no love for the children, this is what we call, "unattached" parenting. They are unattached to their children and completely disconnected from them; or these types of parents may become like dictators in the family, which is referred to as "authoritarian" parenting. This parenting style is comprised of having strict rules that the children must follow, or else, they will be punished. However, we need to keep the balance between being completely unattached (where there is no grace, love, or emotions), and being too permissive (allowing everything, including permitting the children to make their own rules, decisions, and choices). When you are somewhere in the middle, this is what we call loving parenting. In addition to this, when you take a structured approach to parenting, your children will grow up in a structured atmosphere.

St. Paul combined the concept of grace and truth in Ephesians 4:15: "But, speaking the truth in love, [we] may grow up in all things into Him who is the head—Christ—from whom the whole body, [is] joined and knit together" (Eph 4:15,16). In parenting, you need to keep the balance between grace and truth, and to speak the truth in love and grace. When you do this, they will grow up in everything to Him, who is Christ. As I previously mentioned, you cannot divide the roles. You cannot give one role to the father and one to the mother; otherwise, if the children cause a problem, the mother will say to them, "Okay, when your father comes home from work, I will tell him." Why does she not discipline them? Why should she wait until the father gets home? The father gets home from work and the mother tells him, "Look, your children did this and this and this;" so, the father gets upset. He yells at the child and the child goes to his room and cries because his father yelled at him. The mother, then goes behind him into the room and says, "What did you father do to you? Oh, it is okay my beloved son. Your father is a tense person," etc. In this case, the children become confused and do not know what is happening. This is why we have a verse in the Book of Proverbs, "My son, hear the instruction of your father, and do not forsake the law of your mother" (Prov 1:8). In this verse, he speaks about the role of the father *and* the role of the mother. They are both responsible for disciplining their child. Both parents have to keep the balance between grace and truth and be concerned with how they can speak the truth in love.

6. Parenting Boys Versus Parenting Girls

When parenting boys, you need to understand that God assigned males the role of leadership and authority. Because of this, when you are raising boys, you need to plant in them values, such as honesty and responsibility, to be hardworking and trustworthy, and also, how *not* to abuse the authority that was given to them. Teach them how to be servant-leaders. Many wives complain that their husbands are dictators, authoritarian, and abusive of their authority. This is because when these husbands were children, they were never taught how to use their authority properly. Authority is like any gift. It can be used to serve and to help others or it can be used to abuse others. To ensure that when your son grows up he does not become an abusive husband, you need to teach him not only how to be a leader but how to be a servant-leader, because God came as a servant-leader. He said, "The Son of Man did not come to be served, but to serve" (Mt 20:28).

Teach him how to be a leader with a heart of a servant and how *not* to abuse authority. Begin giving him authority, and at the same time, watch and train him in what he is going to do with this authority. For example, point out desirable behaviors to your son. Be a good example to him. Praise good behavior. Make it a point to always try to catch him doing something good. At the same time, do not let bad behavior slide by. The longer a child is allowed to get away with something, the more difficult it will be to break the habit later. Thus, you need to point out the bad behavior in your son and train him on how to get rid of it. Discuss current events with him, depending on his age. Maybe, talk to him about some decisions in the house and teach him how to be able to make decisions. Often, we see that our children are very indecisive when they grow up; they do not know how to make decisions. Therefore, in raising a boy, you need to keep in mind how to train him as a leader, as one who uses authority correctly, but in a humble and loving way.

Because sometimes girls can be very emotional, you need to teach them about healthy and realistic ideas with regard to relationships. For example, some high school girls might be naïve or do not have a realistic idea about relationships and can be easily deceived by any boy. When you talk to them and train them about how to be realistic and discern between right and wrong, between the voice of God and the voice of the devil, you are protecting them from being deceived by others. Train your daughter on how to think well and how to speak up for herself. Train her to care about her inner beauty. Teach her that inner beauty is more important than outer adornment. Girls, often, care more about their hair, makeup, clothes, and outer appearances. However, if from their childhood, you emphasize that true beauty is the beauty of the soul and the spirit, the "gentle and quiet spirit" (1 Pet 3:4), they will understand that inner beauty is more important. Perhaps, you need to study Proverbs 31 with them, which speaks about the virtuous wife. This can become the role model for your daughter.

Teach her how to be able to say "no" because many daughters are shy and struggle with saying "no" and hurting others' feelings. Because the nature of girls is emotional, often they believe that if they say "no," they are going to hurt the feelings of others. That is why they say, "yes," in order not to hurt others' feelings, and that sometimes causes them many problems. God told us, "Let your 'Yes' be 'Yes,' and your 'No,' 'No'" (Mt 5:37). Therefore, we must teach them how to be able to say, "no," to what is wrong and, "yes," to what is right.

We also need to teach our daughters the difference between interdependence and dependence. Some people tell you that dependence is wrong and independence is right, but theoretically, nobody can live independently. All of us depend on one another. The right approach is interdependence: I depend on others and allow others to depend on me. Encourage in her the spirit of giving and sharing, and the ideals of being a caretaker (how to take care of others).

When you deal with your sons and daughters in this way, you will deal with them according to their psychological and emotional needs and psychological structure. We pray that God gives us wisdom in how to follow His model, because He is a successful Father to all of us. Let us follow the model of God in His parenting, in order to raise our children to be godly, righteous, and confident.

B | THE ROLE OF PARENTS IN RAISING CHILDREN

1. A Frightening and Dangerous Reality
2. The Role of Parents in Raising Children
3. The Connection between Spiritual Life and Social Principles
4. Planting the Seeds in the First 4-5 Years of the Child's Life
5. School-Age Children
6. Liberal Parenting
7. Very Strict Parenting
8. The Ideal Way to Raise Children
9. American Culture Verses Egyptian Culture and How Both Relate to Christian Culture
10. Objectivity toward Our Cultures

1. A Frightening and Dangerous Reality

We discover a somewhat frightening and dangerous reality when conversing with our children. Forgive me, but I will speak honestly and bluntly, as it is better to see things as they are, rather than closing our eyes and saying that everything is fine, while this is not true. A sick person prefers that the physician reveals the truth about the illness, even if it were dangerous, so as to take precautions and start proper treatment (and also to avoid contaminating others), rather than for the doctor to say that everything is fine, while the end result is unpleasant.

More than 90% of our children are not attached to our Church. They go to church out of routine, but would rather not go at all. You all know and see that people come late for church. They stand in the back by the doors, so they can conveniently step out and chat with each other throughout the Divine Liturgy. Then, at the conclusion, they come forward with a clear conscience to have Communion, acting as if they have attended the entire Divine Liturgy. They use many excuses, such as not understanding the Divine Liturgy or that it is too long, etc., but these excuses are invalid. We pray short Divine Liturgies in English every two weeks. If the excuse were valid, the children would attend these liturgies, but they do not.

What is even more dangerous than this is 10% of them are doubtful about the Holy Bible. When I discuss certain passages from the Bible with some children, their response is, "Who says that the Bible is true?" These are the same children who come to church consistently. When some of them are doubtful about the Church, and others are doubtful about the Holy Bible, we are dealing with a very dangerous situation, and should not keep silent.

Unfortunately, we pay attention to the church as a building and are more concerned about how to expand and enlarge it as a structure, and how to construct other churches. Certainly, this is good, but who will fill this church after ten or fifteen years if all our children, or a big percentage of them, are not attached to the Church, and it does not matter to them if they go to this church or go to another one? If a percentage of them (be it small) are doubtful about the Holy Bible and our Orthodox Christian religion, and perhaps, some of them doubt God's existence, who will fill this church that we want to expand and enlarge?

2. The Role of Parents in Raising Their Children

What is the role of parents toward the upcoming generations? The church is not the building. It is the believers, because we make up the church. If you are not here, and if a city has no Copts, there will be no churches. We need to direct our attention—as we attend to building churches, we have to attend to building the church as souls and spirits. This is more important. This is our responsibility before God.

Many parents come to complain about their children's behavior, saying, "Our children do not obey us; they answer us back, they retort and they disobey us. These are not the values with which we grew up. This culture is taking them away from us. Help us! Help, church! Help, Abouna[6] [our Father]! We need to restore these children to God and to the Church." Here, I want to ask each of you a question: Who do you think is responsible for this? Who is responsible for our children's lack of attachment to the Church? Who is responsible for the strange actions and behavior we encounter at home?

Most of the responses will center around placing the blame on the community. They will be either: "We live in a western culture with a difficult current, and this is why our children are influenced by the culture," or, "My kids grew up at a time when we had no church. There was no follow up, and so they did not come out as expected."

If we blame the culture and the difficult undercurrent, believe me, the culture has no influence. History, as well as the Holy Bible, witness to this. What happened with Moses? When he was a baby, Pharaoh commanded that every Hebrew son must be killed. Moses's mother was worried about her son, so she hid him in a papyrus basket and threw him in the Nile River. Pharaoh's daughter came, saw him, and adopted him. However, she needed a nurse; so, she called Moses's mother (not knowing that it was his mother), who, then, nursed and raised him, although Moses was raised in Pharaoh's house in the land of Egypt. The people of Israel who were in Egypt at that time were in bondage, in subjection, and in bitter servitude (Cf. Ex 2:2-10). Moses grew up in a strange environment—in a strange culture. However, the Epistle to the Hebrews says, "Moses, when he became of age, refused to be called the son of Pharaoh's daughter, choosing rather to suffer affliction with the people of God than to enjoy

---

6 Abouna: Arabic word meaning, 'our father," a title of an ordained priest, "Father" or "Fr."

the passing pleasures of sin, esteeming the reproach of Christ greater riches than the treasures in Egypt" (Heb 11:24-26).

Moses was raised in a foreign house, with foreign people, and in a foreign family, and yet, this strange community could not influence him. He came out attached to God and to his people. He went to save his people, although he was a prince and was due to be king one day (yet he refused). He "refused to be called the son of Pharaoh's daughter … esteeming the reproach of Christ greater riches than the treasures in Egypt" (Heb 11:24-26).

The current situation in Egypt is difficult; yet people cling to their faith. Look at other denominations around us. You will find them very firm in their religion, teachings, and traditions, although they live in this same culture.

We cannot blame the Church, using the excuse that there was no church, or that the church was small, because the church can only do so much. A child comes to church and only spends a few hours, and yet, sometimes we complain that the length of the Divine Liturgy and Sunday school wasted all day Sunday. When the children come to church, most of them spend their time outside during the Divine Liturgy, and then, attend Sunday school. No one knows if they pay attention in Sunday school or if they spend their time distracting the children next to them. No one knows whether or not they understand the lesson, and then, they go home. This is the time that the child spends in church. How much impact can this hour have on our children? Even if they do benefit, how will this one-hour affect them? Imagine if a student takes a one-hour lecture at school, and after returning home does not study or read. Do you think this student will pass the exam? Of course not! Therefore, the greatest, primary, and final responsibility lies on the family. We cannot blame anyone else but ourselves as parents.

If we look again at Moses, the words that his mother taught him when he was a child as she was nursing, teaching, and raising him are the words that stuck in his mind. When he became a man, he refused to be Pharaoh's daughter's son. When St. Paul praised Timothy in his epistle, he said: "I call to remembrance the genuine faith that is in you, which dwelt first in your grandmother Lois and your mother Eunice, and I am persuaded is in you also" (2 Tim 1:5). Also, in another epistle he says, "Greet the brethren who are in Laodicea, and Nymphas and the church that is in his house" (Col 4:15). This is our role; if we say there is no church, what about the church in your house? What is my role? Have I converted my house into a church?

3. The Connection between Spiritual Life and Social Principles

I also want to clarify another important point: How do we distinguish between social demeanor and spiritual life, or between social principles and spiritual life. Any community believes in social principles. Any person can obey social principles; even country laws are obeyed. Laws prohibiting stealing, murder, adultery, etc., all are social principles. But what constrains these social principles and keeps them from diverting from their correct place? What makes a person control his feelings and emotions so that he does the right thing and keeps off the wrong path? It is the spiritual life. If there is no spiritual life, we cannot demand social principles from people. If there is a proper spiritual life, the proper social demeanor comes automatically, as a result thereof. If you seek good demeanor (respect and obedience) from your son, let me ask you first, before you place such demands on him, whether you have offered him and ingrained within him the spiritual life. If you have not, you have no right to make such demands.

If anyone thinks that he can instill in his children social principles such as honesty, integrity, and love without the spiritual background to support these principles, he may find that the child has these social principles but loses them when he encounters difficulty. He loses control, all these principles start to vanish, and we see a completely different person in front of us. Therefore, we need the spiritual background and a spiritual life to support the social principles, since a spiritual life is the only thing that connects us with God.

Without having a spiritual life, any person who has money and is able to afford life's necessities, such as food and clothing, will not steal. However, if something goes wrong and he is short on money, he will think about stealing. Do you think that if a person has money and is able to eat and drink and buy clothes, then he would not be considered a thief before God? Of course he would be considered a thief, because if he ever needs money, he will steal, or if he has the opportunity to steal, he will steal. On the other hand, a person who maintains principles during both difficult and comfortable times, when life is easy and when life is difficult, this person is blameless before God.

Spiritual life and spiritual principles make this possible. For example, Joseph the righteous was living his life and was not thinking about committing sin. His spiritual relationship with God allowed him, when put in the position to commit sin, to say, "How then can I do this great wickedness, and sin against God?" (Gen 39:9). He refused sin, did not fall into sin, and preserved his spiritual and pure life with God. Joseph's support was his relationship with God; otherwise, if Joseph had no relationship with God, it would have been very easy for him to sin with Potiphar's wife.

Anyone can behave properly in life, but if he goes through difficult times, it can be very easy for him to commit sin, and subsequently, blame life's circumstances. However, if the person has a strong spiritual life with God, he will always be stronger than life's circumstances. If you are attached to God, God will always help you and give you victory. A spiritual life is the supporting backbone to our behavior; I cannot separate spiritual principles from social values. Whoever thinks that he can raise his children and teach them social principles, without rooting them in the Church, is definitely deceiving himself. Satan is also deceiving him as well, and blinding his eyes to the importance of spiritual life.

4. Planting the Seeds in the First Four to Five Years of the Child's Life

In order to harvest fruits, first you need to plant seeds in the soil, for, "Whatever a man sows that he will also reap" (Gal 6:8). Whatever we, as fathers and mothers, sow in our children from their first years, that we will also reap. If I did not sow anything, how can I except to reap anything? Psychologists say that in the first four years of a child's life, the main frame of his personality and characteristics begin to develop. In those years, the child starts to memorize the dictionary. In other words, a child, who at first was not able to speak, learns to speak any language that he hears and understands the meaning of words like water, eat, drink, walk, tired, sleep, etc. Whatever language he hears, he repeats, memorizes, and keeps on his tongue. If he hears English, he will speak English. If he hears Arabic, he will speak Arabic. If he hears Italian, he will speak Italian. If he hears insults, he will insult others; if he hears anger and frustration, he will have a bad temper and be frustrated. If they swear, he will swear. If he sees disrespect and fighting, the child will adopt this image.

During the first four or five years of a child's life, general principles are inherited, imprinted, and engraved in his mind by watching the members of his household. If a child sees those in the household pray, read the Bible, use quiet voices and Christian language, he will learn all these attributes. In addition to this, when we plant our children in church from a young age, when the children play, we will see them imitating things done in church, such as the priest holding the censer. What I am saying is not strange. You all know how when Pope Athanasius was ten years old, Pope Alexander, while sitting in the cathedral, saw him by the shore playing with other children, baptizing them in the water. This was the image imprinted on his mind. It is no wonder that Athanasius became St. Athanasius, hero of the faith. Imagine if St. Athanasius's parents had not paid attention to his spiritual life. He would not have played in this manner when he was ten or twelve, but rather in the disturbing manner of which we all complain.

A very important point to consider is: what have I done with my children during their childhood, in the first four years of their lives? Children look, learn, and imitate. For them, they are discovering a new world—the father, mother, and the family with whom they live. They imitate and apply in their own lives exactly what their families do. When a child finds good role models in the home from the father, mother, and older siblings, this image will be imprinted on the child, making it easy to live a life with God and behave in a good manner. Sometimes, people say that there is no need to be concerned about young children who are one, two, or three years old, because they cannot comprehend or understand anything. This is not true! The child observes, sees, hears, and stores in his mind everything around him. This is very important, because everything the child observes and comprehends in the very first years of his life stays with him for the rest of his life. If the child sees and hears good habits and attitudes, he will develop these characteristics. Therefore, fathers and mothers have responsibilities as role models. [For more on role modeling, see Part I, C.]

5. School-Age Children

We have discussed the importance of the first four to five years of a child's life and the impact of the home on the child during this time. In the second stage of life, which begins at age five or six, a child begins to communicate and interact with the outside community, goes to school, makes friends, and gets involved with them. He begins learning from these children, and they may start to teach him bad habits or strange vocabulary. In this stage, a child also starts to have his own opinion and the desire to have an independent personality. He does not count on what he sees or hears, but rather he has his own personal decisions and opinions. He starts claiming his freedom, and pursuing his opportunity in the world. How can we protect our children during this age? What is our role as parents toward our children from age six until their graduation?

When children begin venturing out into society, we find three types of parents:

1. Very liberal, lenient, and careless parents.

2. Very conservative, strict parents.

3. Parents who are conservative at times of need and easygoing at times of need.

Liberal Parenting

Let us examine these three types of parenting, and evaluate them. The first group favors complete freedom for their children. I do not like to call this freedom, but rather lenience, and there is a difference between freedom and lenience.

a. Lenience

Lenience means the parents are tolerant and approve of anything the children think is appropriate. The children can do anything they want. These parents reject Egypt and are actually vindictive toward Egypt. They have a complex about being called "backward Egyptians." To protect themselves from being labeled as such, they become extremely liberal. They do not mind that their children hang out with any group, go anywhere, choose whomever as friends, or do anything, and they tranquilize themselves saying that they "trust" their children.

b. Trust

Let us discuss trust, and explore if it right or wrong to give our children absolute trust. The Church encourages parents to trust their children.

However, here I am talking about a false claim of trust. There is such a thing as true trust and such a thing as false trust. Parents tranquilize themselves with false trust to give their children freedom in order for no one to say that they are backward Egyptians; they want to hear that they are American, and that they understand American culture and have become part of it.

Is trust earned or given? Certainly, trust is earned, not given. Through their behavior, children cause their parents either to trust them or distrust them. Parents do not freely give trust to their children. I should give trust to whoever is deserving of it, and not to the one who does not deserve it. But if I shut my eyes about trust and I leave my children to do whatever they want, this is wrong. I have to test my children many times, without them realizing it, and then, I can decide if they are ready and deserving of trust or not—whether they earned trust from me or not. This is a very important point.

If you just say that you trust your children, let me tell you something: you trust your children and I trust them, but what is your opinion regarding human weakness? Does human weakness exist or not? Of course, human weakness exists. Take a sin such as adultery, for example. The Bible showed us three excellent characters that fell into this sin:

1. The prophet David, with all his purity, committed adultery. God even said about him, "I have found David the son of Jesse, a man after My own heart" (Acts 13:22).

2. King Solomon with all his wisdom—no one in the world is like Solomon in his wisdom—sinned when women turned away his heart. With all his wisdom, he did not know right from wrong.

3. Samson, with all his strength, fell before Delilah.

These three examples were trustworthy, but they fell because of human weakness. We cannot shut our eyes to human weakness. We cannot say that we will leave boys with girls together without supervision and that we trust them. I am not saying that we should withdraw trust from our children, but that we have to be careful and mindful of human weakness. You trust—this is good, but are you sure that the devil will not fight against them? Of course not! Satan declares war against everyone.

The devil has fought against the anchorites in the mountains who have reached the highest levels of spirituality and caused some of them to fall.

I am not calling for us to stop trusting our children, rather this is a call for caution. Everyone has to be cautious over the children because they are our responsibility, and you will be questioned before God if you are negligent in your responsibility toward them. If you neglect them, you will be held responsible, accountable, and condemned before God. Please open your eyes and take things seriously and objectively. We need to be careful, as the Song of Solomon says, "Catch us the foxes, the little foxes that spoil the vines, for our vines have tender grapes" (Song 2:15). A little fox could get in and bring down your *whole* vineyard that you have planted. If you are attentive to the causes of sin, you will not fall into sin. But if you leave the door wide open for the causes of sin, sin will be very easy.

Let us be realistic and ignore what others say if they call us abnormal or backward. We seek to please God, not to please people. If people give you the label that you seek, that you are American, but you are blameworthy before God, what will your outcome be? Wake up and see if what you are telling yourself is correct or not. Be honest with yourself.

c. Freedom

I would like to further explain the difference between freedom and lenience in order for us to understand the definition of freedom, and so we are also fair with our children when they claim that we do not give them the right to their freedom. Moreover, we need to know whether what they are demanding is truly freedom or lenience. I will give you an example from real life; I do not think anyone can object to the fact that America offers people complete freedom. However, at the same time, there are laws. For example, it is not permitted to exceed the speed limit when driving on the highway. If someone does so, the police have the right to stop him and give him a ticket. He will have to pay a fine, and if he exceeds the speed limit a few more times, his license may be suspended. Can this person demand that he has the right to drive with unlimited speed since he lives in a free county? Certainly not! So, the point I want to make clear is that freedom is not against rules and laws. When a house has rules and a specific system in place and the children have to follow these rules, this does not mean that this is against freedom. Otherwise, federal laws should be cancelled.

It does not work if we permit our children to come and go as they please and to follow or break whatever rule they desire, using the excuse that we want to give our children freedom. When we are being lenient and not providing appropriate freedom, we can call this chaos. However, everything should be organized and in order.

True freedom is inner freedom, as the Holy Bible says, "If the Son makes you free, you shall be free indeed" (Jn 8:36). What is the meaning of inner freedom? Inner freedom is when the person has the ability to control himself from within in the appropriate way. For this reason, it is said in the Book of Proverbs, "He who is slow to anger is better than the mighty, and he who rules his spirit than he who takes a city" (Prov 16:32). This means that he who can rule and control himself is better than a person who rules an entire city.

I can put in place rules and laws and run a country on them, but when it comes to me, it would be difficult to implement these rules, and therefore, I would not be able to follow them. This would mean that inside, I am not free. I am controlled by my desires and lusts. My will is not free. If my will were free, I would be able to do what I want to do, and not do whatever it is I do not want to do. This is true freedom. True freedom is to submit to laws and rules with joy, and to encourage myself to accommodate and adjust to any condition. But the person who is stressed from within, whose will is not free, when placed under certain rules and laws, he would not be able to follow them. Iron collars chain this person internally, and he cannot escape. Otherwise, if he were free from the inside, he would be able to control himself as he wanted and submit to the rules.

Therefore, freedom is different from lawlessness and chaos. Freedom does not mean to not having any rules, procedures, or systems to follow. When our children come and say, "We want to have our freedom," we need to explain to them the definition of "freedom." Ask them, "What does freedom mean?" They would say, "Freedom is that I can do whatever I want, go out whenever I want, and hang out with whoever I want." You have to clarify that this is not freedom, but chaos. If your child is internally free, he will be able to protect himself from anything that is against the rules, regulations, and system of the house. [For more on freedom, see Part I, D.]

d. Right and Wrong according to God's Judgment

This brings us to another important point. What are the criteria for the rules and regulations of the household? What are the rules and regulations to which our children need to submit with satisfaction and the glorious inner freedom of the children of God? Let us discuss the difference between right and wrong, and see what we should accept and what we should reject.

Right and wrong are not what is right or wrong according to our judgment, but what is right or wrong according to God's judgment. If God says that something is wrong and unlawful, and I do not see anything wrong with it, this does not mean that it is right. It means that this thing is wrong and it also means that I am unable to comprehend what is right. The sins and the hardness of my heart may make me unable to distinguish between what is right and wrong according to the biblical definition and the godly perception. A person's reaction to right and wrong differs according to his spiritual stature. For example, if someone committed murder, he may feel that what he has done is a sin and a crime, and that this crime is against God's will. Within himself, he feels guilty and dissatisfied. Even society will prosecute him for this crime.

Someone may get very angry easily and then defend himself by saying, "It is okay for me to react like this. This person got on my nerves and I could not control myself. Would I just keep silent while he insults me?" Well, what do you think about the Sermon the Mount, when the Lord Jesus Christ said, "You have heard that it was said to those of old, 'You shall not murder, and whoever murders will be in danger of the judgment.' But I say to you that whoever is angry with his brother without a cause shall be in danger of the judgment. And whoever says to his brother, 'Raca!' shall be in danger of the council. But whoever says, 'You fool!' shall be in danger of hell fire" (Mt 5:21-22). Many times we use abusive and inappropriate language and our excuse is that these are regular sins and it is okay to use them. We may say, "This life requires this kind of behavior; a person cannot survive in the world without committing these normal sins." No. The Holy Bible says that whoever says to his brother, "You fool" shall be in danger of hell fire.

Therefore, the measure of right and wrong is not what *I* see as right or wrong, but what God sees as right or wrong. The more a person advances in his spiritual life, the more sensitive he becomes toward sin. In the beginning of a person's spiritual life, if he steals, he feels that he committed a sin. When this same person grows and progresses in his spiritual life, merely having the desire to steal or just thinking about stealing something makes him feel that he has sinned. Although he did not steal, for him, the desire to steal is a sin. Maybe, we cannot comprehend this in the beginning of our spiritual lives because we do not yet have the spiritual sensitivity to know right from wrong and whether or not something will please God. One of the Ten Commandments is, "You shall not covet" (Ex 20:17). For example, this can apply to your friend's money. When one gets this desire, he feels guilty, which means his spiritual life has improved and he has become very sensitive. Any small sin affects his heart, because his heart has become more pure.

Another example regarding seeing right and wrong from God's perspective is drinking wine. Maybe you consider that drinking wine in not a sin, although the Holy Bible says, "Who has woe? ... Those who linger long at the wine, those who go in search of mixed wine. Do not look on the wine when it is red, when it sparkles in the cup, when it swirls around smoothly; at the last it bites like a serpent, and stings like a viper" (Prov 23:29–32). It is very clear that God is saying wine is wrong, so how can I justify it for myself and say drinking wine is not a sin?

e. Causes of Sin

There is another point, which concerns things that are not sins in themselves but that lead to sin. We call this the "causes of sin." As a matter of fact, anything that leads to sin, even if it is not a sin, is considered sin. How so? If in the end, this path will lead me to sin, then, from the beginning, it was not right. Sometimes, at the beginning, the situation appears unclear; the difference between right and wrong is not apparent. However, continuing on this path will lead to sin at the end.

For example, consider time. If a person does not take advantage of his time—meaning he has free time but does not use it properly or benefit from it—this is not considered a sin. He does not know how to make proper use of his time, but rather spends his time visiting others, or talking on the phone, or sleeping. This is not a sin. However, free time means an empty mind, and as it is said, "An empty mind is Satan's playground." Therefore, if someone does not use his time properly and take advantage of it, he gives Satan the opportunity to take advantage of it and instruct him on how to use it. Satan will continue offering more plans, such as, go watch TV, or go rent a video, go to this place or that one, etc., and, at the end, because this person does not spend his time properly, Satan will drag him to sin. Consequently, his free time would cause him to fall into sin. This is why our fathers warned us about free time and about how if a person does not know how to take advantage of his time, he may fall into sin.

David fell into sin because he had free time and did not know how to use it. In reality, if each person fulfills all his responsibilities, he will not find any free time. However, sometimes we run away from our responsibilities, and because of this, we have free time. David's army was fighting in battle. His soldiers were getting wounded and being killed, but David chose to run away from his responsibility. His mind was not even occupied with God. He went to take a walk on the roof and Satan approached him, deceived him, led him to desire sin, and he fell. How did this start? It started with free time. David did not know how to spend his time and he decided to take a walk, and Satan used David's situation to lead him to sin. This is the danger of the causes of sin.

What are the causes of sin for our children? Time is a point to consider for them. If we want to discuss the issue of free time, let us ask ourselves a question: Does each father and mother pay attention to how they organize their children's time and how they keep them busy in healthy, practical, and spiritual ways that may benefit them spiritually, scientifically, or culturally? Or do we let them spend their time as they want? It is our responsibility to keep our children busy.

Friendship is another one of the causes of sin. Sometimes, we give our children the freedom to choose their friends without any limits to who they choose. Our excuse is that we trust our children. We convince ourselves that no one can influence them and that they can be friends with anyone because they have strong personalities. They tell us that at the times of temptation, they are able to prevent themselves from committing sin. We believe our children and we close our eyes to the human weakness factor. However, we should not forget about human weakness because we, then, give our children the opportunity to spend time with bad friends that have no values or ethics. They end up going to inappropriate places, and unfortunately, perhaps we go with them. Then we say that we trust our children and, "this is freedom," and our children need to know the difference between good and bad and how to choose.

Some parents do not forbid their children from sin, but punish them harshly if they make mistakes. For example, there can be parents who allow their child to spend time with a friend who smokes cigarettes. The child will learn from his friend and, consequently, he will start smoking, and they will get upset and punish him. If the parents had advised the child about the causes of sin and prevented their son from befriending a smoker from the beginning, he would not have learned how to smoke. Parents have to prevent the exposure of their children to the causes of sin in order to protect them from committing sins. We need to apply rules at home according to the Holy Bible and according to what God sees as right, rather than according to what we see as right. At times, our perception can be different from God's perception.

We need to always be alert regarding the causes of sin, as the Song of Solomon says, "Catch us the foxes, the little foxes that spoil the vines, for our vines have tender grapes" (Song 2:15). This means that prevention is better than treatment. Let us not close our eyes.

7. Very Strict Parenting

We have discussed the first group of parents who are very lenient with their children. The second group of parents is very strict with their children. They deal with them very harshly and do not give them any chances or opportunities to choose or to express their opinions. These parents say, "I said so, and it will be so!" and "These are our rules and this is our system and the children have to submit to whatever we say." Furthermore, the punishment is very severe if the children break any of these rules.

a. Fear

This technique is wrong because it instills the element of fear in our children. The child obeys, not out of love or conviction, but because of fear. As a result, when opportunity presents itself, and the controlling parents are away not present, he goes in a completely different direction. "For every action, there is an equal and opposite reaction" (Newton's Third Law). He rebels because he feels that he has been imprisoned and living in fear. There was always someone giving him orders and he was pressured to follow these orders. Therefore, as soon as he gets the chance to leave the house for college or to travel, for example, he starts doing whatever he likes without considering any rules or values, because all the values instilled in him were orders given without any love or conviction. In this way, in the long run, we hurt our children and do not raise them with the proper values.

b. Weakness

The second result regarding children who grow up in a harsh environment is that they may become weak and develop weak personalities in society. This is because his father acts like a judge at home and his mother like a prosecutor. If the child comes home late one day, they start questioning him: "Where have you been, and with whom?" They make it a big issue and punish him. This is the world in which the child is dealing at home with his father and his mother. Therefore, when he starts to deal with the outside world, he will react with fear and his expectations will be that each person will deal with him in the same ferocious or violent way as his parents. This leads to a weak and unstable personality, and he becomes fearful of people. He struggles and is afraid when talking to someone. Because he is weak, he can also be very easily deceived and bullied by his friends. All of this can lead him to passively submit to them out of fear.

This is not right! This child has a weak and sick personality. Moreover, because he feels different from the other children he meets in school, he withdraws and isolates himself. He does not form friendships and has no acquaintances. He keeps himself in a closed circle, which is his own "self-circle." He becomes an introvert. When you check on him, you find him always depressed and sad. He has no joy or peace because he lives in a home filled with fear, terror, and lack of love, security, and peace. Of course, treating children in this way is not right.

c. How God Interacts with His Children

These children are afraid to express and reveal to their parents what they are feeling inside. They *want* to talk with their parents, but they are unable because they are afraid. Again, this is wrong and God does not even treat us like this. God gives us the right to speak and negotiate with Him, as He did with Abraham. If you think about it, you may wonder how Abraham dared to speak with God in such a courageous way. Abraham said to God, "Far be it from You to do such a thing as this, to slay the righteous with the wicked, so that the righteous should be as the wicked; far be it from You! Shall not the Judge of all the earth do right?" (Gen 18:25). It is as if

Abraham said to God, "My Father, I see that You are not fair about this." Sometimes, if a child tells his father that he does not agree with him about something, his father responds saying, "What is that you are saying to me?" and he may slap his son. However, Abraham stood before *God* and told Him, "Shall not the Judge of all the earth do right?" He went on to negotiate with God about the number of righteous men in Sodom that the Lord must spare the city for their sake. He started with fifty, and God said that He would not destroy the city for the sake of fifty. Then Abraham pleaded with God and asked about forty-five, then forty, and continued to patiently negotiate with God until the number went down to ten, and God said, "I will not destroy it for the sake of ten" (Gen 18:32).

God was very patient with Abraham, His creation. Here, we see God's patience and longsuffering in dealing with His creation. Abraham dared to tell God that he thought He was being unfair, and God did not immediately punish him. Rather, God asked him, "What is it you need Me to do?" Then, God responded and told Abraham that He would do as he requested. God did not say, "What I said is final. I will do as I wish whether you [Abraham] like it or not, and with or without your will." Unfortunately, this is the attitude some parents use with their children.

If we apply this in our children's lives, we will find that many of our children want to have discussions with us but they are afraid and lack courage. What I am saying here does not negate respect between children and parents. Note how Abraham began his discussion and negotiation with God, "Indeed now, I who am but dust and ashes have taken it upon myself to speak to the Lord" (Gen 18:27). Abraham knew his own measure and that his appearance in front of God is dust and ashes.

When a spiritual child does not agree with his parents about certain matters, he should discuss them with his parents without fear and should try to convince them about his opinion. He may start by saying something like, "Dad, I trust your opinions; however, my opinion in this matter is this, this, and that." This should be done with all respect. Otherwise, it will offend the parents when the child says that they are wrong or do not understand something. The commandment says, "Honor your father and your mother" (Ex 20:12). Here, I am talking about freedom of expression. We have to give our children the right to express themselves and their opinions, even if these opinions are different from ours.

Without a doubt, we will hear strange opinions and wrong or inaccurate views. When parents hear a wrong or inaccurate opinion, they should be patient and listen to the children. They should discuss it with them, and correct and advise them. This is what God did with Abraham. The child has to know that he has freedom of expression at home, without being afraid of his father and mother. He must know that he can be honest with them. He should know that if he tells his parents about his mistakes or opinions, including incorrect opinions, they will not punish him harshly; rather, they will correct his point of view. We should not tell them "no" right away and end the discussion. Always have your ears open to your children. This way, parents will be able to keep their children safe and on the right path.

8. The Ideal Way to Raise Children

Parents should neither be too strict, nor too flexible. The question becomes, "What is the ideal way to deal with our children?" There is a story we read in the Synaxarium[7] that reflects the ideal way to raise children. It is the story of St. Anastasia, whose father was a pagan and her mother was Christian. Her mother "brought her up in the teachings of the Christian faith. She was steadfast in her faith and no one was able to dissuade her."[8]

Any method or attempt to raise and nurture children will always fail if it is a method or attempt to raise them away from God. Why? The Holy Bible says, "The fear of the Lord is the beginning of wisdom" (Prov 9:10). "Wisdom" means that our children know how to live properly, know the difference between good and evil, and know what to choose and what to refuse. The beginning of wisdom is the fear of God. If parents spend hours trying to teach and instruct their children about the difference between right and wrong, what to reject and what to accept, how to behave and how to live appropriately, and when to resist outside influences without teaching them to love the Lord, they are wasting their time. The children will not benefit and parents will reap no fruit from them.

---

7 Biography of the Saints in the Coptic Orthodox Church.
8 (Synaxarium: The Martyrdom of St. Anastasia, January 4th—Koiahk 26).

a. Parents' Relationships with God

It is very important to plant in our children the love of God, the fear of God, and religious sense and desires. In doing so, our children will know the difference between right and wrong, and what is acceptable and unacceptable to God. How do we go about this? It is a problem if parents themselves do not have a relationship with God because you cannot give what you do not have. How can parents introduce God to their children if they do not know about God? How can parents teach their children the Holy Bible, or ask them to read it, if they do not read or study the Bible?

One time at a youth meeting, we asked the youth, "What are the issues that bother you or upset you the most in your relationships with your parents?" Several youth complained that when their parents tell them to do something specific because it is the right thing to do, or not to do something because it is wrong, when they ask their parents for the reasoning behind their instruction, the parents do not know. They tell their children, "Go and ask Abouna." Here, parents cannot convince the children that this issue is right or wrong because they do not know what reference or verse to use. The children further remarked, "If the parents do not know the reason, why do they ask us to do this and not that?" And, quite frankly, the children have the right to think this way.

Each parent should build himself up spiritually. Parents should focus on reading the Holy Bible, prayers, confession, and attending church. Parents should concentrate on the salvation of their own souls for their own sake, and not for the sake of their children. The children will then see Christ in them, as it is written, "Let your light so shine before men, that they may see your good works and glorify your Father in heaven" (Mt 5:16). Some parents say, "I just come to church for the sake of the children so they can learn about God's ways." That is not practical, because children will observe that their parents do not apply what they have been taught at church. The dilemma becomes why they should apply the Church's teachings while their parents do not. Therefore, parents should cultivate a personal relationship with the Lord, attend church, read the Holy Bible and the stories of the saints, pray, confess, and take communion. This image of the parents' spiritual lives will be planted automatically in the hearts of the children.

b. Encouraging Our Children to Have a Spiritual Life

The second point is that parents must encourage their children to practice the same things. Encourage your children by making them love church instead of using intimidation. Sometimes parents tell their children, and especially young children, "Do not lie, so God would not send you to Hell." This is wrong. Parents should focus on positive points and teach their children, "If you are honest, God will love you." Do not give children the impression that God only punishes. Rather, teach them to taste and see how great God is, as the Holy Bible says, "Oh, taste and see that the Lord is good" (Ps 34:8).

It is crucial that parents encourage their children to love the Church. Teach children that attending church is something very joyful; it is the house of the Lord. Teach them that when we go to church, we are visiting the Lord, who is the King of kings and the Lord of Hosts, and that the angels surround us in church. Also, in church, we hear heavenly praises, as we say in the Divine Liturgy, "God… who has given to the earthly the praising of the Seraphim."[9] Parents then should ask the children, "Do you not want to be in heaven? The church is heaven on earth."

This way, the children will get to know and love the Church. Encourage children to love the house of the Lord. At home, read the Holy Bible and the stories of the saints to them. Pray for them and with them. Make sure that they go to confession regularly, and take communion. Follow-up and encourage them to fast and to love fasting. Plant in them Christian principles as well as the fact that God is a great God, and that we are so honored and unworthy to be called His children.

One time, Emperor Constantine sent a letter to St. Anthony. When the courier delivered the letter, St. Anthony put the letter aside and continued with his endeavors. His disciples became very excited to learn what was in the letter and asked him why he was not opening it. St. Anthony told them that while they were eager to know what is in a letter sent from an earthly king, he did not see that same level of excitement in knowing what is in God's letter to us: the Bible. Using this gentle approach, St. Anthony taught his disciples that they should have the same level of excitement and love toward the Lord and the Holy Bible, God's word.

---

9 Divine Liturgy of St. Gregory, Anaphora.

In our daily lives, we often do the same thing. When we check the mail and find an important letter from a family or a friend, we may not even wait until we get back in the house to open it to see what is in it; rather, we open it and read it as we are still walking back. In contrast, we find the Bible to be a heavy book that we cannot carry and have no desire to read. That is because we do not have enough love and longing toward God. We need to teach our children how to love God.

Parents usually complain that their children do not want to pray or go to church, "because it is too long," or fast, because "it is too hard, especially at school," or confess, because "Abouna is too strict," and so on. What can parents do? St. Paul said, "Nevertheless, being crafty, I caught you by cunning!" (2 Cor 12:16). What does "I caught you by cunning" mean? St. Paul explained this in another passage in 1 Corinthians, "Though I am free from all men, I have made myself a servant to all, that I might win the more; and to the Jews I became as a Jew, that I might win Jews; to those who are under the law, as under the law, that I might win those who are under the law; to those who are without law, as without law (not being without law toward God, but under law toward Christ), that I might win those who are without law; to the weak I became as weak, that I might win the weak. I have become all things to all men, that I might by all means save some. Now this I do for the gospel's sake, that I may be partaker of it with you" (1 Cor 9:19-23).

Parents need to possess wisdom and patience. Do not introduce spirituality as something the children must accept, or else—like a bad tasting medicine that we used to force down their throats when they were young. If you present spirituality as something your children must exercise against their will or else they will be punished, they will reject both the church and God. Rather, parents should be wise in teaching the children, even if the children resist or reject the teaching. How can we be wise in doing this? It is wise to use indirect methods, keeping in mind that "faith comes by hearing" (Rom 10:17). For example, do not tell a child, "We are going to sit down now and read the Bible together so that you can be a good boy." Maybe he already refuses to listen to Bible stories or anything similar. Instead, if you plan on running errands, ask the child to accompany you. In the car, you may tell him something like, "I remember a story I was reading about..." and start telling a story. For example, you could share the story of Joseph, and how he was faced with many temptations, and how the pressures of sin were surrounding him. You can also expound on how Joseph said, "How can I do this great wickedness, and sin against God?" (Gen 39:9). You may add how much Joseph loved purity and how he had a very pure heart. Your child might respond by saying, "Are you going to give me a lecture?" At this point, change the subject and leave him with the story, knowing that, "My word ... that goes forth from My mouth; it shall not return to Me void, but it shall accomplish what I please, and it shall prosper in the thing for which I sent it" (Is 55:11).

After a few days, you may tell your child something like, "I was listening to a homily about the Nativity Feast, and I heard something very nice," and share it with him. Thus, give children small doses of the word of God. It will touch their hearts. Additionally, you can share your personal experiences with them. For example, tell them about how you faced a big problem at work and did not know how to deal with it. Then, you sent a small arrow prayer, asking God for help, and the Lord responded, and you were able to get out of a tight spot. Tell them that you would like for them to do the same when they face a problem.

Teach your children small lessons, which can be delivered in one or two minutes and in a conversation, not a sermon. After you do this several times, the children will begin to develop an internal spiritual sense and regard for their religion. Eventually, when they face a problem, they will remember what you said and how when you prayed, God answered and helped you get out of a difficult situation. The children may then begin to do the same thing and start praying on their own, without anyone forcing them. At this moment, God will begin His work, and pull them to Himself.

To summarize, if children refuse to read the Bible with you, attend church, or confess, etc., parents should deliver spirituality and religion in small doses, in a pleasant and natural way without force, and use an indirect approach. Therefore, there are no formal sermons or times for teaching the children. You are teaching them every time you interact with them by mentioning stories from the Bible or the lives of the saints, or by reciting a Bible verse that addresses the issue at hand.

To emphasize what we said earlier, it is very important to be filled spiritually to be able to give spiritual messages to your children. It is also important to practice all aspects of the spiritual life and to share them with your children. In this way, you will be planting the fear of God in their hearts day by day. Children's hearts will then change and reject this world, because they will now be children of God and not children of the world. Their inner lives will begin to change. When your children come to you with their problems, explain to them that you often tried to solve your own similar problems by yourself but did not know how. Then, share your experiences with your child and continue by saying that when you got closer to God, He solved your problems and brought you so much peace and joy. After that, ask your child to listen to you and obey you, at least this one time, and to go to his room to pray in private.

Always share with your children the stories of how God intervened numerous times and in different ways and saved you from financial burdens or other problems. Children will no longer refuse or reject God and religion, and these stories will change the false perception that God exists only to punish wrongdoers. They will start to love God and want to live with Him. They will also learn the difference between children and slaves. God told us, "No longer do I call you servants, for a servant does not know what his master is doing; but I have called you friends, for all things that I heard from My Father I have made known to you" (Jn 15:15). Explain that when a child obeys his parents, he does so because he loves them. However, a servant will obey because he fears punishment. That is why God does not want our relationship with Him to be built on fear; rather, it should be built on love because "Love never fails" (1 Cor 13:8). Therefore, when parents plant the love of God in the hearts of their children, this love will never fail. True, sometimes we get tired, or lukewarm, or bored; however, when the love of God is planted in the heart, it will *never* fail.

To briefly review, the first point is for parents to build themselves up spiritually. The second point is to teach our children to love God. However, in doing so, do not deliver spirituality and religion using dry, impersonal, hard, or repulsive methods as if you are forcing bitter medicine down their throats. Rather, teach them to love God and the church, and to love living a godly life.

c. Praying for Your Children

The third point, which is as important as the second, is praying for your children. A case in point is the story of St. Monica and her son St. Augustine.

St. Augustine lived a life of sin. In the book of his confessions[10], he wrote that he committed sin not because he wanted to, but rather to boast about it amongst his friends. He wrote that, on one occasion, they stole food from their neighbor's garden. They stole guava and apples, although they did not need them or want them, and they threw them all away after they stole them. He wanted to rob the neighbor to satisfy a sense inside him, which proved that he could lead his friends and steal without being caught. He reached a very low point in life, and he committed sin just to boast about it. Where was his conscious, knowledge, and the spiritual and religious sense and responsibilities? There was none of this. St. Augustine committed a multitude of sins, including having a child out of wedlock.

His mother, St. Monica, used to pray for him constantly. She poured herself out in front of God and wept for her child. She put his name on the altar in the presence of Bishop Ambrose of Milan (340-397), so, he too, could pray for him. She instructed her son and had many discussions with him, and he belittled her when she talked about God (as per his book *The Confessions*). Because he used to study philosophy at that time, he considered his mother's advice and teaching as nonsense. The bishop, St. Ambrose, used to comfort her and tell her, "God's time will come. Go now; it is not possible that the son of so many tears should perish." That is why St. Augustine is known by the name, "Son of Tears," because the reason for his repentance was the tears of his mother in front of the throne of grace.

Years later, St. Augustine wrote that after he knew the Lord, the teachings of his mother rang in his ears. The word of God will not return void (Is 55:11). Even if your child does not listen to you today, if he belittles you like St. Augustine used to do with his mother, there will come a time when the word of God that you tell your child and the seed that you planted will bring forth fruit. Pray for your child. If he is far from God, pray for him. Stand up and pour out your heart and your tears in front of God and plead with Him for your child. Tell God that your child is His child and that he is the talent that He gave you. Plead with God to teach your child to come back to Him, to love Him, and to repent. Put your child's name on the altar and lift up sacrifices on his behalf, for God to have compassion and mercy on him.

---

10 The Confessions of Saint Augustine.

It is very important that every time you pray, you pray for your children. Lift the name of each child in prayer in front of God. Pray for their troubles, difficulties, and spiritual lives, that God may have compassion and mercy on them and bring them back to Him.

d. Children Need Understanding and Patience

The fourth point is that children need understanding and patience. If you say "no" to something and the child asks, "Why not?" it is very easy to say, "Because I said no;" however, your child will no longer be truthful or straightforward with you. It is much better to be patient, to listen, discuss and negotiate, and try to convince the child. God deals with us, who are dust and ashes, in that same way. When we talk or plead with God for anything, God listens and gives us as much time as we need. We all know the story of Abraham and how he negotiated with God the fate of Sodom and Gomorrah (Gen 18:16-33). God was longsuffering with Abraham and did not brush him off, telling him that he did not know anything. Rather, God was patient and accommodating with Abraham.

Therefore, be longsuffering and discuss the issues that concern your children with them. Keep your hearts open and full of love and kindness, and do not use intimidation. You will never gain the trust of your children with intimidation, but you can gain their trust by love. Be a friend to your children and open your heart to accept them. When children come to discuss an issue with you, surround them with your love and compassion. Listen to their points of view and teach and convince them about the proper way to deal with that issue.

When your child makes a mistake, do not punish, but discipline. To discipline is to show the child the difference between right and wrong, for his own good. To punish is to take revenge. This vengeful attitude is usually apparent when a young child makes an innocent mistake. A young child often does not yet know the difference between right and wrong. Regardless, a parent may become very angry and pour out his retributions on the child, and beat and scold him as if the child knew right from wrong. By doing so, parents displace their anger by pouring out their vengeance on the child. This is wrong.

When we served little children in Sunday school, we were taught that if a child misbehaves in class and the servant felt annoyed and wanted to scold the child or yell at him, that servant should control himself and not do so. If a servant did so at that moment, he would be expressing anger, and the child would feel that he is being punished. The child would not feel the servant's love. Rather, servants should wait until they are calm from within, and then discipline, so the child realizes that the discipline is for his own good and for his benefit. Therefore, as parents or servants, wait until your anger or frustration abates and you are calm, and then, discipline the child so that he does not feel that you are punishing him, but rather, sees that you are building him up.

The child who misbehaves is like a wounded person, who needs tenderness and compassion in dealing with his wounds. Roughness may worsen the condition, and you may lose the child altogether. Remember how tender the Lord Jesus Christ was with the Samaritan woman. When He asked her to go call her husband, she answered, "I have no husband," and the Lord Christ complimented her and said, "You have well said, 'I have no husband'" (Jn 4:17). Despite all her sins, Jesus complimented her for answering truthfully. Likewise, recall how tender and compassionate the father was with the prodigal son (Lk 15:11-32). He opened His arms for the prodigal son, who squandered his inheritance in wild living. When the son returned, he said to him, "Father, I have sinned against heaven and in your sight, and am no longer worthy to be called your son" (Lk 15:21). The father in the parable was so touched and did not let his son finish the statement he had prepared, "Make me like one of your hired servants" (Lk 15:19). Instead, he took him in and forgave him, and told him that he will take him back again and that he is still his child. He then put on a robe on him, gave him a ring and sandals, and slaughtered the fatted calf to celebrate the return of his son.

Be compassionate when you deal with your children. Be compassionate without spoiling them. Learn when to be strict and when to let go, "For He bruises, but He binds up; He wounds, but His hands make whole" (Job 5:18). It requires godly wisdom to discern when to inflict pain and when to give relief, and when to wound and when to heal. Do not let your children fear you, but accept them to yourselves and treat them with love and kindness. Accept their mistakes because these mistakes are due to their weakness and the world's pressures and influence on them. Teach them and discipline them; and when you discipline, discipline by love and compassion and do not punish.

It is imperative to be patient, to listen to them and their opinions and to discuss their issues with them. Try to use logic to convince them, instead of the useless phrase, "I said so!" This way of dealing with children is revolting and does not build them up; in fact, it might cost you your child. Moreover, learn how to befriend your child, so that when something is bothering him, he will find refuge in you and not seek outside sources. Children consult and share their feelings with their friends because they do not find a kind and compassionate heart to listen to them and understand them at home. Believe me, if they find love, kindness, and compassion at home, they will not seek it outside. They look outside for love and kindness because they do not find it at home. The father and mother are busy at work. The time they spend with their children is full of arguments and bad tempers, and parents are impatient with the children; "For what profit is it to a man if he gains the whole world, and loses his own soul? Or what will a man give in exchange for his soul?" (Mt 16:26). Parents then argue that they are working hard for the wellbeing of their children. The question becomes, what will millions of dollars do for them if you lose them? Do not leave them wealth and affluence, but leave them a fortune made of spiritual precepts and godly morals. Children will build their own successful future based on what you taught them.

9. American Culture Versus Egyptian Culture and How Both Relate to Christian Culture

I would like to address some of the questions and concerns children raise concerning us, and whether or not the children have the right to ask these questions.

When parents instruct their young child to do certain things and not do other things, the child's response may be, "You are Egyptians and we are Americans. You cannot apply the Egyptians rules to me, because we live in a community that is totally different than the Egyptian community in which you lived." This point is not correct because there are many things from the Egyptian culture that we do not accept, just as there are many things from the American culture that we do not accept. Likewise, there are things from the Egyptian community that we accept, and there are things in the American community that we also accept. It is not a matter of applying or imposing the Egyptian culture on our children; rather, we apply whatever befits us from both cultures. Therefore, when a child says, "Dad, I am American and you are Egyptian," reply and tell him, "My dear son, we are talking about different concepts in general, not about American concepts or Egyptians concepts. We are Christian, so we are talking about Christian concepts. We choose whatever is good for us as God's children from the Egyptian culture, and whatever is good for us as God's children from the American culture. Whatever is not appropriate for us from either cultures, we do not accept, as children of God." This point has to be clear in their minds, and also in our minds.

Moreover, we need to accept whatever pleases God and reject whatever does not please Him; we need to discuss this with our children. When your child comes to you and says, "I am American and you are Egyptians," reply and say, "Let us not measure it in this way, but rather by God's commandments and the Bible's commandments. What does the Lord want us to do?" If something befits me as a child of God, I will do it, and if it does not befit me, I will not do it, regardless of whether it is Egyptian or American.

10. Objectivity toward Our Cultures

What makes our children refuse the Egyptian culture? Two things cause this rejection. The first is the way we talk about Egypt, and the second is the way we behave in front of our children.

Sometimes, our children only hear the negative things about Egypt, and we never mention the positives, as if there is nothing good in Egypt at all, and we praise the American culture. As a result, when a child adopts something inappropriate from the American culture and we attempt to prevent it, the answer will be, "You are from Egypt," since everything the child hears about Egypt is negative. This viewpoint is inaccurate, and unfortunately, we are the ones who plant these thoughts in our children.

If we look at other communities, we can see how loyal they are to their countries. Loyalty does not mean crediting Egypt with attributes that do not exist, but rather, not always focusing solely on the negative, unpleasant aspects of Egypt. This is disloyalty. One who plants disloyalty to the country in a child, further plants disloyalty to the family and to the Church, and thus, plants in the child a spirit of rebellion. Rather, we need to emphasize to our children that Egypt is our country, that we love her, and that God said, "Blessed is Egypt My people" (Is 19:25), that most of our prophets went to Egypt during difficult times, including Abraham and Isaac—even our Lord Jesus Christ Himself fled to Egypt. Egypt has faith, evangelism, monasteries, martyrs, and saints. Egypt also has negatives, which we will not deny; rather, we need to explain to our children that every culture has positives and negatives. It is not correct to talk negatively about Egypt all the time. This reflects feelings void of loyalty and a denial of gratitude to the country in which the person was raised, and which prepared him to venture out.

When parents do not feel a sense of loyalty, the children are right to say, "If you were not able to live in Egypt, left it, and moved to America, how come you want to apply the Egyptians culture here on us?" They would have a point. We are responsible for how we speak about the Egyptian culture.

If we compare the divorce rate in Egypt, for example, with the divorce rate in America, the Egyptian community, with all its religions, has a lower percentage of divorce than the American community. This reflects which community has higher values and morals. Therefore, the way we talk about the Egyptian culture should be different. We need to be objective, not disgruntled.

We pray that God gives us the blessing of knowing how to deal with our children because it is a great responsibility to raise them according to the will of our Father.

C | TRAIN UP A CHILD IN THE WAY HE SHOULD GO

1. Introduction
2. A Serious and Important Responsibility
3. Parenting Methods
4. Household Atmosphere
5. Role Modeling
6. Spiritual Upbringing

1. Introduction

"Train up a child in the way he should go, and when he is old he will not depart from it" (Prov 22:6). I want to concentrate on two things: (1) "train" and (2) "the way." The word "train" is a verb, indicating that this is an active process. It will not just happen by chance or coincidence; it requires both effort and preparation. The fruit of this effort and preparation becomes apparent along the road. "The way" refers to the path of the particular child, meaning that every child has his or her own way and style. Every child has his own "key" by which we can reach him. Therefore, the wise father is the one who manages to raise his child in the particular way that is suitable for him, and not in any different way.

An important point to consider is how I can discover my child's talents. We sometimes try to shape our children in a particular way that differs from their talents. However, a successful upbringing involves discovering my child's talents, then training him to walk down the path that suits his talents, resulting in his success. By doing this, we make sure that "when he is old, he will not depart from it." For example, in the situation where a father is not convinced with the concept of monasticism, but his son wants to become a monk, this father would tell his son, "No, do not become a monk." Here, the father is not bringing up the child in the way for *that child* that is appropriate to his preferences, or his motives and talents. Instead, he is bringing him up according to the vision that *he* sees for his son. Of course, this is very serious. Many children have failed in their academic pursuits just because we forced them to follow a certain path, which was not their path. We did not see what was appropriate for them and allow them to grow in it.

2. A Serious and Important Responsibility

Raising children is one of the most serious and important responsibilities given to parents. If parents take the responsibility seriously, they will be able to raise godly children, but if they do not, then they will raise children who are bad. It is said that the price of an engineer's mistake is an apartment building and the cost of a doctor's mistake is someone's life. However, the cost of a father or mother's mistake can be the future of their child. If you are negligent in bringing up your children, they may live weary lives full of misery.

If you decide to buy a nice house, you drive around and search, until, perhaps, you finally decide to build your own house by using an excellent architect. Let us assume that you are a father. If your house is not exactly to your liking, it is not important. However, if your children are not according to our Lord's will, they will sadden the hearts of the parents.

We often focus on things like making money for our children and securing their futures, etc. These are all are good things. However, if a father did not make money for his children's future, but was able to give them a successful, spiritual upbringing, he would have made the best possible investment for them. The main goal of a family is raising good children who fear God.

Parenting is also critical because children are the future of the Church and the society. If we raise decent individuals, the Church will continue to be strong and our society will continue to be upright. Some denominations are selling churches due to lack of attendance. The only people who attend are the elderly, because past generations did not care to raise their children in the church, so the children grew up with no ties to the church. There are no youth to sustain the churches, so they are selling them.

Unfortunately, many parents, especially those in the diaspora, and more specifically the ones who are new to the diaspora, get extremely busy upon arrival and do not give enough time to raising their children. This is because when they are new, their main focus is on building their careers quickly. They want to work, to establish themselves, and to save money. Even though they say that they want to do this for their children, both the father and the mother often have demanding jobs, leaving no time for their children. When they come home, they are tired and cannot spend time with their children; they cannot sit with them and raise them in the fear of God. Therefore, they leave their children to receive their upbringing from TV, the Internet, friends, social media, and/or day care. These become the ones who raise our children. As a result, we later find that when they grow up, the children have different values from the ones we wanted them to have. The parents may say, "These are not the children we expected. These are not the children we hoped to see." Why did the children grow up like this? This happened because the parents neglected to perform their responsibilities and relinquished them to others. We left the world to shape them in its own way.

Moreover, in North America, there is no career limit; there is always a chance for growth. This results in a never-ending cycle for parents who are always extremely busy, with limited time for raising their children. Again, the children will end up receiving their entire upbringing from TV, the Internet, friends, media, or day care. This way, it becomes very hard to shape our children in the way that we want. The children are ultimately not shaped by us, but by the world. For example, you might find your children wanting to dress like singers or athletes, since these are the role models available to them continually on television. Their language adapts to the language they hear on television. Later, when these children grow up, they may give us a hard time if they did not grow up in the fear of God. His Holiness Pope Shenouda III of thrice-blessed memory always said, "Raise your children before your children raise you." This means that the child who causes trouble is a source of pain for the father and mother.

As I have mentioned many times, it is better for a father and mother, and better for the whole family, to live in a lower social class and to raise their children in the fear of God, than to live at a higher social standard and, at the end, the children stray away from or from God.

In this section, we will discuss four factors that affect how we raise our children:

1) Method of Parenting
2) Household Atmosphere
3) Role Models
4) Spiritual Upbringing

3. Parenting Method

Our children's personalities and mannerisms are very much influenced by the applied method of parenting. There are four methods of parenting that we will discuss in detail. These four methods depend on a balance between love and control. We either raise our children with (1) authoritarianism (dictatorship and control), (2) permissiveness (spoiling), (3) negligence, or (4) authoritativeness (love and control). It is important to note that parents can switch from one style of parenting to another during life.

The four methods of parenting are illustrated in Table 1. As you can see from the table, love must be accompanied by control. If the parents are extremely demanding without showing any love, it is called "authoritarian parenting." If the parents show love without imposing any control on the children, it is called "permissive parenting." This is where the parents simply allow their children to do anything without restrictions. There are no rules. If the parents show neither love nor control, it is called "uninvolved (or negligent) parenting." If there is a balance between love and control, it is called "authoritative parenting." There is authority from the parents, but this authority is accompanied by love.

In terms of parenting, a combination of an authoritarian father and a permissive mother is not the correct style of parenting. On the contrary, when there is a difference in the style of parenting, the children take advantage of this, which subsequently leads to conflict between the parents. For example, if the father says no but the mother says yes, the father will fight with the mother about how she could agree to something after he objected. For this reason, both the father and the mother should be authoritative in style; both must simultaneously exercise authority as well as show love and compassion.

Table 1. Four methods of parenting[11]

Methods of Parenting	Loving Parent is accepting and child-centered	Unloving Parent is rejecting and parent-centered
Control Parent expects much of child	**Authoritative Parenting**	**Authoritarian Parenting** Relationship is controlling
No Control Parent expects little of child	**Permissive Parenting** Relationship is indulgent	**Uninvolved (Negligent) Parenting**

Before we discuss each of the four parenting methods in detail, let me define what I mean by the words "love" and "control." The word "love" refers to exhibiting warm emotions toward the children. The children must hear the words, "We love you," and they must *feel* that their parents really love them. Often, parents (and especially fathers) say things like, "For whom am I expending all this effort? It is for my children!" This is

---

[11] Adapted from https://my.vanderbilt.edu/developmentalpsychologyblog/2013/12/176/

true, but it is also extremely important to express emotions toward the children and let them know of your love. In the Egyptian culture, it is common to consider the expression of emotion as weakness; but this is not true. It is extremely important to express emotions like love, compassion, and encouragement toward the children. Words of encouragement are very important for the children. Ask yourself these questions: "When was the last time I revealed feelings of love to my children? When was the last time I said an encouraging word? When was the last time I embraced my child and expressed how much I love him or her, and how happy I am that our Lord gave me this gift? "Children are a heritage from the Lord" (Ps 127:3–5).

The word "control" refers to chastening, instructing, disciplining, and following up. "For what son is there whom a father does not chasten? But if you are without chastening, of which all have become partakers, then you are illegitimate and not sons" (Heb 12:7-8). When they do something wrong, I discipline them. Instruction refers to saying "no," even if the children have not done anything wrong. An example of this scenario is when they ask for a toy and I say "no," because I do not want them to become spoiled. I want to teach them that they will not receive everything that they request. I want them to know that life does not provide a person with all his wishes. Following up refers to taking note of their progress. Ask yourself these questions: "When was the last time I took a stand with my children? When was the last time I tried to modify their behavior?" Parents must be very involved in their children's lives.

a. Authoritarian Parenting

In the first style of parenting, there is authority and control but no expression of love, affection, encouragement, or warm feelings. Even if parents have the feelings of love in their hearts, they do not communicate them to their children; the house becomes a very strict dictatorship. The children grow up to feel, "Dad is extremely strict." This approach involves an attempt to completely control the children, making the house feel like a set of guidelines, orders, and laws. It feels like living in a jail or with the police. Everything is either right or wrong, and if it is wrong, the child will be punished. Sometimes the punishment that parents give for a particular wrongdoing is disproportionately more severe than the mistake deserves in order to scare the child so he would not disobey again. Moreover, there are no explanations for the reasoning behind the rules. Basically, there is continuous strictness. The parents always have the last word. Sometimes when commands are given, the father shouts or yells, or says things like, "I said so and it should be so. This is the way I was brought up. You cannot have a discussion with me. I could not raise my eyes to look my father in the eye!"

If there is only strictness and no love, the effect on the children will be one of the following:

1) The children grow up to have very weak and dependent personalities. Actually, they will not have any personality. As a result, other people (at school or at work) can abuse and take advantage of them. This is not compatible with the children of God, "for God has not given us a spirit of fear, but of power and of love and of a sound mind" (2 Tim 1:7). These children will be terrified if anyone yells at them, and will do whatever they are told. This is because they grew up in a home where they were terrified of their parents. They would do whatever they are told, even if it is not correct, since they never learned how to say "no." They rely on their parents, are immature, indecisive, and unable to make their own decisions. They also are unable to say "no," because, in their minds, saying "no," has been associated with punishment, such as physical or psychological punishment. Psychological punishment includes being denied love and kindness, such as when parents stop speaking to their child. However, God said in Matthew 5:37, "But let your 'Yes' be 'Yes,' and your 'No,' 'No.'" Being able to say, "no," has saved a lot of children from many things, such as acquiring bad habits due to peer pressure. If they were unable to say, "no," they would be unable to refuse smoking cigarettes, for example, because they would be afraid that the person offering them the cigarettes would not speak to them again. Being overly controlling of our children weakens them. They may easily fall victim to others who may cause them harm.

2) They become rebellious. As soon as they turn eighteen, they are convinced that no one can tell them what to do. At that age, they rebel against all kinds of authority. I often see children who would come to church with their parents every single Sunday and serve as deacons, up to age sixteen or seventeen. Suddenly, and surprisingly, as soon as they turn eighteen,

stop coming to church completely. Why? Of course, up until the age of eighteen, they were coming to church out of fear. Now that they are eighteen, by law they cannot be controlled by anyone, so they rebel. Not only will these children rebel against the authority of the parents, but they will also rebel against all authority: the authority of the church, sometimes of the government, the school, and even the authority of God. They simply do not want to be under any kind of authority, and they want to do *everything* wrong. Many get involved in drugs and sexual immorality. They have a lot of anger inside them—very strong anger, which is the result of the control of authoritarian parents. The anger is even more intense if their parents were also abusive, physically, emotionally, or verbally. Of course, all kinds of abuse create very intense anger within children.

3) They start searching for love outside the home (especially girls), because there is no love at home. Girls would start to have feelings for any boy who starts to show them any love or compassion. Later, with the very first chance she has to get married, regardless of how unsuitable the groom may be, she will accept the marriage proposal, in order to escape the control of her home. We have seen many girls who, a year or two after getting married, request a divorce, because they got married for this reason. These girls say, "I could not stand living with my parents. The house was hell. I told myself that when anyone came to propose to me, I would leave the fire of this house!" But they leave one fire and enter another fire, and that is why their lives end with divorce and problems.

Even more critically, the image of God gets distorted in the children's minds. How so? When we pray, we address God as, "Our Father." When we say, "Our Father," the mind does something called association. It connects the picture of the father or mother to the picture of God, the heavenly Father. I project the image of my earthly father onto my heavenly Father. So, if my earthly father is extremely strict, controlling and authoritarian, I imagine that God is also strict and authoritarian. My perception of God will be exactly the same as that of my earthly father in his strictness and control. This will result in me not loving God. This is why the Holy Bible warns us against this method of parenting.

I recall once that a priest at one of the churches told me that a 15-year-old boy at his church had started to become an atheist, denying the existence of God. So I sat with this boy to try to understand why he adopted atheism. I found that he knew absolutely nothing about atheism, and that his decision to deny the existence of God was not because he had read books about atheism that distorted his mind with atheist philosophies. At this point, I started to question him about his relationship with his parents, and I discovered that his father was a churchgoer. (Note that I am not saying "spiritual" but "church-goer," since he went to church and took communion *every* Sunday, and kept all the fasts of the Church.) However, he was extremely abusive, both physically and verbally. In addition, he committed "spiritual abuse" against his son. This means that he would use Scripture to abuse his children. For example, after yelling and beating his children, he would say, "The Bible teaches us not to have mercy on our children, and if we beat them, it is okay." The effect of this abuse on the boy was that he started to *hate* God, especially since his father would abuse him in the name of God. This made him reject this "cruel God," [an image which he had conjured up in association with his own biological father] and also deny His existence.

Another time, I was talking with a father and his son when I found the son telling me that he is not interested in the Orthodox Church, and is considering Mormonism. Speaking with him for a while, I discovered that whenever the boy said anything wrong, his father would say, "God will send you to hellfire." Thus, the boy's impression of God in the Orthodox Church is an angry God who is tallying his mistakes in order to justify sending him to Hell. He met a Mormon friend at school, began to talk, and when he told him that he was afraid of God, the friend told him, "No. Come with us. God loves you. He wants you as you are." And so, the boy rebelled against the Church because he was rebelling against his father. I confronted him on this point, telling him, "I see that you reject the Orthodox Church and want to become Mormon, not due to a theological or dogmatic reason, but because you are refusing the image of God that you learned from your father, thinking that this is the image of God in the Orthodox Church." He became silent for a moment, and replied, "You are right, this is the reason." Here, I began to work with the father and told him that he was distorting the image of God for his son, causing him to rebel not only against him, but also against the church he attends. Many times, when our children rebel against the Church, it is due to their rebellion against the authority in the house, or the incorrect image of God that we give our children.

We have found a very interesting connection between how the relationship between parents and their children is reflected in the relationship between those children and God. The relationship between parents and their children is either good or bad. If it is bad, then the children's relationship with God will be the opposite of their parents' relationship with God. For example, if the parents have a poor relationship with God and with their children, the children grow closer to God. If the parents always go to church but have a bad relationship with their children, the children will stay away from God. On the other hand, if the relationship between parents and their children is good, then the children's relationship with God will be the same as their parents' relationship with God. For example, if the parents have a good relationship with their children and with God, then the children will also develop a strong relationship with God. If the parents have a poor relationship with God, but a good relationship with their children, the children will also have a poor relationship with God. Our parenting style influences the relationship between our children and God because our children project the image of their parents onto God.

To this type of parent (the authoritarian parent), God says, "Fathers, do not provoke your children, lest they become discouraged" (Col 3:21). Do not provoke them with control and extreme strictness, because, by doing this, you will be the cause for the failure of your child. This verse is extremely important, which is why it was repeated twice, once in Colossians 3:21, and again in Ephesians 6:4.

Many years ago, a father came to me and complained that his son was being aggressive with him and would threaten to hit him, and that, in some instances, he had to call the police to stop things from escalating between him and his son. I knew this father was very controlling, wanted things his way all the time, did not accept any mistakes, and did not show any type of love or compassion. I advised the father that the next time he and his son get into a similar confrontation and his son was ready to hit him, to hug him. I saw that the father was not taking me seriously and had a smirk on his face, reminding me with what the Holy Bible said in the story of Lot, "But to his sons-in-law he seemed to be joking" (Gen 19:14). The father left and was not convinced; he may have been thinking, "Here I am telling you that my son is hitting me, and I am supposed to hug him?" But this father came back a few weeks later and told me that he had had another big confrontation with his son and his son was about to hit him. He said, "At that moment, I heard your voice in my ear telling me to hug him. I thought, 'I have tried everything else: I beat him, I threatened him, I cursed him, and I called the police on him. Why not try something new and see what will happen? I will just try.'" When he took his son in his arms and hugged him, his son relaxed after being so angry, and leaned on his father's shoulder and cried for twenty minutes. He told his father that he had been waiting for this hug for a long time. It has been twelve years since this happened, and until today, I have not heard of any more trouble between them. The child was thirsty for love and kindness. Children and parents are connected by blood; if we give them love, these ties will erupt and the love within them toward their parents will also flow. On the other hand, violence is a result of lack of love and compassion, or of not expressing that love.

There are at least two reasons why parents deal with their children with too much authority and control. Firstly, it may be because the parents themselves are not satisfied with love, and therefore, cannot give love. I cannot give what I do not have. If the father and mother never knew what love is, and no one showed them love, how can they love others? The next possible reason is insecurity. Most of the people who are abusive and domineering are insecure deep within themselves. They may fear that their children are going to rebel against them. In order to avoid this repercussion, they turn into a lion in the house so that they can guarantee that everyone will follow their orders. Control, then, becomes a way to cover up the parent's insecurity. If a parent has confidence in himself, he will not be controlling or abusive.

This can also be applied regarding service in Sunday school. Once, we were at a youth convention, and I felt that the servants had started to take on the "police officer" attitude. They would see a boy walking with a girl and would start running after him and questioning what they are doing. Then, they would threaten to send them home, etc. I found that this attitude did not yield positive results. On the contrary, the youth started to feel very tired of these retreats and started boycotting them because of the very strict treatment they received from the servants. As a result, I met with all the servants and told them, "If I wanted policing, I would have hired a security firm which would have done a much better job than you! They would have been much better at keeping order at the convention.

However, I do not want police officers, I want servants. A servant will maintain control, but with love. If I were speeding on the highway, a police officer would stop me and give me a ticket as an appropriate punishment. However, a servant's purpose is not only to punish, but to discipline and to help the youth improve and do things the right way." Similarly, the parents' responsibility is to help their children grow in the likeness of the Lord Christ by changing all bad behavior into Christian behavior. This will not happen unless we merge control with love.

b. Permissive Parenting

This style of parenting allows the children to do everything they want. The parents excessively express love and pamper the children, without ever saying "no," to the children or taking any sort of firm stance against them. All the children's requests are granted. They permit everything; the children are actually the ultimate authority in decision-making and the parents' roles are simply to fulfill their commands. Without any kind of control, the children have no rules by which to abide. For example, they choose when to return home; they do not have a curfew (if they want to come home at 4:00 AM, they can). Sometimes, parents do this to be considered nice by their children, or in modern-day terms, "cool parents." They do this so the children will not feel that their parents are old-fashioned, but are modern. Also, this style of parenting is very easy for the parents. If parents simply agree and allow their children to do anything they want, they will save themselves the trouble of arguing and debating.

The problem with this style of parenting is that the children grow up to be extremely irresponsible. When do we see this irresponsibility? You will find that even though the child is smart and intelligent, he gets very bad grades in school. This is because he is spoiled; he goes out and does whatever he wants, and does not study. There is no discipline. He is not used to doing something he does not enjoy, like studying. This is why they fail in school. You will find that these children normally have all the latest gadgets, best cell phones, cars, computers, etc., and at the same time, they are failing school.

In addition, because these children have no responsibility and have no experience in real-life decision-making, they make terrible choices. They may face many hardships and problems due to their inexperience. If they are spoiled with regard to money, they may start to use drugs and get involved in immoral behavior. They often have problems with law enforcement agencies. They find it difficult to finish high school or college. Even if they somehow manage to find a job (normally with the help of family or friends), they usually cannot stay in the same job for a long time and hop from job to job. They quit their jobs very quickly because they are not used to the seriousness that holding a job entails. For example, if they request something from their boss but the boss tells them "no,"—the boss is, of course, not going to spoil them—so, they quit. After all, they are used to being spoiled. Then they would look for another job, and meanwhile Dad and Mom are supporting them financially.

When they grow up, they will not find the pampering they received in their parents' home; rather, they will find that life is full of problems and difficulties. When these children encounter any difficulty, they will fall apart. They may end up with a harsh manager at work, and since they are poorly equipped to handle challenges, they fall apart if they are rebuked; they may not be able to tolerate any criticism or direction, even from their superiors at work. Poetry says concerning these, "The touch of linen scars their hands." They are pampered; they are not toughened by life.

Children who are the products of this type of parenting are also very difficult to deal with in marriage. Their spouses suffer and complain often about them. This is because their irresponsibility makes them a burden, and dealing with them feels like having another child in the family; they need someone to take care of them all the time. They will not look after the children or teach them anything. This is why, in my previous lecture about marriage, I mentioned six types of personalities for which people need to be cautious when choosing their spouses. One of these six types was the irresponsible type, because they are extremely tiring as spouses. [Note: the six types of personalities: (1) someone who lies a lot, (2) someone who is irresponsible and cannot be held accountable, (3) someone who is stingy, (4) someone with an unhealthy attachment to his or her family, (5) someone who is violent and abusive, and (6) someone who does not live a life of purity.]

If you come across someone who is failing academically, or barely passing, and cannot keep a job, most likely this is someone who was brought up in a home where the parents were permissive and spoiled him or her. This kind of love is unhealthy; it is even harmful. When we offer our children love without control, it harms them. This applies to any kind of leader. In any kind of leadership position, we must have love and control. Even God uses both love and control; these two go hand in hand.

This is why, as parents, you need to know that you ought to exercise your God-given authority. Exercise authority with love. This is helpful for your children to become responsible individuals. "The rod and rebuke give wisdom, but a child left to himself brings shame to his mother" (Prov 29:15). Let us explain this verse, "The rod and rebuke give wisdom." The rod here does not imply that we are supposed to beat our children, but it implies exercising control over the children so that they gain wisdom. "But a child left to himself" (when you let the children do whatever they want to do), "brings shame to his mother" (the children bring shame to their parents and the entire family).

"He who spares his rod hates his son, but he who loves him disciplines him promptly" (Prov 13:24). If you are saying that you are exercising no control over your children because you love them, you are mistaken. This verse tells you that if you are not exerting authority over your children, you actually hate them, because your lack of control causes them to become irresponsible, without wisdom, and lacking in discipline.

Another beautiful verse says, "Foolishness is bound up in the heart of a child; the rod of correction will drive it far from him" (Prov 22:15). To explain this: "Foolishness is bound up in the heart of a child," means that we are all born foolish (lacking wisdom); "The rod of correction will drive it far from him," means that the cure for this foolishness is the rod of correction, which is the act of disciplining and controlling the child. Through discipline, the children will gain responsibility and wisdom.

There are different reasons that parents may become permissive. Some parents feel very guilty if they discipline their children or say "no," to them. Of course, this is misplaced guilt. Saying "no," makes these parents uncomfortable and causes them agony. To them, the Holy Bible says, "Do not withhold correction from a child, for if you beat him with a rod, he will not die" (Prov 23:13). Again, "beat him with a rod" does not mean literally beating them, but means controlling and disciplining. This verse is telling you that it is okay to say "no," to your children, nothing will happen to them; it will actually help them gain wisdom. Another reason is that they fear losing their children's love. It is as if they are buying their children's love by approving everything they want. These parents are insecure about their children's love. To guarantee that their children will continue loving them, they do not say, "no," to them.

In other cases, the parents have waited for a long time to have a child and when they finally have him, they want to spoil him. It may also be a reaction to the parents' own upbringing. If one or both of the parents experienced having a very controlling, stern, and authoritarian father, they do not want to see their own children suffer from this severity, and so, go to the other extreme. The result is that the parents give their children love, spoil them, and do not offer any kind of boundaries or control. We see this kind of parenting in the story of Jacob and Joseph. Rachel gave birth to Joseph after a very long time. Jacob waited for Rachel's son, Joseph, for many, many years. When Joseph was finally born, Jacob spoiled him, and he favored him over his siblings.

Therefore, what we have discussed, thus far, shows that we should not treat our children with any extremes. Do not be too strict and aggressive with them, and do not be too lenient and permissive. Both extremes are wrong.

c. Uninvolved or Negligent Parenting

Another extreme that is even worse than the previous two is being completely negligent in raising the children. In this scenario, the parents do not exhibit any control over their children, do not discipline them, and do not express any feelings or emotions toward them. Everyone is living in isolation. The father comes home from work, eats his dinner, then enters his bedroom, or checks his computer or pays the bills. The mother comes home from work and heads straight to the kitchen to do her work. When she is finished, she is exhausted and wants to sleep. The children, each in his own bedroom, have their own TVs, computers or laptops and cell phones. They are disconnected and disengaged. There is no love being given to these children. There are no relationships whatsoever with the other members of the family. No one knows what the other is doing. No one is being disciplined; there are no family gatherings, no discussions, no rebuke, or disciplinary actions. In reality, many of these households are simply turning into being hotels. Technology has contributed tremendously to breaking families apart, causing each one to live in his own world.

This style of parenting yields the worst personalities of children. What would make parents uninvolved? There are a few factors:

1) Parenting requires effort! To maintain control over children and to express love requires active effort from the parents. Sometimes, we do not want to expend this effort. As a result, we start to shift responsibility; the parents want the church to raise the children, and the church wants the parents to raise the children. Everyone shifts the responsibility to someone else simply because no one wants to put in the effort. Eventually, these children will start to cause trouble and will have many issues, which would be a cause not to love them even more. How can I show him love when all he does is bring me [the parent] problems because of things he does at school, or by bringing the police to my house? I am, therefore, causing him to lack discipline by not participating in his upbringing. Then, I have no patience or time to show him love when he starts to cause trouble.

2) Parents have a great deal of stress outside the home. For example, if they are newcomers to the diaspora, they want to build their careers quickly. Their work and their lives are overly stressful, and due to the pressures they face all day at work, they are too tired to spend time with the children at night to discuss their days and guide them or express emotions toward them. When you put a rule in place for your child and he breaks it, and you sit with him and teach him why that was wrong, and he breaks it again, and you spend more time with him, and he breaks the rule a third time, you will find that this is tiring. So, you simply say, "There is no use. If he wants to learn, he will learn. If he does not want to learn, he will not learn," and that is it. You cannot love him because you are upset with the way he is living, and at the same time, you are weary. You do not want to keep making rules only for him to break them and challenge you, so you do not offer love or firmness, and you become totally disengaged from him.

3) When the children were young, perhaps the father and mother did not offer the necessary rearing and care. When those children reached adolescence, they started to wander in the wrong direction: One started using drugs, one started to fail in

school, one started to have girlfriends. The father and mother made several attempts and got tired, and their children did not listen to them. They became annoyed that their children behaved this way. How can parents who are annoyed and unhappy about their children's futures offer any love and compassion? In the meantime, they cannot put any rules in place because the children do not listen. The parents, then, become hopeless and say, "It is enough. I did everything I could. I will not have any relationship with them." Then, they start to completely separate themselves from them.

In this case, the children are truly victims of their parents' negligence. They take the bad traits of both previous parenting styles. They are both rebellious and irresponsible. These children often become alcoholics and drug addicts. Boys often become preoccupied with the party scene and girls often enter into bad relationships at a young age, resulting in situations like teenage pregnancy. Research shows that most children involved in this lifestyle had uninvolved parents.

To these parents, the Holy Bible says, "Behold, children are a heritage from the Lord, the fruit of the womb is a reward" (Ps 127:3). Children are a precious gift from the Lord. If this is your parenting style, then, you are badly treating a gift from the Lord Himself. If someone buys a new car, he takes extremely good care of it. What about your own children who are more important than anything else, and who are God's gift to you? How can you neglect them? You need to put in the effort to raise your children in the fear of God.

Another verse says, "And you, fathers, do not provoke your children to wrath, but bring them up in the training and admonition of the Lord" (Eph 6:4). When the apostle says, "bring them up," he is giving a command. You have to put in the effort to raise children in the training and admonition of the Lord. This is a commandment from God.

Of course, you may have a question here: "If my son is already at this stage, how can I deal with him? My son does not listen to me, is stubborn, and gives me a hard time. I cannot offer him either love, because I am annoyed at him, or firmness. How do I deal with him?" This is a different topic altogether called: "Dealing with Difficult Cases" (see Part I, A) However, I will briefly discuss some things that can help temporarily.

Children, or any of us for that matter, pass through six stages in order to change. And in order to deal with my son in the right way, it is necessary to determine in which stage he is at this time, because the method of interaction differs from one stage to another.

We call the first stage, "Unwilling." This refers to the one who does not want to improve. You tell him, "My son, mend your path, go back to school, leave the drugs, abandon your girlfriend." He does not listen to you. This is the first stage. We call the following stage, the "Dreaming" stage. Many times, while our children are in the, "Unwilling" stage, they do not want to change, and they feel that change is too difficult to achieve. Therefore, for them to change and develop a good personality is like a dream to them. It is possible here for them to move from the first stage to the second. In this case, they will tell you, "I know that I am wrong; however, change is a dream for me. I hope to change, but it is difficult to improve my life. I have reached the point of no return." The third stage is called, the "Willing" stage. He will say, "I can change." Change is no longer a dream for him. However, he has not, yet, started to carry it out.

The fourth stage is when the desire is executed, and this is called, the "Action" stage. He starts to try to change; he struggles, he falls and rises, and falls and rises, and falls and rises. This stage requires continuation and perseverance. We call the fifth stage, "Perseverance," that is, persevering in struggles. The last stage is "Victory," where the change (victory) actually takes place.

When dealing with my child, it is imperative for me to know in which stage he is at the time. How to deal with him depends on which stage: first, second, third, fourth, fifth, or sixth. If my child is in the first stage, if he is unwilling, is stubborn, does not listen to me, and refuses offers of love or firmness, how should I deal with him? There are four steps:

(1) Pray for his sake that God will change him, because you cannot bring that change to him through your words and efforts. Therefore, you actually need heavenly intervention. You always pray for his sake.

(2) Continue to communicate with him and show him that you love him as a person, but you disagree with his behavior. It is important that he gets that message, that as a person, he is important to you, but you do not accept his conduct.

(3) Do not encourage him to do wrong. It is not right to continue giving your child money if you know he is using drugs, or if he uses drugs and goes to jail, that you bail him out and the cycle continues. Here, I am talking about someone who is stubborn and does not listen, and not about a person who is responsive and obedient.

(4) All of us encounter problems. A person is usually ready to listen to God and accept intervention in his life during a crisis. Never miss the moment when your child faces a problem or tribulation. This is the time to intervene and invite the Lord to be among us. God can free us of these problems and bring about a change in our lives. The lives of many people changed when they faced tribulations. For example, Samson did not repent when the Lord was so patient with him. Rather, he repented when he encountered tribulations.

We should not lose hope. Never say, "It is over. I cannot do anything else with my son." No! Even when my child is at the first stage ("unwilling"), by the grace of God, these four steps will materialize with me.

d. Authoritative Parenting

This is the best style of parenting because it involves much love and emotion but also control and discipline when needed. The balance between love and control is very important. You show love, but you should also exercise your authority as a parent.

For young children (before adolescence), you should just give orders (ask them to do things) in order to teach them compliance. When they grow up and become teenagers, do not just give orders, and expect them to blindly comply. At this point, it is necessary to talk to the children and have an active dialogue, wherein you convince and persuade them with the reasons for asking them to do things. Discussion is very important at this age.

The children who come out of households where the parents practiced a balance between love and control grow up to have healthy and balanced personalities. They are able to adapt to society and to any environment. They are successful in school, at work, and in the church service. Also, they are responsible and well disciplined, capable of controlling themselves.

These parents have complied with the Lord's advice when He says, "Chasten your son while there is hope, and do not set your heart on his destruction" (Prov 19:18). This verse refers to the balance that we are discussing. You should not control them until death; otherwise, hold yourself responsible if they destroy themselves. However, you are required to discipline them because there is hope that these children will mature and obtain the likeness of the Lord Christ.

Love and firmness should not be separated, because doing so causes many problems. For example, the combination of a firm father and a loving mother is not a balanced relationship. It leads to the mother being the one whom the children love and who portrays the father as the enemy. Mom would complain to Dad about the children's behavior, but does not discipline them herself. Then, Dad, who may have just come home from a long day and is tired, becomes agitated because of their behavior and takes action, causing the children to become upset. Mom then consoles the children and makes excuses about how their father is tired, etc. Here, Dad looks bad and Mom becomes the hero. There has to be a balance between love and firmness. If the mother encounters a problem, she should take care of it, and if the father encounters a problem, he should take care of it. The father and mother should be in harmony; they must stand together and agree with each other. Even if one parent gives wrong advice to a child, it is better for the child to follow the wrong advice than for you to tell the other spouse that this is wrong in front of the child. If you make the other spouse look bad, this is more damaging than having the child follow wrong advice. So, what should you do as a parent in this case? When you are alone with your spouse, discuss the wrong piece of advice together. After your discussion and after coming to an agreement, the parent who gave the wrong advice should be the one to correct it. It is not right for you to override your spouse. You want respect to exist for both parents.

This issue happens so many times with parents, and sometimes, they do not pay attention to it. Not only this, but spouses encourage the idea that Dad is wrong or that Mom is wrong. The damage from doing this is great.

This applies in all areas. For example, with servants—if the servant in charge saw one of the servants give wrong advice to a child, it is not right to correct him in front of the children. Rather, he should discuss the matter privately with the servant at fault. Then, that servant should personally rectify the matter with the children so that the children's respect for the servant is not minimized.

4. The Household Atmosphere

The second factor is the household atmosphere. Two of the most important emotional needs for any child as he grows up are the feelings of *security* and *importance*. If the atmosphere at home gives the children a sense of security and importance, the children will grow up to be blessed. However, if the house lacks peace and stability, the children develop unhealthy personalities.

There is a very important verse that I want you to understand: "Now the fruit of righteousness is sown in peace by those who make peace" (Jas 3:18). In this verse, the Apostle James likens righteousness to a fruit. The farmer who plants this fruit has to be a peacemaker, and the soil in which this fruit is planted should be a soil of peace. The soil is a metaphor for the household, the farmer is a metaphor for the parents, and the fruit is a metaphor for the children. Thus, if the parents are peacemakers and the household is full of peace, the children will be righteous. In other words, if you want to raise righteous children, you must make sure they grow up in a peaceful house, and you yourself must strive to be a peacemaker.

If we create in the home an environment of safety and stability for the family and the individual, then the children are blessed; however, the absence of this produces troubled children. If the household is full of conflict, fighting and yelling between the parents (to the extent that the word "divorce" might be stated at home), the children immediately start to feel insecure, since they are not sure if this home will continue to be a single united family. Therefore, we have eliminated the first aforementioned emotional need of feeling secure. Also, they start to feel unimportant. They start to feel that they will be distributed between the parents in the same way that all other trivial things such as furniture are, and that there is no difference between them and the furniture. Therefore, we have also eliminated the second aforementioned emotional need of feeling important. Both of these essential emotional needs are lost with divorce.

Moreover, I warn parents, who, at one point, considered aborting the embryo, or if the pregnancy was unwanted, not to share this information with their children. This destroys the child's morale. How can you tell your child, "I did not want you," or, "You came by accident"? You do not have to share this information with your children. As we have said, "Children are a heritage from the Lord" (Ps 127:3-5). How can God give you a gift, and you reject it? It is important for the child's sense of importance; any child wants to feel wanted and loved by his parents.

I recall once many years ago, a mother came to me complaining about her son because he was stealing money. She said, "I do not know why he does this; we give him more than enough money, but he still steals." So, I sat with the boy to figure out why he does this, and I discovered that there are many conflicts between the father and the mother. When they fought, they often told the children things like, "We will get a divorce and put you in an orphanage." As a result of these statements, the boy felt extremely insecure. With his innocent thinking, he resorted to stealing money from his parents and saving the money so that if he were placed in an orphanage, he would have money. This example clearly shows that if the sense of peace is not apparent at home, we will cause our children to develop bad habits, like stealing, as in this example.

Children who grow up in a house that is full of conflict often grow up to reject the idea of marriage. They are terrified of repeating the same suffering that they witnessed with their parents. At the very least, they start to form unhealthy generalizations about marriage. For example, girls may often say things like, "I will not marry an Egyptian man like Dad, because he made Mom suffer. I will marry an American man instead." Of course, generalizations like this are not correct, but this is their thought process. Alternatively, they get married extremely early in order to escape from their homes, regardless of whether the spouse is a good or a bad fit.

There are houses in which you immediately feel peace when you enter; you feel that the atmosphere is very happy, with everyone laughing and being content. However, the houses, which we are discussing here, are very sad and depressing. The atmosphere is always full of yelling, shouting, and swearing. The children who grow up in this atmosphere do not enjoy their childhood, teenage years, or family life. They are put under enormous pressure and stress simply because the parents are not peacemakers. Keep in mind that these lost years will never return. If I have spent all my childhood with these parents, then I have lost my only chance to have a happy childhood. Happiness is important: "Do not sorrow, for the joy of the Lord is your strength" (Neh 8:10). A joyful person has strength, while a sad person lacks strength and does not have energy. Every age for children has its own special joy, but children who are surrounded by negativity do not get to experience this joy. Instead, they live in a depressing environment, which could lead to the child himself becoming depressed or developing an emotional disorder. A major contributing factor to personality disorders is family problems. When a child is raised in a house full of problems, in order to get out of this atmosphere, the child does, what is called, "disassociation," in order to shield himself. In the end, he develops a personality disorder and goes through many emotional problems.

Therefore, parents have to be wiser in keeping their families peaceful. If you have made a commitment to get married and to start a family, then you must do your absolute best to keep your family peaceful. This is the soil in which you will plant your children, and if you want your children to be righteous, it must be full of peace.

A Christian home is where the child wakes up in the morning, sees the parents get up early to pray while holding the Agpeya in their hands and standing in reverence. This image will imprint in the child's mind and will never be wiped from memory. He will know that this is the right thing to do.

Once, a couple was telling me that they have a child who is one year and two months old. The family prays before meals. One time this child's brother ate before they prayed, so this child nudged his brother. The image of praying before meals had been imprinted in this child's memory. He could not even talk; yet this image was imprinted in his mind.

5. Role Models

Our children usually imitate us. They reflect our exact behavior, attitude, values, and morals. Very simply, if parents speak Arabic at home, the children grow up speaking Arabic. If parents speak English at home, the children grow up speaking English. If the parents swear, then the children grow up swearing. If the parents speak aggressively and yell at each other, then the children will grow up to be aggressive and yell at people. If a child notices that the father lies—if someone calls the father, and the fathers asks his son to tell this person that he is not available— the child will learn to use lying to solve issues. His mother may come to complain that her son lies, but this is a normal result, since the child sees his father lie. Therefore, whether you like it or not, your children will grow up to imitate you—exactly. As His Holiness Pope Shenouda III of thrice-blessed memory said, "The child learns the entire dictionary by age four." At age four, the child can communicate with anybody, which means the child understands and has memorized the entire dictionary of his parents. Children even imitate our subconscious movements, facial expressions. and actions.

Just as children learn language from their parents, they will learn everything else. This includes learning faith and spirituality. If a child dislikes church, this makes me ask: Do the parents like church or not? Do the father and mother talk with their children about our Church dogma, and if so, what are they saying? If the child hears the parents say that our Church is complicated and strict, with many fasts and long liturgies, how will this child love Church? These words are engrained in his brain. If the child has never seen his parents holding the Agpeya and standing up to pray, how will he pray?

If the child is born into a family committed to fasting, where the entire family fasts when it is a fasting season, when this child grows up and turns fifteen or sixteen, the church will not need to waste time persuading him to fast. This child has experienced the blessings of fasting in his life. If a child has never seen the parents praying or fasting, and we try to discuss this with the child, we find him arguing a lot and realize that the parents would probably make the same arguments: "How can we fast? What can we eat during fasts? It will be difficult with work." The priest tries his best to find and offer solutions, and yet, they still do not fast. If they want to fast, they will fast. If this person is honest with himself, he will find that these are all excuses. If you want to serve and love God, or pray and fast for God's sake, you will do it. People in your same society, with your same circumstances, are fasting, and they pray and attend church regularly. Why are they able to do it, while you cannot? It is because you do not have the desire.

When the child sees his parents cautious to obey the commandment that says to keep the day of the Lord holy (Sunday) and to get up early on this day to go to church, when he is older, he will go to church early on his own. However, when the child sees his parents too lazy to go to church, trying to find excuses that the church is far, or only attending the last ten minutes, as a result, when the child grows up, the parents will not be able to bring him to church. When the child sees the parents concerned about Communion and Confession and saying that we have to confess and take Communion continually, in the future, they will not need to convince their child about whether Confession is right or wrong, because he already knows what Confession is and why we practice this Mystery[12] [Sacrament]. Moreover, the child will be able to convince others by his experience.

When the parents have appropriate celebrations at home, befitting the Christian home, these are the types of celebrations the child will have. I remember that when we were students, we used to assign subjects in school to saints for their intercessions. For example, we used to say, "This subject is for St. George, this one for St. Mary, this one is for St. Anthony, and this one is for St. Philopateer," and we would ask them for their help and intercession. Because the church was close to home, before we went to school, we used to stop by the church, make the sign of the cross, pray the "Our Father," and light a candle. Before we went to school, college, or work, we would stop by the church. Each one of us, when we were successful, felt that all the success was a blessing, and help from God, and the prayers of His saints. When we celebrated someone's graduation, we would say, "This year, St. Mary, St. Anthony, St. George, and St. Philopateer helped us, and we have to thank them with veneration." We would come together and light a candle before their icons and offer veneration, thanking them for their help. Afterward, we would have a meal together. These were the graduation celebrations. There is no objection to laughing and having a good time, in a Christian demeanor. Do you think that at the graduation parties that are celebrated with sinful activities, there is thanksgiving to God for His help and asking for His help in the upcoming year?

How do you make a new start? On New Year's Eve, some people save the very first minute of their lives in the New Year to ask our Lord to manage it. People who welcome the New Year in an inappropriate way give it to Satan to manage. If Satan will be taking the first moments of the New Year, what will this New Year look like? If Satan will be taking

---

12 "Mystery" is the term commonly used in Orthodox Churches rather than "Sacrament" as it conveys a more accurate meaning that is beyond our comprehension. There are seven Holy Mysteries observed in the Coptic Orthodox Church: (1) Baptism (2) Chrismation, (3) Confession, (4) Eucharist, (5) Matrimony (6) Unction of the Sick, (7) Priesthood.

the first few minutes of the newlyweds' lives, after the Holy Mystery of Matrimony, what will the result be and how will their lives be when they did not give it to God?

In birthday celebrations, we are ending one year and starting a new year. If the beginning of the New Year is given to Satan, with wrong and unsuitable birthday celebrations, do you think that this year will be a blessed year and that God will bless this year? Can I say, "Sweet year with Jesus" (sana helwa ma Yesoo)[13]? Jesus is the only person not invited to the party. Even if He were invited, He would not come.

Where is the Christian behavior in our families, which we pass on to our children? The child who he sees his father and mother drink and smoke at parties—can these parents ask him not to drink or smoke? He grew up seeing that at parties, drinking, smoking, dressing inappropriately, singing, and dancing are practiced, and this is engraved in his mind. Where is the joy? The verse says, "Rejoice in the Lord always. Again I will say, rejoice!" (Phil 4:4). Afterward, when our children grow up and go on the wrong path, we are upset and sad, and then, we run to church asking for help. What have I done? What have I planted? We need to pay attention to our lives. If a child rides in the car with his father and finds all types of song tapes or CDs, and when he sees his father at home up late watching inappropriate things on television, do you think after all this, the father can ask his child not to go to specific places or not to do these things? Consider the way our children dress, especially girls. When they see how their mothers dress at weddings or different events—do you think this girl will dress appropriately? When the parents agree with the way their children dress and say that they trust them, do you think after that, you can reap good fruit from your children? There are many things that parents do, but when their children imitate them, the parents become upset and start to complain.

St. Paul said to Timothy, as a bishop and father to the believers in his diocese, "Be an example to the believers in word, in conduct, in love, in spirit, in faith, in purity" (1 Tim 4:12). This verse can be addressed to parents regarding their children by replacing "the believers" with "your children." Be an example to your children in everything because your children will imitate you in the words that you use, your behavior, your

---

13 This is a common Christian folksong sung in Arabic at birthday celebrations, which means, "A good year with Jesus."

actions of love and dealings with others, your faith and relationship with God, your purity and chastity in your perception of issues, and your meek and gentle spirit. As the Lord said, "learn from Me, for I am gentle and lowly in heart" (Mt 11:29). St. Paul praises St. Timothy's "genuine faith that is in him [Timothy], which dwelt first in his [Timothy's] grandmother, Lois, and his [Timothy's] mother, Eunice" (2 Tim 1:5). This is the influence of role models on the children and grandchildren.

Some parents say, "I will not force my child to attend the church that I attend. I will put all the choices before him. If he wants to attend with the Copts, he can. If he wants to attend with the Catholics, he can. If he wants to attend with the Protestants, he can, because I am open-minded and liberal. I am teaching my children to choose for themselves. I will not force them. I will not force them to be Coptic just because I am Coptic." Here, the parent is tricking himself. He thinks that if he does not influence his child, no one else in the world will. In reality, you are giving your responsibility to someone else, and there *will* be someone else who comes and influences your child, and takes him outside the church and instills other values in him. Furthermore, perhaps these values are the opposite of what you intended to instill in him. Therefore, the idea of leaving your son, not telling him what to do, and letting him choose for himself means that you are abdicating your role to someone else. For a child to grow, he needs a role model. He needs an example.

I read some definitions for the term "role model." The following is one of the definitions, and while it is a little difficult, I liked it very much: "The role model is a psychological process [so it will happen with every one of us, with every one of our children]. It is a fundamental process in growth. [Following the example of the parent is a fundamental process in their growth.] It causes children to subconsciously imitate their parents to a very large extent, not only in imitating the parents' words, deeds, or actions, but also in imitating their parents' motives and intentions that caused them to say these words or carry out these deeds." Note, that the children will not only imitate the external attributes of the parents, but also the internal feelings and motivations that result in the parents' external actions. This happens subconsciously, as if they wear their parents' personalities as a starting point to generate from it their own personalities. The children have to start from a certain personality before they can create their own. Likewise, in using any theory, we always start from a certain theory and then modify it to fit our needs. Similarly, children need to have a starting point from which to generate their individual personalities, and this starting point is always the personality of the parents. They will also discover their skills and talents from the personality of the parents.

Since the role model will shape the personality of the children, the spiritual example set by the parents will shape the spiritual behavior of the children. I will make an interesting observation: Growing up, we all attended Sunday school and were given lessons. How many of us remember any of the specific lessons that were taught to us by our Sunday school teachers at an early age, like in the 5th or 6th grade? We have probably all forgotten these lessons. However, we all remember the personalities of the people who influenced us. We remember the example that they set for us, even though we have probably forgotten their exact words. This example shows us that the influence of the role model's personality is much stronger than the influence of sermons and words. You can lecture your children about the importance of prayer, but if they have never seen you praying, they will never pray. You can lecture your children about the dangers of smoking, but if you smoke, they will never be convinced with the words that you say, since you have not set an example yourself.

This is why being a role model is extremely important. If there is a contradiction between your words and your actions, the children will follow your actions. This is why we always say, "Before you teach, do." This is actually the sermon that is given to any priest on the day he is ordained. We tell new priests, "Pay attention to teaching through your actions more than through your words," because we recognize that his actions are much more influential on the people, as their role model, than his words. For example, Pope Cyril VI did not give many homilies in his lifetime, but the example he set influenced many people. This is the significance of being a good role model.

Once, a young boy came to confess, being very upset because his father yells at him for using the telephone too much. I told the boy that the phone should be used to deliver a message, something important, not for chatting. I advised him to use his time for something beneficial. The boy replied and said, "So why do my parents use the phone a lot? Why is it right for them, and not for me?" I began to defend the parents, saying that perhaps Dad and Mom are using the phone for something important, not to waste time. The child answered me and said, "No, Father, my mother uses the phone for two hours and talks about other people. And then they complain, and ask me not to use the phone!" Of course, I felt embarrassed, not knowing what to say to the child. This is evidence of role modeling.

Another time, a boy went out with his friends and smoked cigarettes, so the father came to me and asked me to talk with the boy. I told the boy that smoking cigarettes is a bad habit and a sin. The boy said, "Father, do not worry. I am not going to get addicted; I smoke cigarettes just for fun." I told the boy, "This is not true, because people who smoke cigarettes cannot quit, and when they started smoking, they said the same thing about smoking for fun." The boy said, "But, I see Dad and Mom when they have a party, they smoke cigarettes, although they do not smoke all the time. Why is it right for them and not right for me?" For the second time, I could not find an answer.

Setting a good example for your children will make you a *"living icon"* for your children. In Orthodox theology, an icon is a window into Heaven, since looking at an icon of any saint is like looking at someone in Paradise. Looking at an icon of the Lord Jesus Christ on His throne is like looking into Heaven. By becoming a good example to your children, you become an icon for your children, since they will see Heaven through you. The religious role model of how the parents worship God has an amazing influence on the children. The parents are forming the religious personalities of their children when they [the children] see the father and mother wake up in the morning to pray and stand before God with reverence, when the father regularly goes to church promptly, enters the church, bows down in front of the altar, and stands in his place with reverence, when they see their mother dress appropriately for church and stand with reverence before God in church. It is not surprising for Zacharias and Elizabeth, who were righteous before God, to be the parents of St. John the Baptist, who was filled with the Holy Spirit while in his mother's womb. Another example of the influence of the religious role model is Jochebed, the mother of Moses, who nursed him for a short time when young, and then, left him. In this short period, Jochebed was able to create and influence Moses's religious personality. St. Paul says, "Moses, when he became of age, refused to be called the son of Pharaoh's daughter, choosing rather to suffer affliction with the people of God than to enjoy the passing pleasures of sin, esteeming the reproach of Christ greater riches than the treasures in Egypt" (Heb 11:24-26). This was the effect of the personality of Jochebed, his mother, and her influence on her son, Moses.

A young child does not actually know God. To him, his parents are god, since he has the feeling that his parents are capable of doing anything for him. If he sees an airplane, he may ask his parents to buy him an airplane because he actually believes that they are capable of doing so for him. Therefore, for very young children, the parents should know that they are like gods. This worship of parents at a young age is a natural result of the child looking for God in the only people whom he knows. As the child starts to grow, he starts to realize the limitations of his parents, causing the worship of his parents to end, and the worship of the true God to develop. The danger in this is that the first perception (or image) of God that is created in any person's mind is the image of his parents. The initial picture a child forms about God is formed through his vision of his parents. Therefore, if the image of the parents was distorted, then so will the image of God. For example, why do some people think that God is very harsh? This is most likely because their parents were too harsh. Some people think that God is so compassionate and that there is no firmness in Him. This may be because their parents spoiled them.

6. Spiritual Upbringing

The final factor is spiritual upbringing. Even though teaching by example as a role model plays a critical role in the upbringing of the child, it does not cancel the parents' active roles in teaching and bringing up their children in the fear of God. This is why, as parents, you must plant spiritual values and habits in your children. How else would a person learn to do good deeds, pray, fast, partake of communion, repent, and confess, do works of mercy, serve, and read the Holy Bible? It must come from the parents. The disciples asked Jesus to teach them how to pray, just like John the Baptist taught his disciples. John the Baptist was a father to his disciples. That is why he was teaching them to pray. You also need to teach your children to pray.

Of course, teaching these habits and spiritual exercises must be done gradually. When you teach your children these habits, make sure to teach them with patience and progression, just as St. Paul says, "I fed you with milk and not with solid food; for until now you were not able to receive it" (1 Cor 3:2). Gradually, teach your children, with patience, how to pray, read the Holy Bible, fast, and do acts of mercy. Also, especially in teaching them service, you need to first discover their particular talents, interests, and gifts, so that when you direct them in how to serve the Lord, they will be successful. For example, a lot of parents want their children to be Sunday school teachers. However, it may very well be that these children do not have the talent for teaching and explaining, but have other talents, such as singing or music, for example. If I make the child teach in Sunday school despite his lack of talent in this field, the child may start to feel like a failure in service. If I encourage him towards serving the Lord according to his musical talent, for example, in the church choir, he will be able to serve the Lord much better. Therefore, we need to direct our children in their service according to their talents and gifts. Do not force your children to do something against their inclinations, but direct them to what suits them. Implanting these habits in our children requires effort from us. It is an active and gradual task.

To plant these habits, we go through three stages: "what," "how," and "why." In the child's first six years, we concentrate on "what." What are the habits that I want my child to develop? I do not concentrate on "how," yet, since the child is too young. Instead, we focus on teaching him what the habits are. I teach him that there are things called prayer, fasting, going to church, taking communion, etc. I do not focus on the details of how these things should be done correctly because the child is still young. The child may stand beside you to pray and be unfocused; this is because he is a child, maybe three or four years old. However, you are instilling in his mind the importance of prayer, that there is something called prayer. It is not time for "how to pray." Instill in him the concept of fasting. You may ask, "Even a five-year-old?" Yes. Tell him, "I am fasting." Maybe he will sneak behind your back and open the refrigerator to drink milk or eat. Close your eyes. This is not the time for "how." You are concentrating on the concept of "what"—the concept of fasting. Even in confession, tell him to go confess. He will not take more than a few seconds and Abouna will not be upset. He will be happy with him. The child needs to get used to sitting with Abouna and telling him things, so you instill in him the concept of confession. Instill in him the concept of charity, for example. Give him a dollar when he goes to his Sunday school class for him to donate to the church.

From age six to twelve, we concentrate on "how" these spiritual exercises should be done. Here, the parents' roles are to teach the child how to excel in all the spiritual exercises. They teach the child how to pray correctly using the Agpeya, how to fast correctly, how to repent and confess on a regular basis, how to tithe to the church from his limited money allowance, and how to study the Holy Bible correctly. The parents start to teach him and train him in how to excel in these spiritual habits. By the age of twelve, he should know how to do all of these things correctly.

From twelve to eighteen, we focus on "why," why it is important to do all these spiritual things. Now, the parents have to explain the reasons behind all these spiritual habits that they have been teaching the child, because at this age, the child wants to understand. Most problems happen when parents wait until the child reaches the age of twelve to start enforcing all these spiritual habits. At this point, the child is already old enough to question why these things are necessary, and since these habits are challenging to follow, he would be inclined to reject them. However, if he had developed these habits at a younger age and experienced their blessings, it is already second nature to him to do these things. Focusing on what the benefits of doing these things are will only serve to strengthen his attachment to these habits. He would say, "Actually, what you are saying makes sense. I experienced this in my life."

This is why the Lord tells the parents, "And these words which I command you today shall be in your heart. You shall teach them diligently to your children, and shall talk of them when you sit in your house, when you walk by the way, when you lie down, and when you rise up. You shall bind them as a sign on your hand, and they shall be as frontlets between your eyes. You shall write them on the doorposts of your house and on your gates" (Deut 6:6-9). This verse shows that you will have an active role in teaching them the Scripture and in planting spiritual habits in your children. If you neglect this spiritual responsibility for your children and you only care that they are successful in school and have money, they will have a poor, lukewarm relationship with the Lord. This weak relationship with God will be reflected in all the other areas in their lives because the Holy Bible says, "The Lord was with Joseph, and he was a successful man" (Gen 39:2). If you want your children to be successful, you must make sure they have a strong relationship with God. However, if you focus on all other measures of success for your children (grades in school, money, etc.), and do not focus on their relationship with God, they will not be successful.

I have explained four factors in this section. The first factor was parenting style, where four parenting styles were discussed and we concluded that the best kind of parenting is the authoritative method because it involves a balance between love and control. The second factor was the household atmosphere. We said that having a peaceful and loving household is a necessity for the successful upbringing of righteous children. The third factor was the role model, and parents serve as role models for their children and children project the image of their parents on God. Therefore, being good examples for our children will allow us to raise spiritual and balanced children. The fourth factor was spiritual upbringing, and we said that parents must play an active role in gradually teaching spiritual habits to their children and must do this in a manner that is appropriate for their specific age.

I want to warn you that parenting is a great responsibility, related to our own salvation. St. Paul says, referring to the mother, "Nevertheless she [the mother] will be saved in childbearing if they continue in faith, love, and holiness, with self-control" (1 Tim 2:15). Therefore, God will hold us accountable for how we raise our children. When Eli the priest neglected raising his children, God punished him. Of course, there are parents who exert great effort into raising their children correctly, but the children corrupt themselves. This is not the parents' fault. So as long as we do our part, God will be happy with us. However, if we neglect our children, we will definitely be accountable before the Lord.

D | SPIRITUAL MATURITY

1. In the World but Not of the World
2. Spiritual Maturity
3. Raising Spiritually Mature Children: Freedom and Decision-Making
4. Raising Spiritually Mature Children: Obedience

1. In the World but Not of the World

Our children are exposed to many external pressures in their lives. These pressures come from the environment in which one is living, the media and its influences, the Internet, non-Christian cultures, or from friends. All these outside influences affect the ability to correctly raise our children. It is very important for parents to have an interest in their children and in bringing them up in a sound, spiritual manner. This is to preserve their Christian principles and continuance in the Christian life, despite all the surrounding circumstances.

The Bible confirms, in more than one place, the importance of the children of God not conforming to the world, despite the fact that they live in the world. As we read in Romans 12:2, "Do not be conformed to this world, but be transformed by the renewing of your mind, that you may prove what is that good and acceptable and perfect will of God." This means that we must not take the form of the children of this world, "but be transformed" to obtain the image and likeness of God. We are created in the image of God and according to His likeness, being transformed into the same image. "Be transformed by the renewing of your mind," means that the renewal of the mind and the acceptance of a new enlightened mind—the mind of Christ, are what help a person to change his image. "That you may prove what is that good and acceptable and perfect will of God." If our children indeed are filled with the Holy Spirit and carry the fruit of the Spirit in their lives, they will have the best protection from all the influences and the external pressures by which they are surrounded.

2. Spiritual Maturity

The problem is that, often, when raising our children, we do not raise them to be spiritually mature. Many of us use the verse, "I fed you with milk and not with solid food" (1 Cor 3:2). They may be adults, twenty-five or thirty-years-old; yet, we still say, "It is okay, St. Paul said, 'I fed you with milk and not with solid food.'" In reality, St. Paul was admonishing his people in this verse, not using it as a principle. In 1 Corinthians 3, he told them, "For you are still carnal" (1 Cor 3:3). This is why there is still envy, strife, and divisions among you. This is why "I fed you with milk and not with solid food; for until now you were not able to receive it".

In Hebrews 5, he reproached the people for their lack of maturity. He told them, "For though by this time you ought to be teachers," meaning that being in Christ and in this faith for many years, they should have been teachers, yet, "You need someone to teach you again the first principles of the oracles of God" (Heb 5:12). You still need someone to teach you the ABC's of the spiritual life, "And you have come to need milk and not solid food," because you are still young children! He then says a serious phrase, "For everyone who partakes only of milk is unskilled in the word of righteousness, for he is a babe" (Heb 5:13). If the principle of "I fed you with milk and not with solid food" is followed, we are, then, bringing up children who will never reach spiritual maturity. If they are children, they will not assume any responsibility, nor can we trust their experience, as St. Paul says, "For everyone who partakes only of milk is unskilled ... but solid food belongs to those who are of full age, that is, those who by reason of use have their senses exercised to discern both good and evil" (Heb 5:13–14). The more a person grows, reaching spiritual maturity, the more he is able to discern both good and evil.

Are we raising our children only on milk? Who among us continues to feed his children milk until the age of young adulthood? They would never grow up to be healthy—hence, the necessity of weaning the child after a certain age, enabling him to eat adult food and to grow up. Nonetheless, often in the spiritual life, we continue in the concept of "I fed you with milk" for many years. This is the reason that we acquire a generation of young people and adults, perhaps with cultural or physical maturity, but lacking spiritual maturity. They are "unskilled in the word of righteousness," unable "to discern both good and evil."

The spiritually mature person, who is able to discern between good and evil, is able to assume responsibility in the setting of freedom, as St. Paul says in Galatians 5, "Only do not use liberty as opportunity for the flesh" (Gal 5:13). So, how could a person become responsible with the freedom that has been granted to him? This is what I wish to speak about in this chapter: How we can raise spiritually mature generations, who assume responsibility, to whom we are able to grant freedom, and when receiving it, do not use it as an opportunity for the flesh.

3. Raising Spiritually Mature Children: Freedom and Decision-Making

Many parents are afraid to give their children freedom lest they misuse it. Nonetheless, if we raise our children in the right way, leading them to spiritual maturity, when granting them freedom, they would neither abuse it nor use it as an opportunity for the flesh. Among the common mistakes parents make is not always bringing up children to become mature, to assume responsibility, to have the ability to make their own choices and decisions by themselves. On the contrary, parents continue to instruct their children on what must be done, making their decisions for them until t

They have grown up and moved out. Doing this is necessary for the first years of the upbringing; because the children are inexperienced, the parents must make decisions for them. However, as the children progressively mature, the parents are supposed to gradually give their children space for freedom, and simultaneously teaching them how to assume responsibility. In this manner, they form mature, spiritual personalities who are able to interact with society and with the outside world, affecting it without being influenced by it.

Therefore, it is not enough to protect children from the present, but when raising them, we need to prepare them for the future, so that when they leave home, they are able to handle the outside world in peace and with safety.

We have noticed that the universities outside Egypt are generally far from the youths' hometowns and that the most perversity they experience is during the first year of university. Many children earn college scholarships, meaning they made the best grades and were outstanding in school; nonetheless, during the first year at university, they can lose it all. Why? It is because they fail to handle the freedom that was given to them when they were living by themselves. They were not prepared for it. They did not have enough maturity to take advantage of this freedom and handle it with enough responsibility. Perhaps the household did not adequately prepare their children for how to handle freedom in a frame of responsibility during this period of time.

In raising children, we must begin by giving them choices, teaching them to choose what is right, and forsaking evil. We must assign some responsibilities to them, teaching and training them to assume responsibility, and to give an account of this before the Lord and the family. We must also teach and train them how to make decisions. Often, we see children who must make a decision, but they do not know how to do so, and they want someone else to make it for them. They would, for example, ask their parents or their father of confession to make the decision, and perhaps the parents would be happy to do so, although it is not in the child's best interest. This shows us that the child is not able to depend on himself or to take responsibility for his decision. It is better to teach the child how to make his own decision and to take responsibility for his decisions.

4. Raising Spiritually Mature Children: Obedience [For more on obedience, see Part I, G.]

In order to lead our children to spiritual maturity, we also need to teach them how to submit and obey those who are in authority and a position of responsibility. One of the biggest problems of our generation is the rebellion against every authority—the authority of the parents, the church, the country, and even rebelling against God's authority. Sometimes, when given freedom to express their opinions, this freedom turns into a slew of insults and inappropriate attacks—a consequence of never learning how to express opinions in the proper manner. Yet, we say, "It is a freedom of speech!" This is because we are not accustomed to assuming responsibility. Even if we do assume responsibility, we are not accustomed to handling it with dependability, due to a lack of an inner feeling of a sense of duty. Thus, it is important to teach submission and obedience to children in their early years to teach them how to obey and to submit to their superiors. It is very easy for a person to rebel. Nonetheless, the mature personality is the one who submits out of love and compliance. However, people sometimes think the opposite, that the rebellious character is the strong one. No, anyone can be stubborn and rebel. The real strength lies in the person who submits with responsibility, love, and compliance.

The point is to teach our children the difference between the obedience of children and that of slaves—obedience out of love and not out of fear. There is a difference between abjectness and submission, where the latter is obedience from free will. With my free will, I submit to the one who is responsible for me. I submit because I love him. I submit because I trust him. An example of submission is when our Lord Jesus Christ said in Gethsemane, "Nevertheless, not as I will, but as You will" (Mt 26:39). St. Paul spoke about the submission of the Son to the Father in 1 Corinthians 15; the Son submitted to the Father in love and trust. Only the spiritually mature person is able to do this.

Thus, we can teach our children the submission of love and not the one of slaves or fear, as St. John says in 1 John 4:18, "There is no fear in love; but perfect love casts out fear." Take heed that teaching obedience to our children is the responsibility of both parents. The responsibility does not only belong either to the mother, or the father, alone, but both of the parents are together responsible for teaching obedience to their children.

a. Some Parents Feel Uneasy Teaching Children Obedience

Some parents feel uneasy teaching their children obedience when using their authority as parents, for many wrong reasons. The first cause of this uneasiness is perhaps feeling that this is against the parents' love for their children. They feel that if they love them, they are supposed to allow them to do as they please, although, in reality, parents who spoil their children and never teach them submission raise a generation of unruly children who have no sense of responsibility. We see that these children most likely fail academically, as they are not accustomed to commitment and submission or to having a spirit of responsibility so that they study, succeed, and excel. The parents raise them in an atmosphere of indulgence. Hence, the child never learns how to become self-disciplined.

Another reason some parents feel uneasy is the fear that they would lose their children's love. They think that by being firm with them, their children may not love them. Thus, they let the children do as they please. This reminds me of the last verse in the book of Judges, when the Holy Bible described the people of Israel: "In those days there was no king in Israel; everyone did what was right in his own eyes" (Judg 21:25). Things were a mess. Everyone was doing whatever seemed to be fitting for him or her. There was no structure or responsibility, nor was there any authority.

In any country, as soon as its authority has lost solemnity, you find corruption. The same applies to the family. As soon as the parents lose their authority, the household becomes corrupted. The household is edifying for the children only when the parents have their authority. The children need to grow up in a home with structure and responsibility. It should not be like Israel in the last age of the Judges when "everyone did what was right in his own eyes".

Often, parents get a misplaced sense of guilt when taking a firm stand with their children in order to teach them obedience and submission. This guilt makes them become lenient. Their conscience is very sensitive and weak. A sensitive conscience has many problems; it forbids what the Lord has authorized. On the other hand, the loose conscience authorizes what the Lord has forbidden. As for the enlightened conscience approved by the Holy Spirit, it sees matters for what they really are. St. Paul describes the weak and sensitive conscience in Romans, "But he who is weak eats only vegetables" (Rom 14:2). The weak conscience is easily defiled, saying that eating meat is sinful, so the individual eats only vegetables and refuses to eat meat! Not only is the weak conscience defiled, but also, it is also easily disturbed when becoming firm with their children, and therefore, they avoid using authority with their children.

Sometimes uneasiness is caused by the parents not having enough self-confidence to be able to handle their children, especially if a child begins to exhibit some stubbornness while still young. This type of parent does not have the feeling of strength and confidence in his ability to handle the child, and thus, he takes the easy way out by leaving the child. Raising children in a positive manner and taking the role and position of a responsible parent requires effort. Therefore, perhaps it is easier to let the child behave as he pleases, transferring the entire responsibility onto the church, saying, "I have sent my children to church and Sunday school." If the child grows up misbehaving, the church is blamed for not disciplining and paying attention to him or her! This is not right. Parents have a role and a responsibility to carry out toward their children. Consequently, if parents do not take this role, responsibility, and authority in teaching their children submission and obedience, the children will grow up to become irresponsible, never respecting any authority.

b. Parents Need to Exercise Authority

Parents must have authority in order to facilitate the healthy growth of their children and the fulfillment of their need for psychological safety. As mentioned earlier, if you live in a country and you feel that the authority of the country is strong and fair, that it has its solemnity and respect, then you feel safe in that country. However, when the authority has lost its solemnity and respect, and has no place, you feel insecure because of the spreading corruption. The same applies on the family level. The more the children feel that their parents are taking on the role of the ones responsible for the household, claiming their authority as parents, the more this fulfills the child's and the youth's need for safety in the home.

Even our Lord, our God, the compassionate, the kind, and meek, deals with us as a Father, with authority over us. He also teaches us obedience and submission to Him. One of the things that comfort us very much is that God is the Pantocrator[14]. This means that He has authority over everything. Every time a person sees difficulties coming to his life, he remembers that the Lord is the Almighty, with power over all creation. Living under the protection of a God who is all-powerful and has real authority provides tranquility and a feeling of safety.

During the month of Paope[15], all the Sunday Gospel readings confirm to us this point of God's authority. The Gospel reading on the first Sunday is about God's authority over sickness, through the healing of the paralytic man. The second Sunday is about God's authority over nature, through the abundance of fish caught. The third Sunday is about God's authority over the evil spirits, through the healing of the man who was blind, demon possessed, and mute. The fourth Sunday is about God's authority over death, through the raising the son of the widow of Nain from the dead. Human beings actually have no authority over these four things. A human being has no authority over many kinds of sicknesses. There are so many illnesses that medicine is still unable to heal. The human being has no authority over nature—standing, along with science, incompetent before natural disasters. The human being has no authority over evil spirits, unless he has received the gift from the Lord of casting out evil spirits; in this manner, his gift is received from the Holy Spirit. However, the ordinary human being has no authority to cast out demons. Also, a human being has no authority over death. Why did the Church put these four Gospel readings for us during the month of Paope—that God, the Son, our Creator has authority over illness, nature, evil spirits, and death? These liturgical readings give us the feeling of security of being

---

14 Greek word meaning Omnipotent God of the universe; Almighty ruler—used especially for Christ, Merriam Webster Dictionary.

15 The Coptic month of Paope is from the 11th of October until the 9th of November (will change in a leap year).

under the care of a mighty God, a capable God, and the Almighty God. Similarly, when our children feel that their parents have authority, they are provided with a feeling of safety and tranquility.

In turn, teaching children obedience and submission, using the authority as a father or as a mother, is the sign of true love for the children. "For whom the Lord loves He chastens" (Heb 12:6). The sign of God's love is that He uses His authority to correct and discipline His children. Similarly, the use of the parents' authority, as a father or as a mother, is a sign of their or love for their children.

When children are taught submission and obedience, especially in the spirit of love and wisdom and not in a spirit of control or of a desire to dominate, they are provided with the ability to grow up with strong personalities. There is a difference between wanting to dominate and control, and using your authority and responsibility as a parent. Using authority in the spirit of love and wisdom remedies the strong will power of our children; it makes them assume responsibility. Moreover, because the children learned obedience and submission at home, they also learn obedience and submission to God, to people in authority, and to anyone in a position of responsibility. They do so with love and out of satisfaction, not out of fear or obligation. Furthermore, the use of this authority, with love and wisdom, not with violence, austerity, or severity, helps in disciplining the children, especially children with strong will power. We call these children, "stubborn." When he is only a few months old, the characteristics of stubbornness become apparent in his personality. How could you discipline this child? You must use your authority. Similarly, the use of this authority makes the children successful academically as well as professionally. The use of this authority disciplines the entire household, allowing for the spirit of peace, love, and joy to reign over the home, rather than the spirit of chaos, dispute, and looseness reigning over the home and among the family.

E | SPIRITUAL DEVELOPMENT OF CHILDREN

1. Love

2. Identity

3. Forgiveness

4. Enthusiasm

5. Answers to Various Questions

What does your child need in order for him to be a spiritual being? Parents transfer God's life to their children, and this is how our children become spiritual beings. The word "life"—God's life—gives us four cornerstones, which are needed in order to build our children's spiritual lives.

    L : Love

    I : Identity

    F : Forgiveness

    E : Enthusiasm

1. Love

For our children to grow as spiritual beings, they have to experience God's love in their lives and they have to be able to share God's love with others. Without experiencing God's love in their lives and without sharing it with others, they cannot become spiritual beings. This is because "God is love" (1 Jn 4:8). This is a very important point. The best way to transfer God's love to your children is by loving them as God has loved you. Think of God's love for you and start treating your children as God has treated you.

In our minds, love is a feeling or emotion; however, when we read 1 Corinthians 13, we do not find a single verse that describes love as an emotion. Rather, all the verses are about love as an action: Love suffers long (verse 4), love hopes in all things (verse 7), love is not provoked (verse 5), love thinks no evil (verse 5), love does not behave rudely (verse 5) and love does not seek its own (verse 5). Did you read anything about feelings in any of these verses? No. These verses address love as an action. Also, St. Paul says, "remembering without ceasing your work of faith, *labor of love*, and patience of hope in our Lord Jesus Christ" (1 Thess 1:3). Therefore, love is an action and not an emotion or a feeling. If love were only emotions and feelings, we would all have a big problem because God tells us to "Love your enemies" (Lk 6:27). How would I be able to develop emotions and feelings in my heart towards my enemy? It is almost impossible. We are all human, and these emotions and feelings do not exist in our hearts. What God is asking here is to perform acts of love toward your enemy, such as to tolerate him, hope for good for him, be patient with him, do not be angry with him, think no evil of him, do not behave rudely with him, and do not seek what is your own before what is your enemy's.

When I start doing these acts of love, God will develop feelings and emotions of love in my heart. No one has control over one's feelings. God gives us these feelings. However, I have control over my actions and my will. Thus, love starts by actions. When God sees how faithful we are in our actions and deeds, He will grant us the emotions and feelings.

When God loved us, He *gave* Himself, "For God so loved the world that *He gave* His only begotten Son, that whoever believes in Him should not perish but have everlasting life" (Jn 3:16). God did not say, "My heart is full of feelings and emotions toward you." Rather, God loved and God gave. He was incarnate and died on the cross for our sakes. The same applies with your love toward your children; express your love in actions. If you love your children, you should be willing to show your love by actions.

Love takes time. Children have to experience your love toward them. You cannot say, "I love my children" while being disconnected from them. This is especially true for fathers. Sometimes, fathers are too busy at work, and consequently, have no relationship with their children. When the mother or the children complain about his absence, the father always responds by saying, "I work so hard and for many hours for you." In addition, many fathers also grew up with disengaged fathers, so they could be repeating a familiar pattern with their own children. Children need a one-on-one relationship with their fathers. Do something for them, such as play with them, take them out, hug them, kiss them, talk to them, spend time with them, listen to them, etc. All these actions will show them that you love them, because love is a relationship. You are in a relationship with them.

How can children experience love toward God? Children call you, "father," and when they pray, they say, "Our Father who art in heaven." If children do not experience the love of their own fathers toward them, this will be projected negatively on their heavenly Father. Children develop a picture or an image of the heavenly Father based on the image they have developed of their parents. This is a very serious point. You are either giving them an accurate or a distorted image of God, because children see God's love in you.

This is the reason that when children have problems with their parents and rebel against their authority, they also immediately rebel against the authority of God and the Church. Consequently, they stop going to church and refuse to talk to or deal with the priest. This is the consequence of rebelling against their parents. Therefore, the first thing parents need to do to help their children establish themselves as spiritual beings is to let them experience God's love in their lives. Facilitate for them the opportunity to experience God's love in their lives.

2. Identity

The second point is identity. The question here is, "What is my identity in relationship to God?" In reality, we have no identity away from God because we are created by God and for God. "For by Him all things were created that are in heaven and that are on earth, visible and invisible, whether thrones or dominions or principalities or powers. All things were created through Him and for Him" (Col 1:16). God wants us to be in His image and according to His likeness. "Then God said, 'Let Us make man in Our image, according to Our likeness'" (Gen 1:26). Therefore, my identity is that I am the son or daughter of God. If I truly see myself as such, this will determine my behavior and how I react in the world.

Joseph the righteous always perceived and understood himself as a son of God, even before the Ten Commandments were given. Therefore, when he was offered the opportunity to sin, he refused to accept the offer. He said, "How then can I do this great wickedness, and sin against God?" (Gen 39:9). I am a son of God! How can I sin against Him? I cannot do this, because I am a child of God. I cannot sadden His heart.

This point about identity is very important because it will protect children from drifting away. This applied to Moses. His identity was that he was one of the people of God. That is why he chose to suffer shame with the people of God rather than to enjoy the pleasure of sin (Heb 11:25). Moreover, Moses refused to be identified as the son of Pharaoh's daughter; that was not his identity. Rather, his identity was that he was one of God's people: "By faith Moses, when he became of age, *refused to be called* the son of Pharaoh's daughter, *choosing* rather to suffer affliction with the *people of God* than to enjoy the passing pleasures of sin, esteeming the reproach of Christ greater riches than the treasures in Egypt; for he looked to the reward" (Heb 11:24-26).

That is our identity! Children should know that they are sons and daughters of God, that they are the light of the world and that they have to shine God's light unto others. When this identity is present and clear before our children, they will not drift away. This identity will determine how they behave in the world.

There were two young children in Egypt who preferred to fail an exam rather than deny their identity as Christians. Their mother had instilled in her two sons that it is better to fail an academic exam, repeat the school year, and suffer shame, than to deny their identity in the Lord Christ. We often sacrifice our identity as Christians for the sake of education, or money, or something else. This requires transformation, as St. Paul said, "And do not be conformed to this world, but be transformed by the renewing of your mind, that you may prove what is that good and acceptable and perfect will of God" (Rom 12:2). When I acquire the mind that I am Christian and I am a son or daughter of God, I will be able to suffer shame, persecution, or hardships in my life for the name of the Lord Christ. This attitude will determine all the steps and actions I will take in my life. Therefore, the question becomes, "What identity are you planting in your child?"

In order for them to know that they are children of God, for you to plant this identity within them, you have to teach your children God's will. You have to sit and read the Holy Bible with them and give them Bible studies. You have to identify the gifts that God planted in them, and how to use these gifts for God's glory. You have to teach them to respect the Ten Commandments and how to apply them in their lives and when dealing with others. God did not give us the Ten Commandments in order for us to memorize and recite them. He gave them to us to live by them. When we ask a child about the Ten Commandments and he recites them, we become very pleased and say, "Good job!" It is good as a start, but he has to be taught how to live by them. The first four commandments regulate our relationship with God and the last six regulate our relationships with others. The Ten Commandments used to be summarized in only two commandments. The first is, "Love the Lord your God," and the second is, "Love your neighbor as yourself." "On these two commandments hang all the Law and Prophets" (Mt 22:37-40).

That is why when someone came to ask the Lord Jesus Christ about how to inherit eternal life, the Lord asked him what was written in the law. To that, he answered that one must love God and his neighbor as himself. Jesus told him, "do this and you will live" (Lk 10:25-28). If I know that I am a child of God, then I will respect the Ten Commandments and I will apply them. Pray with your children, take them to church, and train them to be committed to God and to their relationship with Him. When you establish this Christian identity in your children and a strong feeling of belonging to God and the Church, your children will become spiritual beings.

3. Forgiveness

The third point in their spiritual development is forgiveness. We discussed earlier that there are four needs or cornerstones in developing children's spirituality: **L**ove, **I**dentity, **F**orgiveness, and **E**nthusiasm (LIFE). Why is forgiveness important to our lives and to the building of our spirituality? Why is it a need? It is simply because all of us are sinners. We all sin. Consequentially, we hurt one another whether intentionally or unintentionally. There is no one among us who could say, "I have never hurt anyone in my life." No one would believe it. Similarly, no one can say, "I have never been hurt by anybody." No one would believe that either. All of us have hurt someone and have been hurt by someone. All of us have experienced this, without exception, because all of us are sinners.

That is why all of us need forgiveness. We need to forgive and to accept forgiveness. Therefore, we cannot live a spiritual life without forgiveness. That is why in the Lord's Prayer, God made forgiveness something to be remembered every time we pray, "And forgive us our debts, as we forgive our debtors" (Mt 6:12). If you want to build spirituality in your children, teach them how to forgive and how to accept forgiveness. The best way to teach forgiveness is to forgive your child as God has forgiven you. When children learn that there is forgiveness and when they experience it through the way you react to them, they will learn how to forgive by the example that you set.

When a child comes to you and says, "I am sorry," do not rebuff the child and say, "I am mad at you. Leave me alone now." Instead, immediately respond by saying, "I forgive you." When David confessed his sin in front of Nathan the prophet, Nathan immediately responded by saying that the Lord had forgiven him: "So David said to Nathan, 'I have sinned against the Lord.' And Nathan said to David, 'The Lord also has put away your sin'" (2 Sam 12:13). Compare this with when your child comes and says, "sorry," and you respond by saying, "What do you mean, 'Sorry?' Leave. I am busy right now!" This attitude will not teach forgiveness to children, no matter how many lectures you give them on forgiveness.

Forgiveness does not mean that we do not teach or discipline. "Therefore bear fruits worthy of repentance" (Lk 3:8). When Nathan told David that he is forgiven, he told him that there would be consequences for his sin: "However, because by this deed you have given great occasion to the enemies of the Lord to blaspheme, the child also who is born to you shall surely die" (2 Sam 12:14). After I assure the child that I have forgiven him, in a spirit of love, I have to explain that forgiveness does not mean that there is no discipline. There will be some consequences. Forgiveness means to pardon a debt. There is nothing against the child, now. However, a measure of discipline is needed to teach the child how to grow as a spiritual being and in order to keep this mistake from happening again in the future.

Forgiveness has to be immediate and unconditional. Tell your children that you forgive them. Do not hold onto their prior mistakes. Do not keep reminding the children of their previous sins. God tells us, "For I will be merciful to their unrighteousness, and their sins and their lawless deeds I will remember no more" (Heb 8:12). God promised not to remember our sins. Do not keep reminding your children of their past sins and how bad they are or were. Otherwise, your children will never learn to forgive others.

Encourage the children to forgive one another. When the children fight and argue at home, you have to teach them how to apologize to each other by guiding them in how to say, "I am sorry," and, "I forgive you." In this way, you teach them how to give and accept forgiveness.

Many adults complain that when they argue with their spouses, the other spouse never says, "sorry." This is because when they were young children, they were not taught to apologize when they were wrong. They were not taught to offer and accept forgiveness, and therefore, this flaw stayed with them into adulthood and marriage. That is why it is important to teach young children forgiveness.

If there is a repeated mistake, then without repeating all of his previous mistakes, you can say, "I see a pattern here." You could mention a single incident as a reminder without listing all of the prior mistakes. We have to let go of the past. When we make a mistake and go and confess, the mistake is forgiven. Even if we make the same mistake again, it will be considered a new mistake because the old sin was forgiven.

Let go of anger. Do not be angry with your children and avoid them for days. This does not teach forgiveness. Learn how to deal with the children in a spirit of love and grace to be able to teach them the truth. Withdrawing from your child is not the correct way to discipline him. However, you can discipline your children in grace. Hold a Bible study on forgiveness with the children. Study Chapter 18 in the Holy Gospel according to St. Matthew and the parable about forgiveness. Teach your children that God will be greatly disappointed with us if we do not forgive one another, and that He will not forgive our sins if we do not forgive one another.

Share with the children the stories of the saints, which teach forgiveness. For example, in the story of Anba Abraam the Bishop of Fayum, two people were fighting and refused to reconcile with each other. They came to see him and explained to him what was happening. He asked them to pray with him. He started to pray the Lord's Prayer and when he reached, "And forgive us our trespasses, as we forgive those who trespass against us," he prayed, "And *do not* forgive us our trespasses, *because we do not* forgive those who trespass against us." One of the two said, "Your Grace, that is not how it goes!" So he answered, "Are we going to lie to God?" When children hear these stories when they are still young, they will learn that what they recite daily in their prayers is not just words. "Forgive us our trespasses as we forgive those who trespass against us," must be a way of life.

When your children are angry, listen to their feelings. After listening to their angry feelings, correct them, discipline them, and teach them that this is not the proper way to express anger. Do not shun them and leave, because the child will not learn and understand forgiveness if you act this way. Listen to his angry feelings. It is a good opportunity to teach your child how to express his anger properly. If you leave him, he will never learn how to express his anger in the right way.

Be warm and connected to your children while disciplining them, because disconnection is a threat to their safety. That is the spirit of grace. Remember that when God disciplines us, He does so without disconnecting Himself from us.

4. Enthusiasm

The last need for the spiritual development of our children is enthusiasm. Enthusiasm is derived from a Greek word *entheos*. "En" means *in*. "Theos" means *God*, so "En" + "Theos" = *In God*. So, enthusiasm means be "in God." When we are in God, we will be energetic, enthusiastic, live a godly life, and fight the devil. We become motivated to keep our righteousness and godliness. That is why enthusiasm is very important. People who suffer from depression are completely unmotivated. Sometimes, it is even hard for them to get out of bed or be motivated to do anything during the day. Conversely, the people who are happy and joyful are full of excitement and energy. They are motivated to do many things at the same time. For our children to have spiritual lives and to keep their spiritual identity, they have to be full of energy to fight Satan, and to fight the world and its ungodliness. They will not be excited about their Christianity and they will not be able to fight unless they are full of enthusiasm.

When Nehemiah came to Jerusalem and asked about the inhabitants of the land, he was told that the people had no spirit; they felt defeated and were full of shame.[16] "They said to me, 'The survivors who are left from the captivity in the province are there in great distress and reproach'" (Neh 1:3). Most of the people, perhaps all of them, were depressed. When Nehemiah wanted to rebuild the walls of Jerusalem, he filled the people with enthusiasm. He told them, "the joy of the Lord is your strength" (Neh 8:10). When they were full of joy, enthusiasm, and commitment, they were able to build the walls of Jerusalem. Nehemiah was able to transfer the joy of the Lord to their hearts and to motivate them. Everyone participated in building the walls of Jerusalem. This is because Nehemiah filled their hearts with joy. He motivated them and made them enthusiastic, committed, and dedicated to their relationship with God. Therefore, they were able to rebuild the walls of Jerusalem.

Success always leads to more success. When we succeed in small things, we become encouraged and succeed in greater things. This is why we should fill our children's hearts with the joy of the Lord to make them enthusiastic. We can do this by supporting them through Christian and godly friendships. If our children's friends are spiritual and are

---

16 Cf. Nehemiah, Chapter 1, Old Testament Prophet.

children of God, this will keep our children in a spiritual atmosphere, and consequently, they will be spiritual beings. Therefore, encourage your children to choose spiritual friends.

Teach them how to live a dynamic Christian life. Spiritual life is never static. It is life in action. One of the things that bothers me is when we are in church and decide to sing a hymn. Usually, only one or two people sing! There is no enthusiasm. In Egypt, during the Divine Liturgy, at the time of "Amen, Amen, Amen," the church almost shakes from the people's enthusiasm. Everyone is singing and praying. On the other hand, here, the deacon is the only one singing and praying this part. Where is the enthusiasm? In the liturgy book, this response is titled, "People," and not, "Deacon." Where is the enthusiasm? Why do we not all sing together with loud voices praising God? Why do all of us not act as one? Teach your children to participate. When you pray together at home and you cannot hear your children's voices singing or praying out loud (responding and saying, "Kyrie eleyson," for example), stop and tell them that you want to hear everyone's voice. If children are used to praying out loud and participating in prayers at home, when they go to church, they will participate. The same applies when the children are in Sunday school with their servants. Stop and tell them that you want to hear their voices. When you are singing a hymn, tell the children that we are praising the Lord and that everyone should not only participate, but also participate enthusiastically. Sometimes people are completely disconnected from the prayers. Servants should actively pursue and encourage the children to participate in both prayers and praises. That is how you plant a dynamic Christian life in their hearts.

This is how you teach children to experience the joy of the Lord, the joy of worship, and the joy of being with God. Always teach children that life with God is constantly full of joy, even during times of suffering. Yes, life with God is a narrow gate and a difficult way, but it is full of joy—the joy of the Lord. When they live in the joy of the Lord, the joy of the Lord will be their strength and it will fill them with energy, enthusiasm, and commitment to the Church.

If we are successful in developing these four cornerstones in our children—love, identity, forgiveness, and enthusiasm—they will become spiritual beings.

5. Answers to Various Questions

The Son demonstrated to us the love of God. "For God so loved the world that He gave His only begotten Son, that whoever believes in Him should not perish but have everlasting life" (Jn 3:16). Therefore, when we see the Son on the cross, we are assured that God the Father loves us, to the extent that He gave His only begotten Son to die on the cross for the life of the world.

God the Son sent us the Holy Spirit, who proceeds from God the Father, in order for Him to be in us and to have God's image and likeness in our lives. When the Holy Spirit lives in us, He will transform us to be in the image and likeness of God.

As the Son demonstrated the love of God the Father and sent us the Holy Spirit, parents should transfer God's life to their children's lives. Successful parenting, therefore, is when parents succeed in this transferring process. In your parenting, what image of God are you transferring to your children? Do your children think of God as: 1) very loving and without any discipline; or 2) very cruel, always angry, and upset with me; or 3) "Mercy and truth have met together; Righteousness and peace have kissed" (Ps 85:10)? What image of God do your children have? The image of God that the children develop is the product of internalizing their parents' relationship with them. Through your relationship with your children, they will build a relationship with God. These two elements contribute to building the self-image of your children. Self-image is the way they perceive themselves. Their self-image is that they are Christians and the children of God. That is their identity. In order to develop a godly and spiritual self-image, they have to have a healthy self-image about God and internalize a godly relationship between themselves and their parents.

If we succeed in giving children the healthy and correct image of God, and simultaneously they internalize a godly image regarding their relationship with their parents, the children's self-image, as spiritual beings in relationship to God, will be healthy. In this way, parents can succeed in developing the spiritual identity of their children.

Sometimes, we feel that we need to hide our identity when we are outside of church. We do not have to do this. I have to carry my identity with my wherever I go. Daniel refused to eat the king's food. Why? Daniel was a child of God and was not ashamed to carry his identity with him wherever he was. Our children are sometimes ashamed to identify themselves as "Coptic Orthodox." They hide their identity by saying, "I am Christian" or "I go to a Baptist church," just so they can feel that they go to a *regular* church like the rest of the children. Why? We must teach our children to be proud of who they are. They should be proud to bear witness to the Lord Christ, their Church, and their identity. Look at Muslim children, for example. Despite all the attacks on Islam, young girls wear the hijab and are not ashamed or embarrassed by it, but rather are proud of who they are and of their identity. Furthermore, they demand that others accept and respect them and their religion.

We should teach our children not to be ashamed of who they are. On the contrary, they should be proud of who they are and present themselves with joy and pride—pride in a good manner is pride in the Lord Christ.

There was a question about what our children should do regarding Halloween when celebrated in schools. The child or youth can tell the teacher, "We do not celebrate Halloween." I actually wrote an article about this. In a society that teaches tolerance, often, students are pressured to engage in various forms of festivities deemed as "harmless," even if they do not agree with these principles. If the teacher disagrees, you should talk to him or her and say, "How is it that you teach tolerance, and yet, do not tolerate my child's beliefs? You have to respect my son's beliefs; otherwise, do not talk about tolerance."

We must start with our children when they are young. If we plant all these things in our children, starting from their infancy, it is much easier than when they are fourteen, fifteen, and sixteen years old. However, it is never too late. Perhaps the fruit will not come as early as when I plant these teachings in a younger child who is, for example, two or three years old. It may take much more time and effort, but if we insist on teaching and disciplining them in the way of the Lord, we will reap good fruit. The first point is to not lose hope. If you lose hope about planting and transferring these principles to your child, you will lose your enthusiasm. God, who changed Saul, Moses the Strong, Mary the Egyptian, and others, is capable of changing your child. God is able to work; therefore, do not ever lose hope in your children, regardless of how far they are.

The second point is to create an atmosphere of grace. In this atmosphere, try to establish the truth of the Lord. This may be through discipline, teaching, or learning to bear the consequences of their behavior. Discipline will take great effort from you and they will be very resistant to your efforts. However, in an atmosphere of love and godly grace, gradually, you will be able to see a transformation in the lives of the children.

Maybe the children refuse to pray with you. However, you can use the time that you are with the children in the car or at the dinner table to teach them a story from the Holy Bible or from a homily or lecture that you heard. Try to indirectly teach them spiritual principles and convey the grace of God. If they are not willing to listen directly, try the indirect approach through stories or your interactions with them. If, at a certain point, they do not want to listen directly or indirectly, show them the Lord Christ in you. The children will look at your image and example and will imitate you.

The third point is to be an example and a role model. At the age of fourteen and fifteen, children always look for a role model. Be that role model for your children. When they see forgiveness in you, when they see you praying, when they see that you go to church and worship God in reverence, they will learn these behaviors from you, even without any sermons.

Our church servants in Egypt influenced us greatly when we were younger—when we saw how they were worshiping the Lord in fear and reverence. I cannot forget this image until today. When a 15-year-old wakes up every day and sees his father and mother praying the Agpeya (Coptic Prayer Book of the Hours) together in reverence, this will impact him. Someone told me a very nice story that demonstrates this point. When this person first immigrated to the United States, he lived with his sister and her husband, who were not religious and did not have a relationship with God. This young man was a servant in church and was committed to praying his morning and night prayers. After three months, his sister and her husband told him that they wanted to start praying with him. He did not talk to them about prayer, but they saw him committed to prayer, and they started to pray as a family. There was a transformation in this family. They were adults, but the presence of a godly person among them changed them. We usually say that sin is contagious. Godliness and righteousness are also contagious and can influence others.

We addressed three points: 1) not losing hope, 2) implementing love with control, grace with truth, and disciplining in a warm way, and 3) being an example. I am sure that if you apply these points with your children, you will reap fruit. However, do not demand fruit quickly. Plant the seed and in the opportune time, God will give you a harvest.

Something else to consider is how to intervene in the time of their need. Once, there was a young man who had no relationship with God, and had several sinful relationships. His mother used to come and complain about him to the clergy. We repeatedly tried to reach out to him and to check on him; however, he never returned our phone calls for almost four or five years. The church continued its efforts to contact him regularly by phone, email, and mail, leaving him messages asking about him and saying they would love to see him in church and would be happy if he were with them in the church. They also sent him announcements from the church.

Four or five years later, this young man had problems with his girlfriend and she left him. He had been very attached to her and was going through a hard time because of the break-up. Do you know whom he called first? The first call he made, to seek help and guidance, was to the church. In his heart, he knew that the church loves and cares about him, because for four or five years they were committed to asking about him, even though he never returned their calls. The follow-up in asking about him put in his heart that these people loved him and were worried about him. Thus, he called the church and explained how depressed he was because of the break-up with his girlfriend. The church asked him to come and talk about it. When he went, they did not tell him, "You deserve this, because we told you this was a sinful relationship." On the contrary, the church understood his feelings. There is a difference between understanding feelings and approving feelings. There is a difference between saying, "I understand that you are going through a difficult time in your life," and saying, "What you are doing is okay." Understanding does not mean, "This is right."

The church told him, "Let us pray together." The prayer was said in the following way: "God, You know how his heart is troubled by this break-up. God, You are able to give him peace and joy." The prayers were done in a very nice and nonjudgmental way. Afterword, this young man started to feel some peace. Little by little, he started to grow closer to the priest and the church, and he was invited to attend the youth meeting, which he started to attend, etc. He was still not very interested in religion or Christianity. However, because he was placed in the right atmosphere, a transformation started to occur in his life. On his own, he came to the realization that his relationship with his girlfriend was wrong. He was the one who came to this conclusion. This story happened approximately four years ago and now this young man is very active in the church and serves in Sunday school.

Our children who are apathetic and disconnected will experience hardship in their lives. This is a time where they will need support. This time of hardship refers to any time of need, such as a break-up (like in the aforementioned story), an illness, not getting a certain job, a bad grade on a test, etc. In all these instances, children are vulnerable, and this is the best time for intervention because it is always easy to influence a vulnerable soul. Therefore, during their times of vulnerability, we should show them the love and grace of God in a gentle way without being judgmental. If we are perceptive, do not let the right moment pass, and intervene in a good way, we will be able to transfer God's love and grace to our children.

That is why it is very important to invite people to accept God's grace and love at times of illness or during funerals. However, there is an important point to consider. To be able to intervene at a time of vulnerability, you must have expressed God's love previously. Like in the story mentioned above, the young man received the message that the church loves him because the church continued to contact him, despite the fact that he never returned a phone call for four to five years. We sometimes call someone for five to six months and then stop calling because he did not return our calls. God loves at all times and says, "Behold, I stand at the door and knock" (Rev 3:20). This means that God did not leave the door. Maybe He has been standing at my door for the last twenty years, but if I open the door today, He will be there. He did not leave my door. He was knocking at the door of my heart for all these years, but I kept the door closed in His face. The same applies to church and parents. They must keep knocking on the children's doors (spiritually) and wait for them to open. Do not give up on your child and do not stop knocking on the door of his heart. Knock on the door of his heart with love and patience, and wait. At one point, he will open the door and be ready for the grace of God to fill his heart. As soon as he opens the door, God will go inside and dwell in his heart, and then, no other power will be able to remove God from the heart of the child.

Regarding how to speak to our children about topics such as different denominations, a child as young as nine years old can understand this matter. A parent may need to explain to their child some aspects of church history in a very simple way. They may say something like, "The Lord Jesus Christ chose the disciples and sent them to different countries, including Egypt. St. Mark was the disciple who came to Egypt. The disciples then established churches in different parts of the world, but they all practiced the same way of worship. These churches continued like this for a long time, until the churches split into Orthodox, Catholic, and Protestant." Then, you can say, "Look at the Greek and Antiochian Orthodox Churches. Their liturgies are like our liturgy. Even the Catholic Church has mass, communion, and confession." You could also use the Internet to show the child a video clip of a liturgy from the Greek or Antiochian Orthodox Church, or a mass from the Catholic Church.

During Nativity, you could also show the child video clips and teach him that this congregation worships in this certain way. The child at this age is willing to learn, and you can correct the information he has in his mind. Then, he will learn that the Coptic Orthodox Church represents Egypt and it shares the same theology as the other Orthodox churches. In this way, he will not feel that we are a strange church. When he hears a story or a verse at school, and then, hears the same thing at church and comments about this point, tell him, "Yes, is this not what I have been telling you?" Little by little, he will internalize this in his heart. You could tell him, "The Coptic Orthodox Church reflects the work of the Holy Spirit in the Egyptian people, like the Armenian Orthodox Church reflects the work of the Holy Spirit in the Armenian people and the Ethiopian Orthodox Church in the Ethiopian people. As God works with you, your brother, and your sister, in the same way, God works with the Coptic Church, the Ethiopian Church and the Syrian Church. Every church reflects the work of the Holy Spirit." Simple church history will help him understand how the current church traditions were structured and how and why we practice them today.

We came from Egypt with a complex that we cannot talk about our religion, although we are in the land of freedom. We were not allowed to talk about our religion in Egypt, and we plant the same seeds in our children. We need to be rid of this complex. Also, we should not send our children to school unprepared. We should be proactive and not reactive. Being proactive means that you should send your children to school prepared. Thus, if at school they teach them something secular, Jewish, pagan, etc., they would be prepared psychologically, spiritually, and educationally to face these challenges. Being reactive means that I wait until something happens then react to it. It is much better to be proactive.

When the children come back from school and talk about something, such as Hanukkah, for example, you can hold a Bible study about Jewish feasts in the Old Testament. Then, you can discuss how these feasts are celebrated in the New Testament. All Jewish feasts became Christian holidays and are celebrated with a Christian understanding. In this way, you take the Jewish teaching that the children received at school and convert it to Christian teaching. This is what the Church did in Egypt. It took one of the River Nile celebrations and transformed it into the feast of Archangel Michael. The Church in Egypt *"christened"* the Pharaonic feasts and converted them to Christian feasts. In this way, it becomes a learning experience for the child regarding the Jewish and Christian feasts.

Regarding how to speak to our children about false teachings, in both the Old and New Testaments, we never find God saying that we have to tolerate all teachings and beliefs. We have to differentiate between religion and people, between belief systems and people. We, as Christians, have to teach, with authority, the falsehood of other religions. To protect my children, I have to teach them the falsehood of other religions. However, we also have to teach children that we love everyone. I should love a pagan although paganism is from the devil. I preach Christianity to him because I love him and want him to be saved. St. Paul said, "I have great sorrow and continual grief in my heart. For I could wish that I myself were accursed from Christ for my brethren, my countrymen according to the flesh" (Rom 9:2–3).

If I truly love my brother and I see that he is using drugs, I cannot minimize the addiction and say that I will accept my brother the way he is and accept the addiction. If I truly love my brother, I will try to save him from his addiction. The same applies to my brother or friend, whom I love, who became an atheist, or Muslim, or Jewish, or pagan. Because of my love toward him, I want to save him from the wrong beliefs that will destroy his life and will prevent him from being saved.

Therefore, there is a difference between a person and a belief. The Holy Bible clearly opposed wrong beliefs and wrong teachings. We love everyone and the will of God is for "all men to be saved and to come to the knowledge of the truth" (1 Tim 2:4). If I do not bring this person to the knowledge of the truth, then, I do not love this person. If I tell my brother or my friend, "Even though you are away from the truth, I will not ask you to change because I love you and it is okay to continue to live this away," this is not love. True love is to be saved and to come to the knowledge of truth.

When we talk about the Christian faith, for example, Protestants do not believe in sacraments. Can anyone be saved without baptism or communion? "Whoever eats My flesh and drinks My blood has eternal life, and I will raise him up at the last day. For My flesh is food indeed, and My blood is drink indeed. He who eats My flesh and drinks My blood abides in Me, and I in him" (Jn 6:54–56). When I love someone who is Protestant, should I teach him the true faith, to come to the knowledge of the truth, or should I tell him, "I love you the way you are and do not change"? Then, in the end, he will perish without salvation because he was not baptized and did not take communion? What is true love? We are not demonizing here. We are talking about beliefs and not people. We have to proclaim the truth about religion. I cannot say that the Protestant faith, which teaches that there are no sacraments, is correct. I cannot say that the Protestant faith, which teaches that the Body and Blood on the altar are just symbols, is correct! If you tell your children, "This is the body and blood of the Lord Christ, but it is okay if it is *not* His Body and Blood," that creates confusion for the children. What would your child think? I would be giving him two contradicting messages. I love Protestants, and because I love them so much, I want to invite them to the knowledge of the truth to be saved. But, if I leave them away from the truth, they will not be saved. Where is true love here?

The Catholic Church is more correct than the Protestant churches because it is an apostolic church and practices the church sacraments. However, the Catholic Church has deviated from the truth, with concepts such as the Immaculate Conception, the infallibility of the pope, etc. Sometimes, we have to talk about differences. There are similarities between our Christian faith and Islam! If we focus on the similarities, how can we confront falsehood? The Lord Jesus Christ warned us about false prophets. "Beware of false prophets" (Mt 7:15). He also warned us about false teachings. Therefore, we have to confront this and prove it. It is our responsibility. St. Paul sent Timothy a special letter because he had false teachers in his church. He explained to him how he should confront falsehood.

When our children talk about communion at school and are told that communion is not important, and they come and ask us about communion and baptism, we should not dilute the truth. Sometimes, however, we give a diluted truth that is unclear.

By mentioning all these points, I am not magnifying the problem. I am showing the truth about the falsehood. When I say salvation is through the blood of the Lord Christ and through the Holy Mysteries of Communion [Eucharist] and Baptism, this is not magnifying the problem. I am declaring the truth that I learned from the Church.

F | HOW TO RAISE RESPONSIBLE AND MATURE PERSONALITIES

1. Teaching Children Responsibility
2. A Structured Home
3. Ethics and Morals
4. Decision-Making
5. Free Time
6. The Learning Process
7. Organization and Cleanliness
8. A Spirit of Thanksgiving
9. Dealing with Money
10. Inappropriate Touches
11. Developing Gifts and Talents

1. Teaching Children Responsibility

It is very important to teach our children to be responsible. From my own personal observations, I see that children who are growing up now are not as responsible as in previous generations. I also noticed that many parents promote this because they want to separate consequences from behavior. For example, a child attends a convention with the church and misbehaves. The church follows up by sending a letter to the family, explaining that the child misbehaved at the convention, and therefore, will not be allowed to attend the next convention. Then, the parents argue with the church, "How could you do this? What about love? What about forgiveness?" The notions of love and forgiveness are distorted. *Forgiveness does not negate consequences.* When David sinned, God forgave him. Nathan told him, "The Lord also has put away your sin" (2 Sam 12:13). However, he *also* told him, "Because by this deed you have given great occasion to the enemies of the Lord to blaspheme," (2 Sam 12:14) certain consequences will happen. There is no contradiction between forgiveness and reaping the consequences of one's behavior. When I, as the parent, try to rescue my son from reaping the consequences of his behavior, I separate the behavior from its consequences. In this way, the child will never learn to be responsible and to take responsibility for his behavior.

Say, for instance, a child grows up and gets married outside of the Coptic Orthodox Church and has a Protestant wedding. The Church tells him, "You cannot take Communion." Then, his father says, "You are driving our children away from the Church. Are not these all churches of God? You made my son feel that he is rejected from Church." What I want to know is who rejected whom? Is it the Church that rejected your son, or your son who rejected the Church by going outside and marrying outside the Church? The Church did not reject your son; the Church is saying that what happened is wrong. Your son has to marry within the Church in a sacramental marriage, in order to be able to commune with the Church. The door is not closed. However, with words like, "acceptance," and "tolerance," all these concepts have become distorted. For this reason, I want to emphasize that in order to teach your children to be responsible you cannot separate consequences from behavior. Furthermore, do not try to rescue your children from reaping the consequences of their behavior.

Once, when I was young, I was dressed as a deacon and I was holding the Agpeya[17] upside-down. This means that I was distracted. (If I was standing and holding the Agpeya upside down, it means that I was distracted.) I was in the third grade at the time. I had not noticed that I was holding the Agpeya upside-down, so the deacon coordinator came to me and said, "Look at the Agpeya." So I looked and got embarrassed, and fixed it. After the liturgy ended, the deacon coordinator came to me, and said, "A deacon is like a soldier, like the angel standing around the throne of God. For you to learn the importance of serving as a deacon, you need to spend one month without dressing as a deacon." Of course, I was upset that I would spend one month without dressing as a deacon and I complained to my father. My father did not say, "They are wrong! Go fight with the deacon coordinator or the priest, and send the matter to the bishop or the pope, and send a fax, etc." On the contrary, he did not rescue me, but told me, "What the deacon coordinator said to you is correct. In reality, you were distracted. When you stand in the church and pray, you need to pay attention." My father supported what the deacon coordinator told me. This taught me a lesson—to pay attention when I stand in church. If he had rescued me from the consequences of my behavior, maybe I would not have learned how to respect the church.

Many times, we intervene to rescue our children from reaping the consequences of their behavior, and this is not right. Children need to learn at a very early age that whatever they do has good or bad consequences. Our children are not born with the ability to discern right from wrong. When children behave and obey their parents, the result should be rewarding and proper. When children misbehave, they need to understand that it will result in punishment and negative consequences.

Teach your children to respect other people and their boundaries. Gradually, give your child more responsibility and train him how to do his job properly and how to be committed. Give him a small responsibility, such as cleaning his room, making his bed, organizing his desk, or preparing something for himself. Sometimes, I see older children ask their mothers to bring them a cup of water, perhaps without even saying, "please." Okay, but then what? When will the children learn to depend on themselves?

---

17 Prayer Book of the Hours

We will discuss several things we can do in order to raise responsible and mature personalities. When teaching your child, try to remember the rule to keep the balance between grace and truth and the verse that says, "Train up a child in the way he should go, and when he is old he will not depart from it" (Prov 22:6).

We will discuss several things we can do in order to raise responsible and mature personalities. When teaching your child, try to remember the rule to keep the balance between grace and truth and the verse that says, "Train up a child in the way he should go, and when he is old he will not depart from it" (Prov 22:6).

2. A Structured Home

When a household has its own system and rules, which everyone must observe, this helps in raising mature personalities. It is important to say, "everyone," because both the parents and the children must observe it. This is unless, of course, there is an already established method or system of rules and expectations that may differ between parents and children, but which all members of the family understand. This is in respect to everything, for example, the use of the phone and computer, the time spent watching TV, prayer times and Bible study at home, attending church and Sunday school, and mealtimes and fasting times. The point is that when there is order, structure, and a system at home, it helps in raising mature personalities. When the household is in chaos and disorder, most likely, the children's personalities develop to be irresponsible and immature.

Each member of the household must be assigned a task. Each person must learn to bear responsibility and perform his role at home. In reality, it is their duty to make their beds in the morning, to wash the dishes they use, and to organize their closets and desks. The mother should not be the one who does all these tasks for the children. They must do these tasks themselves. This creates a mature and responsible personality within the child. Besides their personal duties (making up their beds, washing their dishes, etc.), the children should be assigned certain other responsibilities to do at home. They should help with chores around the house, in general.

Sometimes, when I visit young, single people, I enter their homes and find that these youths are very neat and organized. Right away, I feel that these young people came from a structured household. On the other hand, some homes I visit are in total chaos. The clothes are thrown on the floor, and the books and CDs are thrown everywhere. This means that the youth, from whichever homes they may have come, have never learned what "tidiness" or "order" means.

3. Teaching Ethics and Morals

Another way to raise responsible and mature personalities is to teach good, healthy habits, ethics, and morals to our children from a young age. Many of these have begun to disappear from our society. To acquire ethics, principles, and morals when dealing with others are very important aspects in the development of one's personality.

4. Decision-Making

When a child is young, the parents are the ones who tell him what to do. The older he becomes, the more they ought to have him participate in some decision-making, until he reaches a stage where he is able to make his own decisions. As I explained in a lecture about problem solving, the first stage is that I solve his problem. Then, I have the child participate in solving it until I can lead him to solve it by himself. The same applies regarding making decisions. When he is a young child, I make the decision for him, but after that, little by little, I teach him how to make the decision until he is able to rely on himself in making his own decisions.

When I begin to give the child choices, while he is still in the stage of learning how to make decisions, I have to give him an opportunity to choose between two good things. I should not ask him to choose between something bad and something good. While he still has limited experience, if he is asked to choose between something bad and something good, and he chooses the bad thing, I will not agree. Thus, the child would feel that he is a failure. On the other hand, if I allow him to choose between two good things, any choice he makes would be fine. Yet, herein, I am giving him the self-confidence to choose. I encourage him to choose by himself, and in the end, I praise his choice. For example, if we were to begin to study the Bible, I could ask him, "Would you like to begin to study the Gospel according to St. Matthew or St. Mark?" I could just say, "Children, today we will begin to study the Gospel according to St. Matthew." However, it is better to ask him. I want you to give him the self-confidence to understand that he is able to make a choice. So, he might say, "Dad, can we begin with the Gospel according to St. Mark?"

You would, then, praise him for making that choice by saying, "Yes, because St. Mark the Apostle is the one who preached to us (in Egypt)." If he chooses the Gospel according to St. Matthew, tell him, "Great choice, because this is the first Gospel account in the New Testament." Praise your child for any choice he makes because both choices are excellent. Thus, praise any choice he makes, then step by step he will become self-confident.

Sometimes, I meet college students, or young adults that have already graduated, but are unable to make decisions by themselves. They would seek guidance of the priest and insist that he makes the choice for them. They are terrified to make their own decisions and have no confidence in their own ability to make a right decision. They believe that they do not know how to choose. "Please, Father, choose for me. I do not know how to choose." This is because they were not trained, nor did they develop the confidence required for one to make his own choices.

The more children mature, the more freedom you give them. Sometimes, I see a mother that quarrels with her children about how they should dress for church. On the contrary, she should allow them to make the choice. They should first learn how to do so, how to choose suitable clothes for church, clothes that match well together, etc. Afterward, allow them to choose. There may be slight guidance as you train the child. Nevertheless, as the children grow up, give them more confidence and freedom of choice.

When he comes to choose between a good and a bad thing, ask him "What do you think are the positives and the negatives of these two choices?" In this manner, you encourage him to think. Choice, then, is based on analysis. First, I see the choice, and secondly, I assess the positive points as opposed to the negative points of each option.

If, for example, he makes the wrong choice while you are training him (and because you are training him, you do not ask him to make a major decision which might threaten his life), it must not become a big deal. On the contrary, it is a chance to guide him while he still lives in your home, before he leaves it to go to the university or work where circumstances will obligate him to make decisions by himself and he may begin to make bad decisions without having anyone to guide him. At least while the child is still in your home, even if he makes the wrong decision, you are with him and have the opportunity to teach him. Expect that anybody who is being trained to do something new will make mistakes. Thus, absorb these mistakes and begin to teach and train him.

Should you give the child the right to choose, do not take the choice away from him. Sometimes, a mother will ask her daughter to choose a dress to wear at church, then after the girl chooses, the mother would exclaim, "What is this? You cannot wear this!" She should have taught her from the beginning. When you give them the right to choose, you have to respect their choice. Do not take away that choice because it is the wrong choice. This is the reason that in the beginning of your training period, it is better to make your child choose between several good options. In this manner, there is no probability of error when making a choice.

If he says, "I do not know how to choose. Choose for me," never fall into this trap and agree to make the decision. This is often the easiest and fastest solution. However, it never creates mature personalities. So, if he asks you this, give him advice and teach him how to think. Tell him, "Let us think together. What are the advantages and disadvantages of this choice? How about this other choice? What are the drawbacks?" In this way, you are helping him to think and make a choice.

5. Free Time

Another point to think about is how your children may profit from their free time in a mature way, bearing responsibility for time. Perhaps, during their summer vacation or holidays, you could sit with your children and give them a few ideas. We call this, "brainstorming." We think together, come up with ideas of things to do during this vacation, and write down everyone's suggestions. Afterward, ask them to choose to begin working on three to four things. Herein, you are teaching and giving your child the responsibility to choose. When he chooses, he will comply, because he has chosen what he likes the most, rather than having you impose something on him. You could also give him the chance to think about something new that was not said during the brainstorming session.

Often, children come to you complaining of boredom. Teach your child that it is his responsibility to occupy his free time, and that you are ready to help him; yet have him assume this responsibility rather than you solving it for him. Ask him, "What would you like to do? Sit down and think about how to fill your free time. Give me at least five choices, then come to discuss them with me." Again, in this way, you are training him to assume responsibility for how to organize and plan for his life.

To help them fill their free time, why not teach them important things they would need in their lives in the future? Why not give your children a chance to help in the maintenance at home? If you are making or repairing something, allow your children to help you, and teach them. Begin training them. Some parents refuse to let their children participate in this. So, the children grow up; perhaps, get married or maybe stay single, and do not even know how to change a light bulb, do some household chores, cook, clean, sew minor things like a button, do laundry, etc. If you do this, you are preparing your children for the future. As they are doing these chores, encourage them regularly and let them know how proud you are of them and of how fast they learn. Encouragement always has a wonderful effect on children.

6. The Learning Process

Often, as we teach children to assume responsibility, the training process might take a long time. If we ask a child to do something while training him (for example, to make his bed), perhaps the child will not do it with the accuracy as we imagine. He might take a long time to do so. If the child participates in a maintenance task at home, or if you ask her daughter to participate in a household chore, it might be much easier and faster to do it yourself. Yes, it is true that you could do it faster and better yourself; however, you are wasting an opportunity for your child to learn and become a mature person. Remember that when you first began to do these things, perhaps, you did them with much less adequacy than your child. What is done faster and better is not always the right solution.

I thought about how if the Lord wished to help and serve all these congregations of people by Himself—just by Himself, would He be able to do so or not. Of course, He is able. If the Lord wants to preach the word of the Bible to the entire world, just by Himself without human interference or without angels, God is able to do this. Without a doubt, He is able to do this. Often, when our Lord allows us to participate in the ministry, our sins and weaknesses hinder the service. We obstruct God's work. Nevertheless, God invites us to participate with Him in the ministry. Why? He wants to teach us maturity, *even though* when we participate in His ministry, we may hinder it. He does it better than us and faster than us. Regardless, God allows us to participate with Him. If the Lord is doing so with us, we have to do this with our children. We give them the chance to learn and work with us.

7. Teamwork

You also need to instill in your children the understanding that as a group, perhaps siblings together, or children with the father or mother, or with both parents, you can all do something(s) together. This is to encourage teamwork. There is a joke that says, "To make sure that a committee is successful, it must be composed of two members, where one of them is absent. So the other works by himself." Sometimes, a person is able to work by himself but cannot work as part of a team. Accordingly, you need to teach your children the spirit of teamwork. Give them tasks to work on together to develop within them the spirit of cooperation. This requires letting go of the ego, humbleness, and communication. You are actually giving your child many talents and gifts, and you are training him to have new skills: how to communicate, how to be humble, how to understand and deal with people through the assigned task. The purpose is not the task itself, but how to develop the spirit of cooperation between them.

When you are working together, if your son comes up with a suggestion to do things in a different way, do not discourage him. If you did this, you would be suppressing his innovative potential. On the contrary, you should rather encourage the spirit of innovation in him; he thinks and tells you about a different way to do things, and perhaps, this other way is better. If he expresses a wish to perform the task in a different way, why not give him the chance and encourage him to do so?

8. Organization and Cleanliness

Teach your children the significance of time: "redeeming the time, because the days are evil" (Eph 5:16). Sometimes, "time," schedules, systems, cleanliness are not in our vocabulary. The concepts of respecting appointment times, respecting the system, or respecting the cleanliness of the place, often, do not exist. For example, when we are in the church, if a child is not quiet, his father or mother may give him a liturgy book or an Agpeya and a pen to distract him or redirect his attention, but the parent is doing so in the wrong way. The child begins to draw in the liturgy book. This is not right. Some parents allow their children to tear books apart, or write on the walls—this is not right. Thus, we have to teach our children the importance of time, punctuality, orderliness, cleanliness, and to protect public places, like the church. Even if I was in a park, I should not throw paper on the ground. Keeping order and cleanliness of a place is the spirit of responsibility.

Learning how to complete a project in a timely manner is also important. When the child is assigned a project, or if you have given him a subject to research or homework to finish, he should do so on time. He should learn how to finish it ahead of time, without waiting until the last moment and putting so much stress and pressure on himself to finish it because the deadline is tomorrow.

Respecting the law and rules of a place and the system is also important. I, often, feel very sad when I see the traffic in Egypt. Where is the order? A trip that should take twenty minutes, if there were any sort of traffic system, could take two hours! This is because everybody is going against the other, in all directions, attempting to arrive to their destination.

9. A Spirit of Thanksgiving

Teach your children not to have the spirit of complaining. Some children criticize everything all the time. If they attend a meeting, they come out talking about the negative points of that meeting. Their eyes always see what is wrong. The spirit of complaining or grumbling is not a nice one. The Lord, actually, punished the children of Israel because of their grumbling when they were in the desert of Sinai. Children should not always be complaining. Teach them to stay away from the grumbling spirit, and instill in them the spirit of thanksgiving and the spirit of joy, to look at the positive things and to spend a good time laughing together and enjoying each other's company.

10. Dealing with Money

A very important point in creating mature personalities is to teach your child at an early age how to handle money. Often, we either let them spend their money in whatever way they want without any guidance, or we continue making all the financial decisions for them until they graduate. That is why they do not know how to handle their finances when they begin earning a salary. Some people become very stingy and some become careless spenders because nobody taught them how to handle money.

Have a Bible study about what God's plan is for dealing with money. What does God expect from us regarding how to handle our money? Let me tell you some things quickly. First, we are God's servants. We are not the owners of the property. Naked we came into the world and naked we will leave the world (Job 1:21). The Lord is the owner and He has entrusted us with a stewardship. The money I have is not mine; it belongs to God and I am God's servant on earth, just as God commissioned Adam to take care of the earth. Teach your child that a servant must have two qualities, as we read in the Gospel according to St. Luke, "Who then is that *faithful* and *wise* steward?" (Lk 12:42, emphasis added). These two qualities are very important. If you have a business and hire a servant, a supervisor to manage that business, and he does not have wisdom, the business shall not be profitable. If he does not have faithfulness, he will steal the profit from you. In both cases, it will be your loss. Teach your child that we must be wise and diligent when handling money. I should not just expect my parents to support me, such that even after graduating and getting married, I still ask them for money. This is not right. I have to be diligent. As our teacher Paul the Apostle says, "If anyone will not work, neither shall he eat" (2 Thess 3:10).

They also need to learn how to wisely manage the money they receive and spend within their budget. A person who cannot live on 500 dollars will not be able to live on 10,000 dollars. This type of management is important. It is also important to be honest. Often, with economic pressures, one becomes greedy, covetous, and dishonest and may seize any opportunity to steal. Explain to your child that we "use" money but we do not love money, "for the love of money is a root of all kinds of evil, for which some have strayed from the faith in their greediness, and pierced themselves through with many sorrows" (1 Tim 6:10). It is truly possible that the love of money may cause a person to stray from his faith and renounce it.

The Lord expects us to be generous with each other, not stingy. "He who gives, with liberality… he who shows mercy, with cheerfulness" (Rom 12:8). God also expects us to be content and satisfied with what we have. "Be content with such things as you have" (Heb 13:5). One of the most beautiful verses about being satisfied is what St. Paul said in Philippians, "for I have learned in whatever state I am, to be content: I know how to be abased, and I know how to abound. Everywhere and in all things I have learned both to be full and to be hungry, both to abound and to suffer need" (Phil 4:11–12). "I have learned" shows that it is something that needs to be taught; there is training. As parents, we are supposed to teach our children to be content with what they have, so that they are not always looking for a better cell phone, better car, better computer, etc. These are some principles, so you may hold a Bible study with your children on the subject of money, and discuss God's plan for money in the family and with individuals.

Do not spoil your children with money. No matter how rich you are or how many resources you have, you must, nevertheless, put restrictions. Pampering may spoil your children. When the children reach an age where they could begin to have some discernment, start giving them a small allowance and follow up with them on how to use it. Teach them how to pay tithes from this allowance. Also, teach them how to buy some of the things they need. Even though you may be able to buy them these things, this teaches them the spirit of responsibility. Explain to him that he will buy a certain item from his allowance; if he spends his allowance without buying this item, do not buy it for him so that he may learn how to handle money and manage it wisely.

If his brother needs something, teach him how to help his brother generously and with liberality. By doing these things, you instill in him how to take the right measures and how to manage his money well. Teach him how to make a budget, even with the small amount of money he receives as an allowance. Teach him how to save, even if he only saves a small portion. Talk to him about the benefits of savings. Warn him about the dangers of borrowing and the importance of spending and living according to one's abilities. Some people get in trouble and borrow loans without paying them back because as young children, nobody taught them about this. Warn him that he should not just borrow money from his brother every time he desires something. Otherwise, he will continue to borrow, fall in debt and be unable to pay it back. If the parents pay his brother back, the child will never learn. Teach him that this is not a good practice. He should be content with what he has, and spend according to the allowance he receives.

At a young age, even if his family can afford to provide for him, why not allow him to work? I often feel that work gives a child a sense of responsibility and makes him more mature; it turns him into an adult, who is ready to assume responsibility. He would also have the opportunity to deal with the outside society. Most of our children [in the Southern Diocese], starting from high school, work even if their families are able to provide for them. So the children bear responsibility. However, this is not to be at the expense of their service at church, their relationship with the Lord, their time at home, or their schoolwork and education. If it does not interfere with those things, there is no reason why they should not work if there is a chance to do so.

11. Inappropriate Touches

A very important point is to teach the children to never allow anybody to touch them in an inappropriate way. We often hear stories in which the parents were not aware that anything even happened. Teach them to firmly refuse that anybody touches them in the wrong way. In the case that anything should happen, they must come and inform you *immediately*. No matter who that person is, if he is from the household or is a relative, they must come and tell you so that this abuse is stopped immediately because children often suffer greatly. When a person begins to hurt them, often the abuser threatens them ("If you speak, I will do this or that to you"). The child, then, becomes unable to speak and keeps these things suppressed inside of him. The abuse goes too far, leaving deep psychological wounds, which sometimes cause personality disorders. From a young age, children *must* be taught that nobody is to touch them inappropriately.

If someone crosses this boundary, your child must inform you immediately so that you can intervene. Of course, you must intervene seriously and wisely. Do not ignore the situation. Sometimes, when this happens by a relative, the parents begin to think that this is going to cause a major problem or scandal, so they keep quiet and let it go. No. You need wisdom, seriousness, and intervention. When your son comes to tell you about it, do not blame or scold him. If it is your daughter who is telling you about something that happened to her by force, most likely it was by force without any fault on her part. Sometimes, when we blame the children, we make them suffer psychologically. Do not blame them; rather reassure and comfort them. As I have said before, when children feel that they have strong parents who protect them, they feel confident. Assure them that everything is fine and that you will intervene firmly, with love, wisdom, and seriousness to end it. This is an important point that I hope you pay close attention to it.

12. Developing Gifts and Talents

One of the important points when teaching our children responsibility and developing within them mature personalities is to nurture their capabilities and gifts. How does one do so? When they work with you at home or when they play together, observe them, and try to discover their talents and capabilities. Perhaps one is talented in art, music, sports, or manual work. Discover these talents and capabilities and develop them for the glory of God. Teach him how to use it for the glory of God. Also, help your children to acquire new talents. Some talents exist in us and require development, and certain talents are acquired. Moreover, do not pressure your children so that they become distracted between many activities, as well as studying, so that they no longer have time to spend at home, or to pray, or to go to church. Moderation is good. Do not allow the many activities to be on account of their time with the family, or their time to rest, and of course, more importantly, on account of their relationship with God.

The goal is to create mature personalities. Raising children requires effort from parents. Some people let their children just grow up, simply living in the house, and that is it. This is not right. When you want to build a house, you begin to plan what you want it to look like; you choose all the details, how you want the windows to look, how you want the door, the doorknob, the lamps, and the light bulbs. You choose everything, so the house comes out the way you expect. The same applies to raising children. You need to plan for every small stone. St. Peter the Apostle said, "as living stones, [you] are being built up a spiritual house" (1 Pet 2:5). You have to choose everything in your child's life. In the end, our children will grow up with mature personalities, responsible personalities, personalities that glorify God in their lives. Such children are those to whom the word of the Lord Jesus Christ would apply, when He said, "You are the light of the world ... that they may see your good works and glorify your Father in heaven" (Mt 5:14,16).

G | SUBMISSION AND OBEDIENCE

1. Allowing Children to Express Their Opinions
2. Teaching Children to Accept Responsibility for Their Mistakes
3. Do Not React Out of Anger
4. Supervising Children's Behaviors
5. "This is Enough" and "This is Inappropriate"
6. Respecting Privacy
7. Teaching Children to Obey from the First Time
8. Maintaining Respect for Both Parents

1. Allowing Children to Express Their Opinions

I want to emphasize that teaching our children submission and obedience does not at all contradict with giving them a chance to express their opinions and have an opinion that is different from ours. For example, your child may disagree with you about something. You have to give him this opportunity to disagree. Our Lord, the Pantocrator, gave His children the chance to express their opinions and to have an opinion different from His. For example, Abraham stood and said to the Lord, "Shall not the Judge of all the earth do right? ... Would You also destroy the righteous with the wicked?" (Gen 18:25,23). The Lord, who commanded us to obey and submit to Him, also permitted us to discuss with Him, disagree with Him, and express our opinions to Him. Once, the Lord told Moses to leave Him alone, as if Moses was holding God! "Now therefore, let Me alone, that My wrath may burn hot against them and I may consume them. And I will make of you a great nation" (Ex 32:10). Then Moses pleaded with God not to do this, saying, "I pray, blot me out of Your book which You have written" (Ex 32:32). Do you know what happened? The Lord listened to Moses. He did not destroy the nation. He punished them and accepted Moses's intercession.

Why does God do this? He does things like this so He can teach us how to use authority with love, humility, and wisdom. Just as it is important to use your authority as a father or as a mother, I am emphasizing as well the need to completely avoid domination and control, and give our children a chance to express their opinions, or even to disagree with us.

2. Teaching Children to Accept Responsibility for Their Mistakes

Often among the things that cause parents to begin to be disturbed, and not know how to act, is when they hear that their child has become involved in a problem. This could be a problem at school due to misbehavior, a problem at church, or even a problem with the country and the law. Often parents rush to defend and justify their children's mistakes. They also attempt to pressure those in authority to alleviate the consequences or the discipline. For example, if a child misbehaves at school or church, and the ones in authority discipline this child, many parents go to school or to church and argue, attempting to blame the authority figures and remove the discipline or the chastisement. They would defend their child even if he were at fault. These parents do not realize that they are losing a chance to teach their child the responsibility that comes with making a mistake. They are losing the opportunity to instill the spirit of responsibility in their child, and to teach him or her that there is such a thing as accountability, which is giving "an account of your stewardship" (Lk 16:2). When one misbehaves, this mistake has consequences.

If you do not allow your child to bear the consequences of a mistake, you are teaching him to misbehave and to be undisciplined. In this manner, why would he stop misbehaving? Often, our involvement in order to alleviate the discipline of our children harms them, prevents them from acquiring the spirit of responsibility, and prevents us from creating a generation that is spiritually mature. Therefore, if you hear that your son is in trouble, at school, at church, or with the law, what are you supposed to do? First, search for the truth of the matter. See whether your son is at fault or not. If he is indeed at fault, teach him to take responsibility for his mistake. Teach him to say like the thief on the right side said, "And we indeed justly" (Lk 23:41). This was part of the reason for the justification of the right-hand thief, because he accepted the responsibility of his mistake and confessed it.

If you think about what the Holy Mystery of Confession is, it is accepting responsibility for your sin. When I go to confession, I am saying that I deserve punishment. I deserve the punishment of death. However, I come desiring God's mercy. God died on the cross, because He loved me and redeemed me, to give me His forgiveness and purify me with His sacred blood when I partake of Him, and thus, I am cleansed of my sin. However, confession is so called because I confess my faults and that I deserve the punishment of death, because the wages of sin is death. Thus, this is a chance to teach your child to take responsibility and admit his mistake.

I was thinking about what the difference was between David the Prophet and King Saul. David maybe committed sins that Saul never committed. David committed adultery and murder. However, why did the Lord say about David that he is, "A man after My own heart" (1 Sam 13:14)? As for Saul, of whom the Bible never mentions that he committed adultery, the Lord rejected him! This is because David took responsibility for his mistake. When Nathan came to admonish him, saying, "You are the man!" (2 Sam 12:7), he *immediately* said, "I have sinned against the Lord" (2 Sam 12:13). However, Saul did not learn to take this kind of responsibility. During the war with Amalek, the Lord asked Saul to kill all the sheep and flocks (1 Sam 15). But Saul kept the well-fed sheep. The Lord sent him Samuel to rebuke him and Samuel asked him, "Have you fulfilled God's commandment?" Saul began to lie and to avoid answering the question. He was unable to say, "I have sinned against the Lord" as David said. He said, "No, no, everything is in order, I have obeyed the voice of the Lord." Then Samuel asked, "Then what is this noise I hear? What is this bleating of the sheep in my ears?" Saul answered, "These will be used to sacrifice to the Lord your God!" Samuel said, "What makes God happier—obedience or sacrifice? What delights God? In obeying His commandment, or in breaking it to offer burnt sacrifices?" Saul was still unable to say, "I have sinned against the Lord." Rather, he said, "Honestly, I feared the people" and he continued to give justifications and excuses. He never learned to accept responsibility. Most likely, when he was a young child, his parents did not teach him how to accept the consequences of his mistakes. Maybe they would defend him whenever he made a mistake. This is why he grew up not knowing how to say, "I have sinned against the Lord," as David said.

If you examine the issue and discover that your son is indeed at fault, teach him to take responsibility for his mistake. However, if you find that your son has been wronged, it is a chance for you to teach him how to handle injustice with courage, wisdom, and maturity, and how to defend himself. Nevertheless, do not do this task for him (unless he is a young child). You have to help your child develop courage, that he may learn how to stand up and defend his rights. He needs to learn to defend himself, for example, and say, "This is wrong. There is injustice in this matter." Do not do this task for him; otherwise, you will not allow him the opportunity to learn how to handle injustice, and he will certainly face injustice in his life. Therefore, you can teach him how to handle the situation with courage—because the Lord has given us the spirit of power—and also with wisdom and maturity as well, so that he does not make a mistake while defending himself and bring upon himself a great punishment.

In either case—whether he is at fault or whether he has been unjustly accused—it is an opportunity to teach your child maturity, to take responsibility, and to deal with society at large.

3. Do Not React Out of Anger

Regarding how to teach our children submission and obedience, if your child misbehaves—for example, you gave him an order or asked something from him, and he did not do it, or he behaved badly with you or with his siblings—how should you react? How should you teach him submission and obedience? How could you teach him the spirit of responsibility?

First, I tell you that you have to control your emotions and restrain yourself. Otherwise, your reactions would become harmful and hurtful because you would be responding emotionally in anger and irritation. Therefore, if you find out that your son misbehaved, you must first be sure to stay calm. Have confidence in yourself. Be sure that you are interacting with your son on a foundation of love, and not on the basis of releasing your anger or revenge. Often, when our children make a mistake, the parent becomes very angry and irritated and responds in order to just release the anger that is inside of him. Sometimes, the parent reacts in order to take revenge on the child who is at fault and misbehaved in this way. Something that will help you control your temper is to remember that the problem is not *your child*. The problem is his conduct and behavior. If you were to view your child as the problem, you would attempt to destroy him, because he is "the problem;" and you would pour out all your wrath upon your child, and not on the problem itself. However, when you say that the problem is his behavior, you and your son would stand together and cooperate to deal with the problem and solve it. Your child is your beloved one, whom you want to rescue from the problem (i.e., his misbehavior and his conduct).

What should you do if deep within you, you do not feel confident and you feel that you are unable to handle the situation and that it is getting out of control? Pray to the Lord and ask for His help. Then, deal with your child with trust and out of duty and with authority, even if you feel the opposite inside your heart. If you act with the aid of God and with trust, responsibility, and authority—the authority given to you by God as a father or mother—be sure that your child will respond to you.

When you deal with your child, remember that nobody is perfect; you are not perfect. Thus, do not expect perfection from your children. We, even, say in the Psalms, "If You, Lord, should mark iniquities, O Lord, who could stand?" (Ps 130:3). The Lord does not expect perfection from us. He demanded perfection from us when He said, "Be perfect" (Mt 5:8); however, the Lord deals with us knowing our weaknesses. One of the phrases that I really like in the Absolution Prayer[18] is when we say, "O Master who know the weakness of men as the Good One and Lover of mankind." So the Lord knows our weaknesses and He deals with us on this basis.

Do not allow Satan to put negative, destructive thoughts in your mind. Avoid these feelings when you are teaching your children submission and obedience. If you find any of these feelings inside your heart, you will find it difficult to use your authority to teach your children submission and obedience. Some people feel desperate and say that they failed in raising their children, but avoid saying this. Others may say, "I have a great feeling of guilt; I failed to achieve my best with my children." So they have a major feeling of guilt, not knowing how to handle the situation. Another may say, "I am ashamed of them, because of their failure and depravity." Or "I am so angry toward them. I cannot stand seeing them." On the other hand, we may begin to blame others. The father would say that his wife is the reason for the children's failures. The wife may say that her husband is the reason for the failure. You may also begin to take the children's misbehaviors in a personal way, not in an objective way, as if it were directed toward you personally. Of course, this would add to the anger inside you, if you say, "I know—my son is challenging *me*." Maybe he is not challenging you; perhaps, unfortunately, he grew up with the wrong temperament and with a difficult character. However, he is not challenging you personally; he is just rebelling against every authority— your authority, the authority of the law, the authority of the church, and the authority of God. Once you begin to accept and interpret the situation in a personal way— "he is challenging me"—this causes you to become emotional and filled with anger, and it will prevent you from being able to deal with your son in a sound manner.

As such, it is good to expect that your children will have problems. They will not be perfect. Adam and Eve were under the direct protection of God. He was their Father. Nevertheless, they fell into sin. So it is good to be realistic, and to expect that our children may cause some problems. Perhaps when we were their age, we also caused some trouble. That is for sure! If you expect perfection in your children, and expect that

---

18 Prayer of Absolution to the Son, Divine Liturgy of St. Basil.

they should never make mistakes, as soon as they do, you find yourself distressed. You lose control of yourself, you lose control over your nerves, and you become unable to handle the situation. But, if you expect that problems may occur, you will handle the situation in a better way. You will have more control and restraint of your nerves. You will be able to deal with that situation with your son, to get past it, and to lead your son toward spiritual maturity and teach him submission and obedience.

Remember that you also have weaknesses. Remember that you have often attempted to better yourself, and even though you made sincere attempts, you have failed several times. How many times did we go to our fathers of confession in real repentance and regret? How many times did we stand up during New Year's Eve and make promises to God and then, break our promises? As such, if despite our true and sincere attempts and our genuine intentions, we may fail, why would the world end if my child misbehaves or makes a mistake? In addition, parents may begin to doubt the child's sincerity about his intentions, and tell him, "You are a failure. You will never improve," etc. Every person is in need, should continue to learn, better himself, and grow until the last day of his life. Look at the mistake that your child makes as if it were an opportunity to learn.

When someone upsets and distresses us, rather than becoming annoyed by his or her existence in our lives, we can view it as a school to learn longsuffering, tolerance, forgiveness, and mercy. How would I be able to learn longsuffering if I only deal with the righteous and saintly? How could I learn and grow in endurance if all the people with whom I encounter never make mistakes? Thus, when a person has a problem or is in a difficult situation, it is good to look at it as a "school." The Lord is taking you to a school to learn a new virtue. The same applies if your child behaves badly; look at the situation as a chance for him to learn something new.

Often, when our children behave incorrectly or get themselves in trouble, we become angry. The reason for this anger is the unwillingness to deal with the problem. The person is not willing to take care of the problem. Of course, it requires time and effort to do so, and this is what makes him become angry. However, if you look at it as a chance for learning and benefit, what St. Paul says in Hebrews 5:14 would apply to your child: "Those who by reason of *use* have their senses exercised to discern both good and evil" (emphasis added). Perhaps if you looked at the situation as a chance for learning, you would not get angry.

Your reaction to your child's mistake is very important because your responsibility does not consist in just punishing your child when he makes a mistake. Your responsibility is more so to teach and train your child with love and wisdom when he makes a mistake. Again, when my son makes a mistake, my responsibility is not just to punish him. It is rather also to treat him and help him improve himself, training and teaching in love and wisdom.

I want to tell you that even if by means of a mistake, your child *tried* to provoke you or irritate you, you must have control over yourself and over your nerves. If you lose your temper in any situation and you do not control yourself, you shall lose that situation. Believe me, from personal experience, I lost every situation in which I lost my temper and was unable to control my emotions. The more a person controls his temper, restrains and contains himself, the more he will be able to win. (Although we are using the term "win," we are not in a battle. By winning, I mean that we benefit from the situation, and it ends positively for all parties involved).

Because of this, even if your child attempts to irritate or provoke you, or if he really *did* mean it against you, personally, you must not lose your objectivity. Many people came to our Lord Jesus Christ to try to catch Him with a word and to provoke Him, and to inflame Him. But our Lord Jesus Christ dealt with them with amazing objectivity. For example, once they accused Him with a terrible accusation; maybe none of us would accept this accusation. They told Him that He casts out demons by Beelzebub (Mt 12:24). How hard, how difficult, and how harsh is this accusation! What did our Lord Jesus Christ do? He handled the matter and the accusation, with objectivity. We did not see Him become enraged and lose His temper. He answered them, as St. Peter says, "Who, when He was reviled, did not revile in return" (1 Pet 2:23). Thus, the Lord told them, "Let us analyze the situation in an objective manner. Does Satan wish to spread his kingdom or does he wish to ruin it? He surely wants to spread it! Then, is it possible that a devil would cast out another devil? If one devil casts out another, how would his kingdom stand? I will give you another reason. Do your children, not the twelve disciples and the seventy-two apostles, also cast out demons? If Beelzebub is with Me, if the ruler of the demons is with Me, by whom do your sons cast them out? Therefore they shall be your judges."[19] Herein, you find that our Lord

---

19 Cf. Mt 12:27

Jesus Christ dealt with the situation and this accusation with objectivity and amazing serenity. He did not lose His temper, He did not get angry, and He did not become defensive.

Similarly, in order for you to turn the situation into a chance to learn a lesson and to benefit, you must have the ability to control yourself when your child attempts to irritate or provoke you. Remember that each situation shall turn to goodness in the end if we deal with it in the right manner.

4. Supervising Children's Behaviors

Another important point in the subject of how to teach our children submission and obedience is to follow-up with their behavior, especially at a young age. There should be a type of supervision. For example, if your child is still in elementary school, it is not right that you allow him to sit at the computer and go on the Internet. Perhaps, you also put a TV in his room and he can watch whatever he wishes and do whatever he wants. There must be follow-up and wise supervision, so that you may be able to stir up, direct, train, instruct, and advise him.

When you follow up with your children, do not let the purpose be only to look for their mistakes. Let the purpose be to look for their good and fine deeds, to praise and reward them, and to encourage them. This way, your children would not be annoyed that you follow-up, observe, and supervise them. Your children would be annoyed and distressed when they feel that you supervise them only to catch their mistakes and punish them for these. If the child were to feel that in this supervision, you see that he behaved correctly and encourage and reward him for his behavior, the child would be happy and would want you to follow-up with him. He will know that his parents will encourage the right behaviors as they also discipline the wrong behavior. The child will also feel that you are being fair. You are not severe and always against him.

What I am saying is useful for anyone who has responsibility or authority, for example, Sunday school servants and priests. St. Paul the apostle instructed Timothy the bishop to let those "who rule well be counted worthy of double honor" (1 Tim 5:17). This means that when Timothy follows up with servants and priests, he must not just follow-up with those who make mistakes, to rebuke them in front of everyone so that the rest also may fear. Rather, he should also follow-up with those who rule well and grant them double honor. This balance is very important. So, if your child does something good, reward him. Similarly, if he misbehaves, you have to intervene and attempt to stop the mistake with a spirit of love and responsibility.

5. "This is Enough" and "This is Inappropriate"

When you see that your child is misbehaving, note the tone and intensity of your voice. Speak with firm love, not with enraged anger. When a young child is doing something wrong, it is recommended that you tell him, "This is enough," instead of saying, "No, do not do this." The reason for this is that usually, when you use the word "no," the child may answer you back saying, "No, I *will* do it." Then, you may become stubborn with each other. However, when you tell him, "This is enough," you do not give him a word he could reuse against you. Our Lord Jesus Christ even used this phrase. Before going to the cross, He told his disciples, "he who has no sword, let him sell his garment and buy one" (Lk 22:36). They thought He was talking about a sword. Of course, the Lord Jesus Christ did not mean an actual sword; otherwise, He would not have told Peter, "Put your sword into the sheath" (Jn 18:11). "So they said, 'Lord, look, here are two swords.' And He said to them, 'It is enough'" (Lk 22:38). He meant, "Enough about this subject."

When your child grows up a little more, instead of telling him, "This is enough," which may come as an order given to a young child, maybe you should change this phrase and tell him, "This is inappropriate." What is the difference between "this is enough" and "this is inappropriate"? "This is enough" is an order—stop. Do not do this again. And if you have taught your child to obey you from the first time (as I will discuss shortly), then the child will stop. You will not enter into a discussion with him. The phrase, "this is inappropriate," is useful with those who are older because it may become the beginning of a discussion between the two of you, regarding what is suitable and what is not suitable.

St. Paul set four very important points in order to be able to discern between good and evil. He said, "All things are lawful for me, but all things are not helpful" (1 Cor 10:23). Not everything is suitable for me. The second point is that "not all things edify" (1 Cor 10:23). Thirdly, "I will not be brought under the power of any" (1 Cor 6:12), which means that nothing will control me. The fourth point is that I should not be the cause of offense to anyone (1 Cor 10:24). When you tell your child that this behavior is inappropriate and he asks you why, tell him because our teacher St. Paul the Apostle said, "All things are lawful for me, but not all things edify, not all things are appropriate, nothing controls me, nor do I become a cause of offense to anyone."

Many people wonder what is wrong with drinking alcohol. The Lord Jesus Christ turned water into wine at the wedding of Cana of Galilee. So, what is wrong with drinking alcohol? All things are lawful for a person and Christianity does not forbid wine; it forbids the *misuse* of wine. If you were to enter into a discussion with your child about whether or not to drink alcohol, when you apply and discuss St. Paul's four points, you would find that it is possible for alcohol abuse to occur; wine could take control over the person. No alcoholic became an alcoholic by saying, "My goal is to become an alcoholic within three years!" Surely, when he started drinking, he thought that alcohol would never control him. Nevertheless, at the end, he fell and succumbed to alcoholism. Therefore, it does take control over the person. It may also be a cause of offense to others. This is the reason that alcohol does not edify. Many physical diseases are caused by alcohol. Therefore, it is not befitting for us, as children of God. Even though we do not forbid these substances, they are not befitting for us as children of God. Thus, when you tell the child that it is not appropriate, it is an opportunity for you to enter into a beneficial conversation with him and to teach him. Note that my goal from the very beginning is to raise a mature personality that can take responsibility.

6. Respecting Privacy

Another point in teaching our children submission and obedience is that in order to develop mature, responsible personalities, you have to respect your children's privacy. However, especially at a young age, respecting their privacy does not cancel your right to monitor this privacy at any time, if necessary. Your children must know that this is your right as a parent who is responsible for them and who shall give account for them before the Lord. This certainly requires wisdom. When you respect your children's privacy, this allows them to develop a sense of self-esteem and responsibility. You are giving them a responsibility, and they are dealing with it. You respect them and their privacy.

If you find that the children have started to behave with absolute secrecy and have started to create ambiguity around themselves—if they never allow you to look at their cell phones, they will not allow you to turn on their computers, etc.—most probably this secrecy is concealing a hidden mistake. Because of this, before buying a cell phone or a computer for your child, you must first agree with him on the following rule: You will respect his privacy, however, when necessary, it is your right to oversee these private matters *for his protection.* When he learns this, and you agree about it, this will create a sense of responsibility in your children. They know that their parents can at any time look through their cell phones, desks, books, computers, etc.

7. Teaching Children to Obey from the First Time

You must train your children to obey you from the first time. Often, and I shall clarify how, we make the children obey us only when we become angry and raise our voices, but if you just ask him to do something, he will not do it. As soon as you yell or become angry and raise your voice, he starts to respond to you.

What should you do if he does not respond to you from the first time? I will explain this in the next section, but I want to tell you that you must handle the situation immediately, with gentleness, but with firmness. Explain to him that his disobedience has its consequences. An example of this is when the Lord Jesus Christ came to wash Peter's feet. Peter found this very difficult and said to Him, "You shall never wash my feet!" (Jn 13:8). "Never", with finality. Our Lord did not beg him or discuss it with him. The Lord said, "Okay. Should you choose this, that I do not wash you, you have no part with Me." He immediately explained to him the consequences of his attitude. What happened to Peter? He changed his attitude. He said, "Lord, not my feet only, but also my hands and my head!" (Jn 13:9). So, the Lord corrected the situation a second time and told him, "He who is bathed needs only to wash his feet" (Jn 13:10). What I want to focus on here is how God dealt with Peter's disobedience the first time. It was done right away. He did not repeat the order to Peter many times. If He had done that, He would have been training Peter to obey at the tenth time, not the first time.

Let me give you a summary of the incorrect way we deal with our children when they do not obey us from the first time. You give the order or make the request. If he does not do it, you tell him, "Look I am giving you a second chance." If he does not do it, you then tell him, "This is the third time I am asking you to do this." If he still did not do it, you begin to negotiate with him, "Okay, so what will you do?" If he still does not do it, you begin to warn and threaten, saying, "I will not give you your allowance," etc. If he is still disobedient, you begin to change your tone of voice; you begin to beg and nag, "For my sake, please go with your sister just this one time." If he does not listen, you start to give him a lecture about obedience and manners and bring all the Bible verses that can teach him obedience. If he still does not listen—now we are at step eight—you attempt to bribe him; you tell him, "Look, if you go with your sister, I will buy you this. Did you not ask me for the iPod? I will buy it for you! Just go with her." You try to bribe him so that he listens to you. If he does not listen to you, you begin to yell and raise your voice. And if he still does not listen, you hit him at the end.

I am not saying this is the correct way. I am saying that you must teach them to obey from the first time, or in the end, you find that parents get sick of the whole process, give up, and do it themselves. In reality, if you are using these ten steps, you are most likely teaching your children *disobedience*! You are not teaching them obedience and submission. It is within your ability to train your children to obey you while you are calm, without needing to raise your voice or shout. And it is *also* within your ability to train and teach them to obey you only when you raise your voice. This is your responsibility.

Of course, using these ten steps creates an atmosphere of tension in the family, which is neither right nor healthy for any of the family members. Because of this, it is very important to teach your children to tell you, "yes" politely, with love and submission, and to say it from the first time, knowing that obedience and submission bring blessings into their lives, knowing also that disobedience has consequences and that they will bear the responsibility of their disobedience.

If you ask them to do something that they have never done previously, prior to making your demand, you can explain to them what you expect from them. However, this explanation is not an opportunity for an argument or discussion. At the same time, if you ask for something and they politely ask if it is possible for them to postpone it for a little bit, or if, for example, their mother requested something opposite to what you requested, listen to what they are saying, and afterward think and make a wise decision that is suitable to the situation. The Lord Jesus Christ did the same thing. Once, there was someone who seemed to be disobeying the Lord Jesus Christ, but the Lord dealt with him in a different way than He did with Peter. When the Lord Jesus came to John the Baptist and asked John to baptize Him, John tried to prevent Him, saying, "I need to be baptized by You, and are You coming to me?" (Mt 3:14). Here, the Lord Jesus did not explain to him, as He did with Peter, "If you did not baptize Me, this or that will happen." The Lord Jesus said to him, "Permit it to be so now, for thus it is fitting for us to fulfill all righteousness" (Mt 3:15). Then John consented.

This is also a great lesson on the humility of John the Baptist. Often, one thinks that if he *insists* on his humble opinion, this is humility. For example, a person may insist on being the last one to take communion. He allows everybody to come before him, then, at the end, there are two humble people left, who want to take the "lowest place." Each one insists that the other goes before him, and they hold up communion, and each one thinks that he is humble. Insisting on your opinion is not humility. It is a type of stubbornness and ego—an ego that hides behind humility. However, when John the Baptist told Him, "Lord, I cannot!" and He said to him, "Permit it to be so now" (Mt 3:15), John consented, because he had learned obedience and submission.

If you make a request of your children and they respond impolitely, immediately explain to them that this is unacceptable and this way must not be used when dealing with one another. In addition, as I will explain shortly, this inappropriate manner has its consequences. However, before giving an order, remember the expression that says, "If you wish to be obeyed, then ask for what is possible."

8. Maintaining Respect for Both Parents

Sometimes, we face another problem when teaching our children submission and obedience. Disagreement between the parents, or if the couple criticizes one another in front of the children, teaches the children to disobey both of them. When they find that their parents always disagree, fight, or criticize each other, the children, at the end, may not obey the father *or* the mother. Do not ever think that when you criticize the mother in front of your children, that they will obey you. On the contrary, they will not obey you, or her. If you wish for your children to learn obedience and submission, have a discussion with your spouse and come to an agreement on your method of raising the children. When you discuss this subject together, you will certainly find points of agreement and points of disagreement. Benefit from the points of agreement and come to a consensus together, *with love and humility*, about the points of disagreement. Humility is very important, because it is what makes you both give up your opinions and be able to come to an agreement.

If you find that your spouse is giving an order that you consider unacceptable or using a method of discipline that you do not like, you may feel like you want to interfere to save the child from the situation. However, usually your interference harms your child more than if you had stayed out of the situation. If you were to privately speak to your spouse about the order or discipline that you consider unacceptable, this would be more beneficial for your child than if you were to interfere and undermine the authority of the other spouse in front of the child. Moreover, more often than not, one spouse's disagreement with the other spouse's method is not objective, but due to a personal reason, i.e., there is a problem between them. It is possible that one spouse's perception is that everything the other spouse is doing is wrong because one is not at peace with the other and there are marital problems between them. This is why one spouse criticizes everything the other does.

Your interference may also cause a problem between you and your spouse. Then, you would still have your child's problem, but also a problem between you and your spouse. At the same time, the children would see that you are fighting over the method of raising them. So, if you see something where there is disagreement between the two of you, control yourselves; be patient until both you are alone together to discuss this situation and reach an agreement together on the subject. Or, if one spouse finds the other spouse doing something not in agreement with the other, that spouse could begin to speak in a general way, without addressing the other spouse directly, but addressing everyone, and saying something like, "Let us calm down, now, and discuss this subject later." Here, you are not criticizing your spouse but addressing everyone. However, come to an agreement with your spouse first that this will be something that may be used.

There is only one exception to the rule of not undermining the other's authority: *If you your spouse is abusing any of your children* (for example, if the father is severely beating the child). One might say, "If I get involved, I may get hurt myself!" Nonetheless, if your spouse is severely hurting your child, your immediate interference is necessary. If this abuse is repeated, or if it becomes a habitual method of one parent, *you must involve the church and professionals to help you stop this destructive method with our children.*

H | DISCIPLINE AND EDIFICATION

1. Six Essential Principles to Establish in the Home
2. Discipline, Punishment, and Chastisement
3. Discipline According to the Holy Bible
4. As a Parent, Are You Disciplined?
5. The Theology of Discipline
6. Incorrect Methods of Discipline
7. Discipline is a Method of Teaching
8. Ten Possible Steps to Take When Disciplining
9. Suitable Methods of Discipline
10. Suitable Methods of Discipline for Each Age

    Until Age 1 ½ (12-18 Months)

    Ages 1 ½ –3 (18-36 Months)

    Ages 4–12 Years

    Ages 13–16 Years

In the previous section, we spoke about how we can teach our children submission and obedience in order to develop in them spiritual maturity and the ability to accept responsibility. The purpose of this is so that when we give them freedom, they will know how to handle this freedom in a mature and sound manner.

This section covers discipline and edification. However, before speaking about the subject of discipline and edification, we must first set some essential principles when dealing with our children, because without the existence of this foundation, perhaps edification and discipline would cause a *reverse effect*, and not have the effect we seek.

1. Six Essential Principles to Establish in the Home

The first principle is to establish a relationship of love and respect between you and your children. Your relationship with your children is the key to your authority as their parents. Do not keep telling your children, "I am your father, you have to respect me… the Bible says 'Children, obey your parents in the Lord.'" No. Your relationship with your child is what will grant and win for you this authority, and what would make your child obey and submit to you, because he trusts and loves you.

If your relationship with your children is based on threats and fear, your children will rebel against you. If they do not rebel against you visibly perhaps because of fear, they will, at least, do so internally, in their hearts. As such, before thinking about discipline, establish a relationship of love and respect with your children.

I want to tell you that the home is supposed to be an image of heaven, of paradise. Your home is not a battlefield where all parties fight with each other. It is an image of paradise on earth, a paradise of love. Build a relationship established on love and respect. Say, "please," and "thank you," as you would with your colleagues and friends. Interacting with your child with politeness and respect will not lessen your position or your authority.

Also, even when you punish or discipline, do so in an atmosphere of love and respect, and not in an atmosphere of anger and agitation, as I previously explained. Thus, this is the first principle: that you create a relationship of love and respect with your children.

The second principle is to have a regular Bible study with your children about the verses that refer to raising children and the role of children and parents. This is to help the children understand what the Lord expects from them as children, and that God has entrusted the children to their parents' care. He said, "Fathers, do not provoke your children, lest they become discouraged" (Col 3:21). When a child clearly understands the complete picture, he will, then, accept to become obedient and submissive in love and enthusiasm. However, never use these verses when you are angry, such that you declare God's wrath toward them. This would most likely cause your children, at least internally, to rebel against God, especially if the father is hardhearted. The child may wonder how God is asking him to submit to such a severe father. The result would be that the child would begin to not love God.

For the Bible studies, you could begin by doing one about honoring parents. Refer to H.H. Pope Shenouda's book, "The Ten Commandments." This is one of the best books that articulate the issue of honoring parents (the fifth commandment). You may hold another Bible study about obedience; the verses are in Ephesians, Colossians, and First Timothy. Obedience is part of honoring. Honoring one's parents also includes caring for them and their needs, and treating them with respect and appreciation. There could be another Bible study regarding "Discipleship to Our Parents," explaining how to become a disciple to one's parents and learn from them. The Holy Bible does not simply ask us to obey and honor them, but also to become disciples to them. The Lord asks us to learn from our parents. We acquire from them valuable instructions, as the Book of Proverbs says, "For they *will be* a graceful ornament on your head, And chains about your neck" (Prov 1:9; Cf. Septuagint).

The third principle is to become a role model. How do you treat your own parents, the children's grandparents? How do you treat your parents-in-law? The children will see this. When you tell them that God commanded us to honor our parents, and they see that you do not treat your parents or in-laws with the same respect, honor, obedience, and submission and learn from them, the children will say, "Mom and Dad say one thing and do something else." As such, be a role model. You want to teach your children how to take responsibility. Part of this, as I mentioned earlier, is admitting mistakes, bearing the consequences, and apologizing.

When you make an error, as a parent, do you admit your mistake? Do you accept responsibility and apologize for it? You want to teach your child maturity and how to deal with society, which may contain injustice, criticism, or offenses—just as they criticized Christ and said that He casts out demons by Beelzebub, the ruler of the demons (Mt 12:24). The child looks at you to see how you react when others criticize you or how you deal with people when they give you advice.

Are your expectations for your children different from your own behavior? Perhaps you spend seven or eight hours every day on the computer; yet you want your child to only spend half an hour. Do you want your child not to smoke, while you smoke? Do the children see in you a desire for growth and self-improvement? Or do you just want your children to become better, while it is not important that you also improve? Is there ambivalence in your own life? Is what you say different from your behavior, and what you do in your life? Be a role model.

The fourth principle is to reward and praise your children's good behavior. I addressed this point a bit in the previous section. Do not be satisfied by simply punishing mistakes, but also praise and reward good behavior. The fifth principle is to discipline with love and compassion. Remember that the purpose of discipline is improvement, and not revenge or to release anger. As such, when you discipline your child, do not embarrass, or humiliate him by calling him such things as a "failure," and saying every possible harsh word. Do not offend him in the presence of his siblings, relatives, cousins, or friends. They say that discipline with anger, agitation, and rage harms the children more so that not disciplining them at all. In certain instances, if you do not punish them, this is better than if you discipline them with rage and anger, embarrassing, insulting, and even humiliating them.

The last principle is that the more the children grow and develop, the more freedom you must begin to give them, decreasing your authority over them gradually. This is to allow them to develop and reach maturity. This way, by the time they leave home, they will have enough maturity to make decisions and sound choices.

After having stated these six principles as a foundation for our relationship with our children, we will begin talking about discipline and edification. First we will discuss what discipline is and if, as a parent, you are disciplined. We will also discuss the *Theology of Discipline* as well as what to do when my child misbehaves. I would like to emphasize again that the purpose of discipline is reformation and growth, and for the child to reach maturity. Even for St. Paul the Apostle, when he took a stand with a sinner in the city of Corinth in 1 Corinthians 5, the purpose of this discipline was "that his spirit may be saved in the day of the Lord Jesus" (1 Cor 5:5). The purpose of any form of discipline is correction; it is not just about punishing the mistake. "For the Son of Man did not come to destroy men's lives but to save them" (Lk 9:56). Therefore, discipline is given to us by God to use in order to "save men's lives," for the purpose of improvement.

Often, our children's misbehavior is their subconscious tool, which they use to attract their parents' attention when their parents have become preoccupied and are not giving them enough time. The children, therefore, begin to misbehave and act out, simply to attract the parents' attention, as if this were their way of saying, "Give me time! Give me attention and care!" Perhaps, the children's misbehavior is a form of protest against the parents' method of raising them, if parents are always using negative and sharp criticism. The children attempt to misbehave in order to express their disagreement and as a type of protest or rebellion against it, being unable to say that they refuse this treatment.

2. Discipline, Punishment, and Chastisement

Many times, punishment is inappropriate or disproportional to the mistake made in that it is stronger and more severe than necessary. Discipline, however, should always be proportional to the mistake, because it is done out of love and with love. Discipline is not based on one's anger in comparison to punishment, which is usually driven by anger. Discipline is always edifying, while punishment can be destructive to others.

Discipline is not only characterized by chastening; rather, it consists of both chastening and education. In other words, discipline is broader than chastening because chastening occurs only as a result of wrongdoings. Sometimes, you say, "no," to your child, even though he has done nothing wrong. It is said out of love, to discipline and prevent spoiling. For example, your child asks for a toy. Knowing that he has a plethora of toys and giving him yet another one would be spoiling him, you refuse to buy him the new toy. In this case, you are neither punishing not chastening the child, since he did nothing wrong, rather, you are disciplining him to prevent him from being spoiled.

I remember when we were Sunday school servants, and sometimes, a boy would cause trouble. We would tug his ear. Our servants used to tell us, "If you are irritated and upset internally because of the trouble he is causing, you are wrong to squeeze his ear, since this would be an act of expressing your anger. You need to be calm from within, so that when you squeeze the boy's ear, you do it gently with a smile and explain to him his mistake." Then, the action would not be an expression, or release of anger.

Why should we discipline our children? It is because they are very valuable to us. Because of His great love for us, God does not leave us to wander according to our own minds, but chastens and disciplines us. Because He loves us, He does not want us to go astray. Our children are very valuable because they are God's gift to us. When disciplining your children, you need to emphasize the fact that they are very valuable, very dear, and very close to you, and that you love them so much to the extent that you cannot leave them solely to their own will so they do not hurt themselves.

3. Discipline according to the Holy Bible

There are many verses about discipline, especially in the Book of Proverbs. I will choose three verses to demonstrate the means by which we ought to discipline. The first verse is in Proverbs 13:24, "He who spares his rod hates his son, but he who loves him disciplines him promptly." Here, the Lord does not mean corporal punishment; the "rod" refers to discipline. Some people believe that love should not include discipline, saying, "I love them; I cannot discipline them." The Holy Bible says the opposite: "He who spares his rod hates his son, but he who loves him disciplines him promptly." If you really love your son, you have to discipline him.

The second verse is Proverbs 22:6, "Train up a child in the way he should go, and when he is old he will not depart from it." The word "train" refers to discipline leading to good character, which requires training and exercises. Moreover, "he" in "the way *he* should go" refers to the child—train up a child in the way *that child* should go. This means that creativity and understanding are needed in order to know the proper way for each specific child. It is not just one method for every child, and wisdom is needed to discover what is proper for this specific person. For example, disciplining a shy child may differ from disciplining a fearless child. I would treat a child that is timid differently than I would a bold one. The parent's part is to discover the most suitable way to deal with each individual child according to the child's needs and abilities.

The third verse, to which we will return and which is well known, is Ephesians 6:1-4 with a special emphasis on verse four. "Children, obey your parents in the Lord, for this is right. 'Honor your father and mother,' which is the first commandment with promise: 'that it may be well with you and you may live long on the earth.' And you, fathers, do not provoke your children to wrath, but bring them up [discipline them, train them] in the training and admonition of the Lord." Verse four, "And you, fathers, do not provoke your children to wrath, but bring them up in the training and admonition of the Lord," is the verse on which we will focus, particularly on the two elements, training, and admonition.

4. As a Parent, Are You Disciplined?

There is an Arabic saying that means, "How can you give something that you are lacking?" In order to be able to discipline your children, you yourself must be a disciplined person. If you are lacking discipline, it will be a great challenge for you to discipline your children.

Lacking discipline constitutes a lack of boundaries in your life with yourself—a lack of self-control. There are, of course, many areas for self-examination to see whether you are disciplined or not. For example, do you possess self-control with food? In regard to money, to what extent are you disciplined? How do you handle money? These questions can reveal to you whether you have self-control or not. Regarding time, do you have control and are you disciplined with your time? In gratification, are you one of the people who seek immediate gratification or can you delay it? There are some people who, when they need something, they must have it immediately; they lack patience. This is immediate and instant gratification. On the other hand, there are others who, when they need something, they wait patiently until it comes in the proper time. In the area of responsibility and accountability, do you take responsibility for your behavior, or not? Do you hold yourself accountable or do you try to find excuses and self-justifications? In order to be a good parent and to discipline your children in an effective way, you need to start with yourself, to be a disciplined person. We may discover that we are disciplined in certain areas, but not in others. It is very important to discover the weak points in our lives in which we are not disciplined, and to try to work on them. Usually, disciplined parents bring up disciplined children that grow up with the same spirit and mind.

5. The Theology of Discipline

Ephesians 6:4 says, "And you, fathers, do not provoke your children to wrath, but bring them up in the training and admonition of the Lord." Looking at the phrase, "of the Lord," leads us to a discourse on the theology of discipline.

a. God is Love

Our God is a loving God. God is love.[20] In His love, He is concerned that we become the people He wants us to be and who we need to be. Therefore, God disciplines us because He loves us.

b. God is Involved in Our Lives

Second, God is also involved in our lives. He is not detached from us. He is not the God who is far away from us, up in heaven, and we are on earth, disconnected. Yes, He is above us because He is in heaven and we are His creation, as we say, "Our Father who art in heaven," but God who is above us in heaven, became *with us*, Immanuel, "God with us." He is now also abiding in us through His Holy Spirit, whom He sent to live *in us*: You are the temple of God and the Holy Spirit abides in you (see 1 Cor 3:17 & 6: 19). In other words, God is above us, because He is our God, God is with us, because He is Immanuel, and God is living in us, through the Holy Spirit. God is involved in our lives, because He loves us.

We read in Proverbs 3:12, "For whom the Lord loves He corrects, just as a father the son in whom he delights" and in Hebrews 12:6, "For whom the Lord loves He chastens, and scourges every son whom He receives." In the same way, because you love your children, you need to keep this in your mind. You need to keep the hierarchy and the structure of the family. As parents, you need to be on a certain level and your children need to be on a different level. You are the parents and your children are under

---

20 1 Jn 4:8.

your authority. If authority is reversed in the family, you cannot discipline them. At the same time, you are with them, and you are involved with them. Through your love, you are also inside their hearts. Just as God is above us, with us, and in us, you need to keep these three dimensions with your children.

You are above them because you are the authority figure. You are the decision-maker in the household, not the children. Many times, we see that the authority is reversed: the children make the decisions and the parents execute. God does not allow this in our relationship with Him, because if He allowed us to make the decisions and He is the one to execute them, it would not be for our benefit. Therefore, God reminds us in every prayer of, "Our Father who art in heaven," that God is in heaven, He is above us, He is our Creator. However, this does not mean that He is far away from us, but He is with us and in us. Although you are the authority figure in the household, you are not disconnected. The children are not afraid of you. They are not scared, to bring up issues with you; rather, they can talk to you. Yes, there is a hierarchy. However, the children feel that you are with them, sitting and playing with them on the floor, going out with them, and carrying them. At the same time, you are in their hearts with love. However, all of this does not negate, nor forbid that you are the parents and they are the children. Thus, the respect of the hierarchy and the structure are maintained.

c. God is Just

Third, God is just. By nature, He acts with justice. That is why He appointed a day for recompense, in which He will give each one according to his deeds. People often ask how this loving God can throw people in the lake of fire and brimstone (Rev 20:10,15). There is no contradiction. God is just and God is love. People who will go to Hell do so as a result of their own choice. They made the choice to separate themselves from God. In other words, they choose this fate for themselves; it is not God who sends them there. In the same way, you need to be just with your children. There is no contradiction between grace and truth and there is no contradiction between love and justice. Sometimes we say, "No, I cannot see my child cry. I cannot deprive my child of anything. I cannot see my child in need of something and withhold it from him." You are actually hurting your children if you think or behave like this. If you do not discipline inappropriate behavior, the children will continue in it.

Since there is justice, bad behavior is disciplined, but in the same light, good behavior is rewarded. It is important to pay attention to both sides. God rewards everyone according their deeds. Many times we discipline wrong behavior, but we neglect to reward good behavior. This is wrong. Just as you discipline and punish the bad behavior, you also need to reward the good behavior.

d. God is Sovereign

The last point regarding the theology of discipline is that God is sovereign. God is in a position of authority over us. However, although He is sovereign, He gives us the freedom to make choices and He respects our free will, even when we make wrong choices. Yes, many times, God lets us reap the consequences of our choices, but He respects our choices, even the wrong ones. Sometimes, as parents, we do not respect the choices of our children, even their wrong choices. There is a difference between *respecting* their choices and *approving* their choices.

Sometimes, when the child makes a wrong decision, the parent engages in a power struggle with him, which can result in one of two consequences. The first situation that may occur is that I break my child to the point where he may say to himself, "Yes, sir, I know the law. I know that there is a certain age in which I can call the police on my father so that he would not be able to tell me what to do." The child would continue to listen to you, but be filled with anger and hatred, until the age of eighteen. Upon reaching that age, on his birthday, he calls the police on you, and at this point, ends your authority over your son. You have filled him with rebellion against authority. This is one outcome of entering into a power struggle.

The other extreme is that your son will win, causing you to yield to his opinion. Once he wins the struggle and you yield to him, the authority gets reversed in the home. Now, the children are the authority figures and the parents listen to them. This will cause the children to become irresponsible. They will never learn how to take responsibility. My advice to you is to never enter into a power struggle with your children. Who will break whom? Many parents just want to break their children, but this is incorrect. For children who are older, (at least fifteen or sixteen years old), give them choices, explain to them the consequences of their choices, and be consistent. If they make a wrong choice, just remind them; they should be free to make their choices. Then, at the end, be consistent. Let them risk the consequences. (This does not apply to younger children).

Our Lord Jesus Christ taught us this. In the parable of the prodigal son, when the younger son decided to leave his father's house and go to a far country, the father respected his decision, although it was a wrong one. I am sure that the father explained to his son the consequences. He told him, "You will go, you will be happy for a certain period of time, and then you will run out of money. Your friends will leave you, and you will be humiliated." But the son chose to go to the far country. When he got there, he saw that the things his father told him would happen did indeed happen.

There is a key verse in this parable that, sometimes, does not catch our attention. "And he began to be in want … and no one gave him anything" (Lk 15:14-16). The phrase, "no one gave him anything," is very important in this parable. When he started to be in need, no one gave him. "But when he had spent all, there arose a severe famine in that land, and he began to be in want. Then he went and joined himself to a citizen of that country, and he sent him into his fields to feed swine. And he would gladly have filled his stomach with the pods that the swine ate, and no one gave him anything" (Lk 14:14-16). The following verse says, "But when he came to himself" (Lk 15:17). Let me change something small in this parable: The father heard that his son started to be in need, and we know the father is rich. This is clear when the son said, "How many of my father's hired servants have bread enough and to spare" (Lk 15:17). The father was rich to the point that his servants would throw out leftovers. If the father had said, "My son is very poor. I will send him some food and money. This way, he will feel my love for him and he will come back," would the prodigal son have returned? He would not have. That is called "harmful" love.

Sometimes, when a child speeds and gets a ticket, his father pays it for him. Then, he speeds again, gets another ticket, and goes to his father so he can pay it. Then, he speeds a third time and his father pays it again. Afterward, his license gets suspended and the father has to pay for a lawyer on the boy's behalf. Here, the father is repeatedly rescuing him and preventing him from reaping the consequences of his bad behavior. In reality, the father is challenging God's plan because God put a rule in place called, "the law of sowing and reaping" (see Gal 6:7). Whatever you sow, you will reap. However, in this example, the father says, "No, God. I will let my son sow, but I will reap instead of him." I always say, if I sow thorns, and someone else gets hurt while reaping them, what will stop me from sowing thorns if I am not the one getting hurt? What is going to stop me from sowing them is when I actually hurt myself. In summary, do not get into a power struggle with your children; God does not get into a power struggle with us. God explains to us the consequences of our behavior, and then, gives us choices. When we make wrong choices, we reap the consequences. But, of course, God does this in a loving way; the balance between grace and truth is very important.

When the son returned to his father, the father was waiting for him, received him with joy, and did not let him say, "Make me like one of your hired servants" (Lk 15:19). That is grace. The son knew for sure that if he returned, his father would not make him feel ashamed. On the contrary, he would receive him with joy and merriment. Also, David says to God, "If You, Lord, should mark iniquities, O Lord, who could stand?" (Ps 130:3). God does not discipline us for every single mistake we make, because if He did that, all of us would be constantly suffering. In disciplining your children and letting them reap the consequences of their choices, there is a big space for God's grace. For example, when we look at Samson, the first, second, and third times he fell in sin, God saved him. He would be drowning in sin, and God's Spirit would dwell upon him and he would kill the Philistines. This is astonishing! However, after a certain limit, God said, "No. Samson will learn from reaping the consequences of his wrong decisions." What I want to say is, you should not let your children reap the consequences the first time they do something wrong. There is balance between grace and truth and keeping that balance is very important in disciplining your children.

To review the four points of the Theology of Discipline: God is loving, God is involved, God is just, and God is sovereign.

6. Incorrect Methods of Discipline

"Fathers, do not provoke your children to wrath" (Eph 6:4). Provoking or embittering your child happens when you use the wrong style of discipline. There are three incorrect styles of disciplining that will provoke a child to bitterness and wrath:

1) The first type is called **permissiveness**, which is when I allow my child to do whatever he wants to do. Many times we think that this is love, but permissiveness is actually a *lack* of love. If your child does not know how to drive very well, but comes to you, begging and complaining that he wants to drive, and you give him the keys saying, "Here, son, take them. Because I love you, you can drive the car"—what would happen? The child could hurt himself, and maybe, injure or kill himself or others. Would that not be the outcome? In this situation, can we call it love if the father gives his son the keys to the car? It is the same concept when you let your son, in his immaturity, lead his own life, as if he is driving his own car. The person that drives the car is the one that directs the path on which he is going. When you let him make his own choices and decisions, you are letting him lead the "car" of his life. If he is immature and does not know how to drive well, meaning not self-discipline, you are destroying him and killing him. In this way, you provoke him to anger and to wrath because you bring bitterness to his life. Sometimes, children need guidance, as well as someone to guide them. If the parents do not take this role, without a doubt, there are many people who would like to guide your children. It just depends who would take that role. [This parenting style is discussed in more detail in Part I, C.]

2) Another style is called **authoritarian** parenting, which is when parents are completely in control of their children. They do not give them any choices and do not train them to make decisions. Sometimes, children that grow up in this environment turn out to be one of two personalities. They either become rebellious or negatively compliant, meaning that they become very weak and are always afraid. You notice they have an unstable or shaky personality. They become unable to stand before their teachers in school and speak properly. There are two brothers from Egypt, Andrew, and Mario, who are 7th graders. They are very young, but they have power and courage. If they had been subservient, they would have been afraid to fail their course. With all courage, when they went to take an exam, they wrote

on it, "I am Christian," and returned it to their instructor. They both failed and were allowed to retake the exam. When they entered to take the exam for the second time, the same thing happened. They wrote, "I am Christian" and returned the papers. They are only in 7th grade, and they have courage, strength, and resilience. They were able to stand up for the truth. Sometimes, older people are terrified to behave the same way these two children did. If the parents were authoritarian and raised their children to have fear, they would have been afraid and would not have done what they did. Sometimes, when we control and dictate to our children, we shape them into becoming subservient. They are not strong enough to say the word of truth. [This parenting style is discussed in more detail in Part I, C.]

3) The third incorrect style of disciplining is **inconsistence**, which can mean different things. One type of inconsistency is saying something and not following through with it. For example, you may tell your child, "If you do *this*, the consequence will be the *that*," but, you are inconsistent. Another type is inconsistency between your words and your behavior. The children notice the difference between who you are and what you want your children to be. That is why I mentioned at the beginning that if you want to discipline your children, you yourself must be a disciplined person. Inconsistency could also be in giving contradicting, double-messages. If you tell your son, "I really do love you," however, all your actions do not show this love, the child gets confused and is unable to reconcile the messages you are sending. Do you really love him or you do not love him? They did a study on schizophrenic children and found that a large percentage, more than 80% of these children received contradicting messages from their parents in early childhood. They wanted to resolve the contradicting messages but could not, and they became schizophrenic. Sometimes, we harm our children when we send them contradicting messages. We put them in a state of confusion. The child starts to question if his father really loves him or not, since all his actions show

otherwise, and sometimes to solve this confusion, the child's mind enters into a state of schizophrenia.

7. Discipline is a Method of Teaching

Discipline is a method of teaching. Note that we always hear about the *disciples* of the Lord Jesus Christ. We do not say "students" or "pupils" even though "disciples," "students," and "pupils" are all translated from the same word in the Arabic language. A pupil learns passively, by being fed. A student learns by studying, which is why he is called a student. A disciple learns by discipline. Therefore, discipline is a method of teaching. For the parent, it refers to teaching the child. For a child, it is a method of learning. In the Book of Isaiah, there is a prophecy about the Lord Jesus Christ that says, "The Lord God has given Me the tongue of the learned" and "He awakens My ear to hear as the learned" (Is 50:4).

Disciplining your children includes educating them, that is, teaching and training them. If you want to plant a certain virtue in your child's life, you need to explain it and to train him in it, and to tell him how to perform it. Often, we punish or discipline our children without teaching or training them on how to keep the rules we want them to follow. Discipline is not just punishment; you can discipline them when you spend time explaining to them the rules, values, and principles that you want to plant in their hearts. Also, you train them, as the verse says, "train up a child" (Prov 22:6). Theoretical explanation is not enough. It does not make sense for a medical student to go out and perform surgery once he finishes his classes. First, he has to go through rotations to learn from and be trained by the more experienced. The educational part of discipline is the explanation; afterward comes the training, which is the opportunity to apply what they learned. Therefore, explain the rules to your children, train them, and be flexible. If you feel that the child is still unable to comprehend a certain rule, feed him with "milk," until he is mature enough to eat solid food.[21] Education is meant to happen gradually. Teach your child step by step.

In the process of educating, children go through three different stages. The first stage is "what," the second is "how," and third is "why." The first six years in your child's life is the time for the "what" stage. What are the principles that you want to plant in your son? During the first six years,

---

21 Cf. 1 Cor 3:2: St. Paul's analogy to spiritual maturity.

do not focus on "how" to do them because his mind will not absorb this. It is not time for "how," but at least teach him the principles. Ages six to twelve is the time for explaining how to excel in these principles. Then, the next stage (ages twelve to eighteen) is the time for "why." The child's brain matures and you can explain the reasons to him.

Thus, the educational part of discipline is very important. Before you get your driver's license, you have to be educated. You study the manual, and after you learn all the rules, you are tested on them in order to get your driver's license. Once you get your license, this means that you know the rules and if you violate any of the rules, the officer can give you a ticket. No one would hand you a driver's license without explaining the rules and regulations. Similarly, you cannot punish your child for doing something wrong, if you never explained or trained him in why it was wrong. You need to explain the principles to him and train him to avoid mistakes, and if he still falls, then, there are consequences. Discipline should have a purpose, which is to bring up a godly child.

8. Ten Possible Steps to Take When Disciplining

If your child makes a mistake, you do not need to take all ten steps. Let us take only what we need in each situation.

a. The First Step

The first point is to calm down! Never punish when you are angry or furious. You have to be deeply calm internally. Some say if one is furious and angry, he should wait twenty minutes in a peaceful place with the intention of calming himself. Then, he will be able to calm down. However, a person must not further irritate himself, by thinking about how such a thing could have happened, and with other such negative thoughts. The person would then never calm down. However, if one were to sit alone and pray, open the Bible, or sing a hymn to calm his soul, he would be able to calm down no matter how enraged he is.

Ask yourself, have you lost control of your temper or are you still in control of it? If you find that you have lost control of your temper, bow down and pray, asking for help from the Lord so that the result of the conversation between you and your child, and the result of the discipline, may be good. One option, if you find that you are furious, is to ask your child to go to his room for a while, to give yourself time to calm down.

This would also make him feel that he did something wrong. Then, call him back to talk.

b. The Second Step

The second step is to evaluate what happened. Stop and think about the mistake. Analyze it in an objective manner. There may be reasons for his misbehavior that you would need to understand and examine prior to disciplining. Your child, whom you may think is being disobedient, may be just four or five years old. He may be suffering from a type of mental handicap or disorder; this could be the reason for his poor comprehension. As such, you are punishing him while this is the best he can be. For example, some children are unable to memorize three things in a row. If you gave them three orders, they would not be able to absorb all three of them. Therefore, there may be a more profound reason; yet you are punishing without knowing the real reason.

Once a father told me that his son used to refuse a specific type of food. His father thought that the child was spoiled and he used to punish him. The father later discovered that his child suffered from an allergy caused by that food. Whenever he ate it, he used to suffer a lot. This was the reason that the two of them went into episodes of stubbornness and rage against each other. The father wanted to force the child to obey him, and the child was unable to do so because he was not feeling well. In addition, the child was unable to explain because he was too young to understand his symptoms. This story illustrates the reason that before you begin to punish or get irritated with your children, you need to understand whether there are any other reasons for what you call, "stubbornness," or "disobedience."

Another example is if your child was holding a cup but it fell from his hands and it broke. Ask yourself, was this misbehavior done willfully and out of stubbornness on his part or was it unintentional? Suppose, for example, something fell from his hands and broke unintentionally. This situation does not need rage or punishment. It does not require discipline. Perhaps it just requires me to teach him how to be more careful. Though we are adults, things fall from our hands and break as well. I have seen parents who punish their children severely if they break something. Why?

See if your child is perhaps ill. Perhaps, he is tired. Perhaps, he is exhausted or stressed because of exams. There may be a reason for his misbehavior. Understand his situation. Perhaps, *you* [the parent] may be the reason—your desire to be in control and to rule over him. It may be your austerity in the way you treat your child that could create a kind of rebellion. Thus, you would be punishing him for an error that you caused, due to your severe harshness and wish to be in control and dominate. Perhaps, as I previously mentioned, you are not giving your child enough of your time. The child may be behaving in this manner to attract your attention. The child's behavior may also be a reaction to problems between parents or the fighting and tension that exists in the household. Would we punish a child while we are the cause?

Perhaps, the child has problems at school with his friends, or any other type of problem such as children making fun of him. Perhaps, the child does not feel safe enough to come and tell his parents what happens to him, because if he told them, they may scold him: "If you were respectable, the other children would have respected you," etc. The child does not feel safe, and at the same time, he has a problem, which is making him anxious and causing him to behave in this manner.

Perhaps, the child was raised with a guilt complex, despite having done nothing wrong on his part. For example, many parents tell their children, "All my problems with your mom are because of you!" Here, you put a load of guilt on your child, while it is not his fault at all! Maybe this feeling of guilt is what causes him to misbehave.

Maybe you criticize him so frequently that the child has begun to believe that he is indeed a failure and a bad boy that must be punished. Once I was praising a child by telling him, "When I talk to you, I feel that you are a mature and wise person." The boy was surprised! He said, "Wow, nobody ever told me anything like this." He did not believe it, although he really was a good boy. This means that nobody ever praises him; he never hears a good word from anybody. He was under the belief that he is a failure and does not deserve any praise and that he must be punished.

Ask yourself if the command you gave or the demand you asked of your son was clear to him. Was this request suitable to his capabilities and abilities, or maybe you asked him for something that is far greater than his capabilities?

After having asked yourself all these questions, you may discover that your child does not need punishment, that he just needs love and compassion. He needs you to become closer to him and to help him

Childhood: Discipline and Edification

get rid of all the erroneous and negative feelings that have accumulated inside of him.

If your child misbehaves, then, while you are calm, and after you have studied the situation and examined what happened, and after you have asked yourself all the questions mentioned above, sit alone with your child, just the two of you. Do not embarrass him in front of his siblings or relatives. Sometimes, when I visit a family, they seem to find it the only chance for them to complain about their child. Sadly, the child would then be very upset, "Are they going to ruin my image in front of His Grace who came to visit us at home?" Sometimes, it is not wise that we begin complaining about our children in front of others. Why not call the priest before he comes to visit to give him an idea about the problem happening with your child, so that the priest could, perhaps, sit privately with your child and talk with him? Do not scold and criticize him in front of others. When you sit privately with him, you will make him less defensive and he will not be focused on simply defending himself. It would enable him, if he really did make a mistake, to be able to say, "I truly did make a mistake, Dad, I am sorry." However, usually when you embarrass him in front of others, he will continue to defend himself, regardless of whether or not he is in the right.

c. The Third Step

The third step is to discuss what happened with him. I said *discuss*, meaning *listen* to him. Let it be a discussion. Do not turn the meeting into a lecture, in which you list his mistakes and their consequences. But discuss with him what happened. Tell him, "I want to know from you, my beloved, what happened in that situation?" If the child begins to speak in an improper way, as I said before, do not accept this. You may say, "Look, I see that you are not calm, so go to your room and calm down first, because it will not work for us to talk while you are irritated or talking this way. It is not possible for us to talk in this way." I often do this. When someone, for example, calls me on the phone and there is a problem that is bothering him in church or in the service, or if he asks to see me and comes in very irritated and angry, I tell him, "No, it is not going to work for us to talk this way. You need to calm down first so that we can talk. I cannot discuss anything in this kind of atmosphere. Calm down completely, and then, we can talk." And if the person insists on talking, I keep repeating my words, "Calm down so that we can talk. I am going to have to hang up until you calm down so that we can talk." The person agrees at the end and calms down. Do not accept that your child talks to you in an improper way. You must also deal with this kind of situation with gentleness and love. You do not need to yell at him; you just need to repeat yourself and say, "We cannot have a conversation while you are talking in this way. Go to your room, make the sign of the cross, calm down, and when you are calm, come back and we will talk together."

As you are saying these things to him, note the tone of your voice and the words that you will use with him in the discussion. When you talk to him, speak with firm love and seriousness. Often, in order to get out of the situation, children attempt to make fun and joke about it. Make it clear to him that, "No. Now, there is something wrong, and we are discussing the matter." Make the discussion serious. This does not mean that you have to be angry or furious. When you are talking with him, do not show any hatred; do not insult him. Do not say words to hurt him. Rather, explain to him the mistake. You may show him how much pain and disappointment this mistake caused you personally. This is the method that St. Paul the Apostle used when he explained to the Corinthians how sad he was after hearing about the sin that took place in Corinth. He told them in 2 Corinthians 2:4, "For out of much affliction and anguish of heart I wrote to you, with many tears." Of course when they learned that their shepherd is sad and is writing this letter to them with much affliction, anguish of heart, and many tears, this made them also sad.

It is often beneficial that the child feels saddened and sorry for his misbehavior. This is what St. Paul says in 2 Corinthians 7:8, "For even if I made you sorry with my letter, I do not regret it; though I did regret it." In other words, "I do not regret that my letter, in which I rebuked the Corinthian sinners, caused you to be sad, despite having regretted it because I never wished to write you a letter using such language." But why did you not regret it, our teacher Paul? He says, "For I perceive that the same epistle made you sorry, though only for a while" (2 Cor 7:8). This means that the sadness was temporary. "Now I rejoice, not that you were made sorry, but that your sorrow led to repentance" (2 Cor 7:9). Thus, there is "godly sorrow," which leads to repentance. "For you were made sorry in a godly manner, that you might suffer loss from us in nothing" (2 Cor 7:9). Then, he says a wonderful verse, "For godly sorrow produces repentance leading to salvation, not to be regretted; but the sorrow of the world produces death" (2 Cor 7:10). Thus, if you plant feelings of sadness in your child, this will help him to produce repentance, "leading to salvation, not to be regretted" (2 Cor 7:10).

However, sometimes people exaggerate the sadness and sorrow, to the point that they break the child's heart and he feels that there is no more hope. Do not do this. You must be realistic. Moreover, do not use this method for every mistake—major or minor; otherwise, it defeats its purpose with time. The child might even feel that his father is not being genuine with him. When the situation is indeed sorrowful and sad, or something major, you can make him know how much it saddened you.

As much as you can, stay away from words that lead to desperation of the heart. You may destroy his spirit. The goal, as we said, is *correction*, not *destruction*.

With young children, and often with adults, it is not beneficial to ask them, "Did you do this?" The answer to this question is either, "yes" or "no." It is likely that he will lie and say, "No, I did not do it," to defend himself. Rather, tell him, "I want to hear your point of view about this situation." Do not say, "Did you hit your brother!" Ask him, "What happened between you and your brother today?" Here, you are not giving him a chance to lie. "We want to talk about what happened today."

Do not ask young children, "Why did you do this?" Usually, a child acts out of inexperience; he does not have an evil, inner motive behind his misbehavior. He misbehaved out of immaturity, childishness, and inexperience. St. Paul says, "For everyone who partakes only of milk is unskilled … for he is a babe" (Heb 5:13). If you ask him, "why," he may just answer, casually, "I wanted to." How would you answer that? Asking "why" is something we can ask someone who is older.

When your child comes to explain to you his point of view, do not interrupt him. Be a good listener. Understand the truth from him. Understand his point of view. Look at the situation from his point of view. One time, I was very upset with someone. Then, I thought to myself, "Why did this person behave in this way with me?" I imagined myself in his place; I actually wrote it down, but I was writing from his point of view. I imagined myself in his place, and I started to explain why I behaved this way. Believe me, as soon as I finished writing, the discomfort and irritation that were inside of me vanished completely. Why? Because what occurred was that I understood the situation from his point of view.

There was surely some truth or some logic as to why he had behaved in that way. Therefore, do not simply look at a situation from your own point of view.

Never enter into a power struggle between you and your child about who would break whose word. If you enter into a power struggle and your child disobeys you, your authority would be shaken. Nevertheless, expect that, often, no matter how fair-minded you are with your children; they may still be upset from the punishment. St. Paul the Apostle said this: "Now no chastening seems to be joyful for the present, but painful; nevertheless, afterward it yields the peaceable fruit of righteousness to those who have been trained by it" (Heb 12:11). So, sometimes, no matter how fair you were with your child, he may still be upset from the punishment he received, which is okay. There is nothing wrong with that. If he did not get upset, he would not adjust his behavior. He must feel upset in order not to repeat the mistake again.

In this conversation, teach your children to accept responsibility and bear the consequences of their mistakes. Help them to develop a conscience that is alive and enlightened by the Holy Spirit, who inspires them to judge themselves before others do.

We said that the goal is improvement. Ask your child, "My beloved, what can we gain from this situation?' This is what I mean by suggesting that it be a conversation, not a lecture. Allow him to think; discuss with him. Ask him, "If you find yourself in the same situation again, if your brother did the same thing with you again, what will the alternatives be? How will you treat him?" Here, you are allowing him to think and to find alternatives, so that, when he finds himself, once again, in the same situation, he would behave differently. Do not give him the answers. Let him think about it by himself. If you give him the answer, he will forget it. But if he thought about it and came to the answer himself, he would keep it and apply it. If he tells you, "I do not know what to do," tell him, "Okay, think about it until tomorrow and we will talk again then. Try to think of other options. If your brother behaved in the same way with you, how could you react to that behavior?" Give him a chance to think. You can give him some hints; tell him, "I will tell you about something Abigail did with David. Read that chapter in the first book of Samuel and see." You may give him a hint like this to help him reach the answer.

d. The Fourth Step

A very important point is that if your child is lying, you have to deal with it. If a child grows up accustomed to lying, this becomes a major problem. Try to be sure of the truth from others. If the problem happened at church, you could ask his Sunday school servant, for example. If you find that the child indeed did something wrong and then lied, then he committed two mistakes. Therefore, when you administer the consequences, give him two punishments. This is what the Lord did with David when he committed adultery and then committed murder; he received a punishment for the adultery and another punishment for the murder. Do not give two punishments for one mistake. Each mistake must be punished, but do not punish twice for one mistake. The psalm says, "If You, Lord, should mark iniquities, O Lord, who could stand?" (Ps 130:3). Do not continuously punish your children for every mistake. This is why I said not to expect perfection from our children.

If you have no proof as to whether or not the child lied about a situation, never tell him, "You are a liar;" otherwise, you will oppress him. You would also be pushing him to lie the next time. If you were unable to be sure whether or not the child lied, allow the situation to pass. However, if you know from previous experiences and you are sure that your child is in the habit of lying, and you discovered the truth about the situation at hand, and you were 95% sure that he lied, treat him as though he had lied, although you are not 100% sure, but you are 95% sure. Why? To tell him that all the previous lying that he did caused people to lose their trust in him, and he needs to gain back people's trust once again. There is a story they used to tell us a long time ago when we were in elementary school about the boy who was swimming and kept saying that he was drowning, but he was lying. Once he was actually drowning and nobody came to his rescue.

Often, young children do not lie on purpose. However, they may imagine stories and tell you fairytales as if it were a game. Deal with it as if it were a game, not a lie. Maybe if you tell him, "This is a lie," the child would not have in his mind that it is a lie, but rather a part of his wide imagination. Thus, the child is just imagining and telling stories; it is a kind of game he plays. Therefore, do not deal with it as if it were a lie.

e. The Fifth Step

The next step is to give the suitable punishment according to the age, gravity, and type of mistake, surrounding circumstances, and personality.

f. The Sixth Step

The next point is to expect and raise your child with positive reactions. Do not accept that when you give him a punishment, he would turn, slam the door, and leave the room. Do not accept such behavior. Teach your child to say, "I am sorry." If your child does not learn to say, "I am sorry," he would never know how to confess in the correct way. He would come and justify his mistakes; it would not be in a true spirit of repentance. What will happen when he grows up and gets married? So many women complain to us that their husbands never apologize. He never came and told her, "I am sorry," because he did not learn to bear the consequences of his mistakes from his childhood.

If your child cries in front of you, never weaken or change your stance. It is okay for him to be sad; but sadness that does not produce death. On the contrary, it is godly sorrow that "produces repentance leading to salvation." St. Peter the apostle wept bitterly.

If you are explaining to your child what his punishment will be, and afterward, the child does something like slamming the door, do not allow the situation to pass, but deal with this behavior as another mistake. However, before dealing with it as a mistake, ask yourself the following questions to be sure you are not doing an injustice to your child: Is his reaction caused by my austerity? If I am severe and/or unable to make him understand well, he may get up and slam the door in my face. Is this reaction caused by my severity? Have I followed all the steps mentioned above? Was I dealing with him in love, or with anger and rage? If you acted in an appropriate way with your child, and then, this was his reaction, wait until the child calms down and then, call him back. Explain to him that this reaction is unacceptable and give him another punishment for his reaction. Do not do this until the tension subsides, so that the child learns that his reactions must be acceptable. This is a chance for him to learn. If, for example, he did something like that at work and slammed the door in his manager's face, he would be fired. So, this is a chance to teach your child how to behave politely and how to control his reactions, even if he is responding to something he does not accept. Later, explain to him that any inappropriate reactions will not be tolerated.

g. The Seventh Step

The next step is to stand up and pray together before ending the conversation. Ask him to pray first. When he prays, ask him to ask God at least three things: First, he needs to apologize to our Lord for the mistake he made. Second, he needs to ask God for forgiveness. Third, he must ask help from God to overcome this point of weakness. You pray afterward, thanking God for providing an opportunity for repentance and forgiveness.

Emphasize God's love and that discipline is a form of His love. Also, emphasize God's forgiveness and His acceptance of sinners. Stress the importance of repentance and confession. Encourage him to go afterward and sit with his father of confession and confess his mistake. "If we confess our sins, He is faithful and just to forgive us" (1 Jn 1:9). Stress to him the importance of partaking of Communion because "the blood of Jesus Christ His Son cleanses us from all sin" (1 Jn 1:7). Lest he fall into desperation, assure him that we all have our weaknesses and that nobody is perfect, and talk about the importance of striving, "forgetting those things which are behind and reaching forward to those things which are ahead" (Phil 3:13). The importance of the spiritual struggle is to get rid of our weaknesses.

h. The Eighth Step

The eighth point is that after having prayed, take your child in your arms, and hug him so that he knows you are not seeking revenge. You are doing this, and you love him. Assure him that you love him, and that you have already forgiven him, as long as he has complied in the right manner. The Holy Bible says, "And if he repents, forgive him" (Lk 17:3). Reconcile with him, and show him your love.

i. The Ninth Step

The next point is that after this, you have to follow up with your child. If, for example, he offended his brother, teach him to apologize to his brother and ask for forgiveness. If he took something that was not his, teach him to return it, like Zacchaeus who, when he treated people unjustly, said, "I restore fourfold" (Lk 19:8). To remedy the results of one's mistakes is one of the ways of taking responsibility.

j. The Tenth Step

The last point is to *forget the situation*. "Their sin I will remember no more" (Jer 31:34). "As far as the east is from the west, so far has He removed our transgressions from us" (Ps 103:12). If the Lord does not remember our sins, you, also, having admonished your child and given him the punishment, forget the situation. Do not keep mentioning it to your child tens of times, nor every time you see him reminding him about it, "Do you remember when you did this?" No. It is over; forget the situation, so the child would feel your love.

9. Suitable Methods of Discipline

Often, parents who were subjected to cruelty and severity in their youth from their parents completely reject the principle of disciplining altogether. They consider it to be a type of cruelty. Of course, there is a difference between disciplining with love and tenderness and disciplining with cruelty. When I was reviewing the questions I received, I found a question asking me how there could be authority without cruelty and control. There is a great difference between someone having authority, and someone using this authority to control and abuse and to force his or her own opinion.

The Lord gave us authority for the sole purpose of using it to protect those who are under our authority. For example, when the Lord gave authority to the clergy in the Church, it was to be used for the protection and care of our children. When the Lord gave authority to the father and the mother, it was to be used for the protection and care of their children. The same is supposed to be applicable for the authority in the country: it is to protect citizens and people.

Often, people, who are in a position of authority, hurt others and misuse their power. This does not mean there is something wrong with authority itself, but the mistake is that of the person that abuses it. This is why the existence of a system that holds the responsible people accountable is very important, lest a misuse of authority takes place leading to the harm of others. What I want to say is that if a father or mother has been exposed in their youth to cruelty, they must deal with these feelings that exist inside of them. However, they should not refuse the principle of disciplining at all, as this refusal is not beneficial to their children.

Our teacher, St. Paul the Apostle, says in his letter to the Hebrews, "Now no chastening seems to be joyful for the present, but painful; nevertheless, afterward it yields the peaceable fruit of righteousness to those who have been trained by it" (Heb 12:11). Even though at the present time, discipline is not joyful, but actually painful, it is useful for our children. Explain to them that it will be painful.

Sometimes parents reject the principle of discipline if they have only one child or if they have only one boy. Also, they may refuse to discipline children for whom they waited a long time. This is also not useful for the child. It may lead to spoiling, which may corrupt the child.

We shall discuss some useful methods of discipline. As I mentioned earlier, you have to choose the kind of chastening suitable for each child based on his or her personality. You have to know that your child would appreciate this way of chastening before choosing something like this.

a. Education

First—and, perhaps, you may be surprised that it is considered discipline or punishment—is education. Remember that the purpose of a discipline, as I mentioned earlier, is correction. It is an opportunity to teach why a particular action or decision was wrong. I will give you a general example: Sometimes, when a person gets a traffic ticket, they tell him to attend a course consisting of several classes on defensive driving and the points on his license will be removed. Regarding your child, you may, for example, ask him to do research. If your child curses a lot, ask him to research the subject of cursing and teach him how to search for the verses that talk about cursing in the Bible. Have him start to talk about the seriousness of cursing and how it deprives a person from the heavenly kingdom, etc. The purpose of this exercise is to encourage him to deeply examine his weakness and attempt to overcome it.

You are accomplishing more than one thing by having him research and study. First, you are making him open the Bible and study it. Second, you are making him understand, by himself, the danger of the sin or the error he made, directly from the Bible. Third, you are making him figure out exercises to overcome this weakness in his life. Of course, you may give him names of some books that discuss the subject of the "sins of the tongue." He may research the Epistle of Saint James about the sins of the tongue, etc. In other words, discipline does not necessarily need to be something that hurts the child or makes him sad. No. It could be a chance to teach him, to give the child positive discipline so that he begins to work on researching this subject. It is, thus, a chance for him to benefit. Of course, he should present this research to you by a certain time, etc.

It is important to teach your children not only what *not* to do, but also what they *should* do. When we speak about cursing, the Bible says, "Being reviled, we bless" (1 Cor 4:12) and "Bless those who curse you" (Mt 5:44). Teach him not to only stop cursing—to stop cursing is just one part of it—but also that what is more important is to bless others. I bless the person who offends me, who curses me or who swears at me, rather than curse back. In this manner, I am helping the child to mature and grow spiritually. This is why I am reiterating not to let the only method of education you use be punitive and cause sadness and pain to the child. Let it not be the first thing that comes to mind when your child makes a mistake. Rather, use training. For example, after having completed this research, start to praise him for it. Praise his effort in this good research about the sins of the tongue, which he accomplished. Training, advising, guiding, and complimenting can all help your children to get rid of their mistakes, and to grow and be spiritually mature.

When you are interacting with your children, do not assume that every mistake they make is caused by disobedience. Perhaps your children are doing the best they can; however, they do not know how to comply with what you asked. For example, you asked him to do research, but you did not show him how to do it. So, he brought a sheet of paper and wrote down the sins of the tongue: Cursing, lying, and swearing, and the Lord is upset with these mistakes. Then, he presented this paper to you, saying, "Here is my research." Do not tell him, "You are a stubborn child, and you do not want to respect what I asked you to do; you do not listen to what I say!" Perhaps you asked him to do something he does not know how to do. He may not know what it means to research a certain subject. If he is in first or second grade and you asked him to research the sins of the tongue, perhaps he does not know how to do it. However, if you explain to him, and show him how to use the Bible Index (and now with the help of the computer, searching on the Internet makes this much easier), this will help him achieve his task. You may also tell him about certain chapters, or give him names of some books that are suitable for his age. Teach him how to begin doing the research.

Do not assume that your children are disobedient. Perhaps they are doing their best but they do not know how to accomplish what you asked. This is why it may appear to you that they are not listening to what you say. Train them first before assuming that they are disobedient to you.

Train them and explain to them how to work on the research before falsely accusing them or punishing them for their disobedience.

One of the ways to educate a child is to ask him to set apart a specific time to pray for the sake of the issue at hand. Explain to him that in order to overcome the sin of anger, for example, he needs divine assistance. The exercise you would give him is to spend a certain amount of time every day praying. You may begin with him and explain to him how to pray and how to ask for divine assistance, how to read certain psalms, and how to memorize certain ones. Tell him, "As soon as you feel that anger is beginning to grow inside of you, read this psalm." For example, pray the psalm that says, "Make haste to help me, O Lord" (Ps 69), or "I will lift up my eyes to the hills" (Ps 120). Again, do not give your children an order, but show them how to do it. Tell them which psalm they should read. Give them time to memorize it, and explain to them that when they begin to get any feelings of anger, they should begin to pray this psalm to calm themselves and not fall into the sin of anger.

As you give them the exercise to help them overcome the point of weakness, encourage them, and tell them that you trust them and that you trust that they are able to accomplish this task with great success. For example, when you ask your child to research a topic, encourage him. Tell him, "I know that this research is not too hard for you to do. I trust that you are an intelligent and hardworking person. I trust that just by looking in those books and researching these chapters, you will be able to prepare a wonderful research paper." Encourage your children and give them self-confidence because this will also help them accomplish your request with competence.

Sometimes, the child may try to do the research wholeheartedly several times and in a sincere manner, but at the end, the result is weak. Rather than blaming him because the result is not according to your expectations, it is better to compliment his sincere attempts to accomplish your request. He truly attempted to accomplish your request, although the result did not come out the way you expected. Show appreciation for his effort, that the child sat down and brought the books, even if the end result was not as expected.

Another point is to compensate the children, in general, not just when they stop the negative behavior, but also when they do something positive. For example, perhaps the problem you are attempting to remedy is that one child is frustrating his brother. You gave the child several exercises and he stopped annoying his brother. This is good. However, when he begins to do something positive with his brother, I want you to encourage this point. As I said, it is not enough that a person stays away from the error, but there is also a focus on how to grow positively. Thus, it is not enough to just stay away from the mistake; he must also grow in a positive direction. Therefore, reward your children for their positive effort.

I am using the term, "reward," because there is a difference between a "reward" and a "bribe." A reward is part of a system that has a target, which is to teach your children good habits and to expel bad ones. For example, if a child swears at his siblings, or fights with them, you encourage him to stop these fights. At the same time, when he attempts to be positive with his siblings, offering them love and cooperation, you reward this behavior. There is a system that you are following with him, with good habits that you want him to acquire and bad habits that you want him to eliminate. Thus, you encourage these good habits through compensation.

On the other hand, a bribe is used just for a specific situation. For example, if you are going to church or to a certain meeting, or if a guest is coming to your home, you might be tempted to bribe your child just for this situation. You may say, "There are people coming today to visit us. If you behave properly, I will give you something special [whatever that may be]." Herein, you are not helping him develop good habits; you are bribing him for the sake of a certain situation or for the sake of behavior in a certain situation. Usually, when children hear this, they know that this guest is important for the parents; so, they begin to threaten you in a negative manner: If you do not do what they want, they might embarrass you in front of your guest. Thus, do not raise your children on bribes. Teach them the habit of improving their behaviors, in general, as this is your goal (to improve their behavior and help them develop mature and responsible personalities).

Do not wait until your children reach perfection to compensate them. As soon as you see any improvement in their character or behavior, begin to compensate and praise this improvement. This encourages them, as the Holy Bible says, "Comfort the fainthearted" (1 Thess 5:14).

A chart used to keep track of good behavior is a useful, illustrative tool. For example, the parents could put stars every day the child behaves correctly. When the child sees on the chart that he received several stars, and after several stars he will receive a reward, or his allowance will increase, etc., or that something will be taken away from him because he misbehaved, this could help him. This is used in what is called, "Behavioral Therapy," to cure children's behavioral problems.

As I mentioned earlier, it is very important that you develop in your children the habit of critical thinking. Rather than telling your child, "I see that you are making this mistake, and you must improve in this," ask him, "What do you think the areas are in which you need to improve? What do you think you need to do to improve in this matter?" This approach is better than telling him, "You are bothering your brothers while they are studying. You are wasting their time. You annoy them," etc. Ask him, "What do you think the points are that you need to change in your behavior at home?" He would give you examples. Then, ask him, "How could you overcome your behavior by using these points?" You may give him some hints to have him answer you correctly. When he gives you an answer, tell him that you expect him to live up to what he has just said. In this manner, his confidence is growing. *He* is the one who said what he must do, and *he* is the one to comply.

Promise your children that you shall help them with all your capability to reach their goal to improve. Notice the difference: now it is not *your* target and the child is carrying it out. This target has become the *child's* target; he wants to reach it and you are helping him. Thus, the child is not doing you a favor. He will not say, "I changed my character for your sake." Of course not—who is the one who benefits? He is. Thus, it is wise to make the improvement his target. He is not doing it because this is what his dad wants. He is not changing himself because this is what his mom wants. No. He sees that this is what he needs and you are the one helping him reach this target.

If there is a common weakness that you and your child share—for example, if your child is irritable and is often short tempered, and you have the same problem (you also are irritable and short tempered)—then, there is nothing wrong with working together on these shortcomings. When the child makes a mistake, and you are talking to him about the subject of nervousness—you want to agree together on discipline to overcome the issue of anger—so, you may tell him, "By the way, I also suffer from this. I also lose my temper and become nervous. Let us work on this together; let us pray together. We can read the book written by His Holiness Pope Shenouda about anger together, and study it together." This is also a way to teach the child how to assume responsibility. In this manner, the child has learned the spirit of responsibility from you; he learned from you how you try to eliminate your faults. At the same time, you are also helping him get rid of this fault in him. It is a very helpful strategy to use so that your child can see that you want to endeavor with him. Even our fathers the monks use this idea. When a Father Confessor or an elder in the monastic community finds a novice who is striving against a certain weakness—the novice is crushed and defeated from this weakness that is in his life. We read in the Paradise of the Fathers that the elder monk would say to him, "My son, even I am being fought with the same thoughts. Let us fight together." It encourages the beginner when he is not the only one dealing with the issue; often, a person thinks that he is the only one that falls into this sin, and all the other people are saints, and he is the only sinner. This makes a person fall into despair—feeling defeated and filled with a downcast spirit. However, when you tell him that we are all exposed to this type of battle, we all fall in this struggle, you are encouraging him, and helping him feel that he is not alone in this fight. Rather, we will struggle together, and the Lord shall reward us with triumph.

As I mentioned earlier, use verses and stories from the Holy Bible. Hold a Bible study about the subject that is the cause of the problem you are tackling. These are all very important matters in learning.

Another point is to ask your children about their input, rather than giving them a list of instructions. If the weakness is that your children move around a lot at church, become disobedient, or cause a disturbance, etc., rather than saying, "We are going to church, and I expect you to behave in such and such a way," sit with them and say, "We are going to church. How do you think we should behave there?" When it comes out of their mouths, it becomes their own will and decision. You should, then, encourage and praise them. Say, "You are right; we must behave in this way. I will watch you today and I will be happy to see you behaving in that manner."

Sometimes, when dealing with young children who still do not grasp matters properly, they may not understand. For example, if the child is bothering his brother and you tell him "Do not annoy your brother," he may not understand. If you tell him, "Let your brother study," he still may not understand. However, attempt to distract his attention with something else. This is called "redirection." You are redirecting his attention to something else. You attract his attention by bringing him a game or something else to do, rather than to focus on his brother. When you give it to him, you find that he is attracted to it, and he stays away from his brother. In this manner, he allows his brother to continue studying, etc.

Therefore, this first method of discipline is education, and we covered several points on this subject.

b. Hitting (is NOT acceptable)

The second point is the subject of hitting children. Is spanking considered one of the acceptable methods of discipline? The truth is that hitting and causing physical harm is completely rejected. The verses in the Holy Bible that talk about using "the rod" for disciplining speak about the principle of discipline, in general, but do not refer to inflicting physical harm. The most a father or a mother could do is a light slap on the child's hand if he misbehaves. Unfortunately, some parents hit their children severely and brutally. This breaks the child's inner spirit. It leaves deep wounds that may require years of healing. We never encourage beatings. As I said, the most you could do is to slap a child on his hand, without inflicting pain— nothing more. Any beating or inflicting pain is completely rejected.

c. Time-Outs

One of the methods of discipline is what we call, "time out." You ask him to stay in a place in the room for a certain period of time. Of course, in order for the child to respond, when you use the method of time out, short time-outs are more effective than longer ones. You could use two to three minutes with very young children. With those who are a little bit older, you could use around seven minutes. When you attempt to use time-outs, you must not begin to count the allotted period of time while the child continues to run and jump around. You are supposed to begin to calculate the two or three or seven minutes when he starts to comply by being silent and quiet and when he stops moving around. By doing this, you are teaching him how to become disciplined. When you give him an order, he is obligated to carry it out.

There is another way to use time-outs. You can begin with six minutes. If the child responds right away and immediately becomes quiet and calm, after three minutes, you may tell him, "Because you responded from the first time, your time-out ended after three minutes." In this way, you teach him that when he responds to the punishment the first time and shows a good response—his reactions are positive and correct—you will reward him. The wisdom behind this method is that you are giving him a reward (a shorter period of time in time-out), even as you discipline him.

The same idea is often followed in prisons, when someone is released earlier than the sentenced prison time for proper behavior. It is the same psychological concept: how to use that period for the purpose of rewarding, while still punishing. In this manner, you encourage the proper behavior.

d. Grounding

There is another form of discipline, or exercise, which we call grounding. It means that you make the child sit alone in his room for a period time, or he must stay in his room for one day, or he cannot leave the house to attend specific social outings for a certain period of time, or something [e.g., cell phone, computer, car] is taken away from him for a set time. Usually, shorter periods of time are more effective than longer periods. If, for example, you told the child not to leave his room for two days, this would be, of course, a long period of time for the child. After a while, he would forget the mistake he made and the reason for the punishment. He would think about how severe his dad is, and how much his mom treats him badly, etc. Therefore, he comes out, after these two days—that is, if he has remained in there for the two days—filled with anger. If he has not stayed in his room for the two days, your order has not been carried out. Thus, the child has learned to undermine your authority at home. This is why shorter periods of time are more effective than longer ones. The exception to this is in the case of a big mistake, which needs a longer period of punishment. If you will keep him in his room for an entire day, it is better if you prepare a program for him to follow while he is in his room so he can benefit from the time. Agree together about a program for him to follow during that time.

After having specified the period of the punishment (for example, that he will stay in his room for several hours), he would come out, and then, you would sit together and discuss how he would not make the same mistake again in the future.

There is another good method to use regarding grounding, which is to not to specify a specific period of time (for example, that he will stay in his room for three hours). Instead, tell him, "Look. Go to your room. When you are ready to accept responsibility for your behavior in a polite manner, you may come out and apologize for it;" or, "When you are ready to apologize to your brother whom you have insulted [or hit], and ask him to forgive you, then, you may come out of your room and do that." In this scenario, you are putting the responsibility of specifying the period of his punishment on the child. If he comes out after half an hour, or after ten or fifteen minutes, and goes *politely* to apologize, then, the situation can be over. I say, "politely," because it should not just be a duty. He must come out feeling responsible, saying, "Indeed, I wronged you. I am sorry; please forgive me. I promise I will not do this again." This is the goal I want to reach. The purpose of punishment is reform. If the child will really do this after fifteen minutes, then there is no need to keep him in his room—punished for three hours. This is another method, which teaches the child to take responsibility, make a sound decision, and come out of his room after having thought about his mistake to apologize to the person he offended, and asking for forgiveness.

e. Forbidding the Child from Certain Activities or Taking Something Away

Another one of the methods of discipline is to forbid the child from participating in certain activities. For example, you may take away from him a certain toy that he likes for a period of time; or, if he is older, you may take away his cell phone or computer for a while. I am saying, "for a while," because the punishment must be for a specified amount of time, *or until the behavior changes*. You should tell him exactly what it is that you expect from him concerning his behavior. Do not be vague. Say, "I expect [this and this and this] from you." Therefore, when he does these specific things, the punishment would end at that time, and you would give him back the object that you took from him. However, the punishment must be specified, either for a certain period of time or until the behavior changes. In general, shorter punishment times are more effective, except with major mistakes that really require longer time to produce remorse and transformation.

It must be noted here that it is not recommended to punish by taking away a certain reward that the child has earned. For example, you told him to do research. He did it, and you rewarded him for it. If he makes a mistake, do not then take away this reward; otherwise, you will shake the child's confidence in you. He may say, "Dad is looking for any reason to take away the reward he gave me," and thus, he would not believe your promises in the future. You may take away anything, other than what you have promised him and given him as a reward, and which he earned with his diligence and by carrying out your request.

f. Chores

Chastening or discipline may also be in the form of asking your child to do certain tasks at home. Sometimes, when someone has broken the law, the sentence may not be prison time, but rather community service. The person is asked to volunteer in an area of public service at a place for a certain number of hours. When he completes these hours, he would have carried out the sentence. The idea behind this type of sentence is that it helps a person form a more mature and grateful personality, and directs him toward doing positive work. When he does this, he learns virtues and gains experiences. Thus, the punishment becomes a chance for reformation, a chance for edification, growth, psychological maturity, and maturity of the personality. Often, people think that discipline must be something that hurts the child. No, not necessarily. The purpose is reformation more so than pressuring him to make him suffer. Therefore, you could assign him to help you with some extra chores at home, as part of the consequences of his misconduct.

g. Competitions

You may also make a kind of competition between the children. For example, if your children get up late for church, you could tell them that the one who wakes up late on Sunday will help the one who wakes up early to clean his room. In this way, you are punishing and rewarding simultaneously. Receiving help is rewarding the child who got up early. The one who woke up late is being punished by having to help his brother or sister in a certain task he is supposed to do by himself. Thus, the benefit of this discipline is to punish and reward at the same time. You reward the good behavior and at the same time, you punish the bad behavior.

h. Repairing Damage

Another one of the methods of discipline is to ask your child to fix what he has damaged. If he has made a mess somewhere, he could clean this area. If he has broken something, out of negligence and not by accident, he may use part of his allowance to repair what he has broken. In this way, you are teaching him one of the ways of taking responsibility. Even though the amount he is paying out of his allowance is not a considerable amount—for example, if something would cost $100 to repair and he pays only $1 or so—this, nevertheless, teaches him to take responsibility. I made a mistake, so I accept the responsibility for my mistake. This is what Zacchaeus did.[22] As a tax collector, he was treating people unfairly, but when he met with the Lord Jesus Christ, he said, "Look, Lord, I give half of my goods to the poor; and if I have taken anything from anyone by false accusation, I restore fourfold" (Lk 19:8).

i. Letting Him Reap the Consequences of His Behavior

Finally, you could simply let him reap the consequences of his behavior. This is another form of discipline. For example, a child gets several speeding tickets, and the father pays the first few times. After the second time, he tells his son, "No. *You* have to pay the ticket from your own money. Work for a few more hours and pay it yourself." You may tell me, "He will not work and will not pay it, and then, there will be an arrest warrant for him!" I would respond, "Your son is irresponsible, and if you rescue him from his irresponsibility, he may never learn to be responsible." It is very sad to have the situation go as far as having an arrest warrant get issued, but this could be the only way from him to learn to be responsible, which could be heartbreaking to parents. It was heartbreaking for God when He handed Samson over to the Philistines, who blinded Samson and made him work for them. However, that was the only way for Samson to repent and return back to God. Sometimes, the only way for returning back is for the child to desire to eat the "pods that the swine ate," yet, find that no one gives him anything (Lk 15:16). Letting a child reap the consequences of his behavior and not intervening to rescue him is, in itself, an effective method of chastening.

10. Suitable Methods of Discipline for Each Age

There is not only just *one* way to discipline your child; you have to think about what the best way is. Perhaps you try one way and it does not work. Thus, you need to try another way, which may still not work. Then, you need to try a third way. Discipline begins in infancy. Infants know that you respond to their crying, which they understand, not on the logical level, but on an emotional level, too. For this reason, the recommendation for babies under one year old is for parents to issue a firm, "no," or redirect, distract, or remove the child from the situation. When a child does something specific and you move him from where he is and bring him somewhere else, that is a method of discipline for this very young age.

---

22 Cf. Luke 19:1-10

a. Until the Age of 18 Months

In the first year and a half in the life of a child, there are only two effective things:

1. **Redirecting**: Attract his attention toward something else. If he is playing with something that he should not, take him to an appropriate toy to distract his attention from the first object. This is as much as he can comprehend. He cannot understand more than this.

2. **Positive reinforcement**: Reward the good behavior. If a child stays calm, you can take him and hug him and tell him, "I am pleased with you; you made Dad happy because you were quiet in church." The more you encourage him for the positive behavior, the more he will think, "Dad likes this; Mom likes that." Encourage positive behavior.

All the other things I mentioned will not work before age one and a half; for example, sending him to his room, putting him in time-out, setting some rules with him, or taking away one of his privileges. If you take away a toy from him at this age, he will still not understand what that means.

b. Toddlers: Ages 18 – 36 Months

From ages one and a half to three, in addition to positive reinforcement and redirecting attention, there are two other things that could benefit a child:

3. **Time-outs**: Teach him to stay quiet and not move for two or three minutes. This was used in the past when a child was being punished. He would have to stand facing the wall, but this is of course harsh for the child. However, you could ask him to stay in his place without moving for a certain brief period of time according to his age. He could begin to learn and understand that he did something wrong. At this age, just asking him not to move while he is sitting in his place for a certain period of time, makes him conform to your request. At this age, two or three minutes are more than enough. You do not need more than this. Some people say that time-outs should be one minute per year of age.

4. **Verbal Instruction and Explanation**: Explain to your child that what he did is wrong. You explain to him and say, "This is wrong and unacceptable." You need to instill in his mind what is acceptable and what is not.

At this young age, you can also require the child to apologize for what he did. To teach responsibility, you could set a timer, tell the child that it is bedtime, and expect the child to clean up any messes he has made before he goes to bed.

c. Ages 4–12 Years

From ages four to twelve, which is the age of learning, progressing, and training, everything that we have already mentioned works: requiring the child to apologize, positive reinforcement, trying to redirect his attention, and explaining positives and negatives and what you expect from him. Asking him to stay still without moving for a certain period of time will also benefit him. Grounding the child and taking away some of his privileges or forbidding him from certain activities can also work. To begin to set some rules at home and explain to him that breaking them would have consequences will work with him. Starting from about age nine, assigning him extra chores and work at home would also work as discipline.

This is the best age to teach your children everything you want to impress permanently in their minds. Children, between the ages of four and seven, are more impressionable, and therefore, easier to teach than those between ages eight and twelve. The more a child grows up, the more resistance there is to learn.

d. Ages 13–16 Years

From ages thirteen to sixteen, children have grown up; so, using time-outs and redirecting attention to something else will not work. They are too old for this. However, all the other procedures can be effective. Moreover, requiring that your son or daughter work to pay for damages or debt can also work.

In conclusion, parenting requires effort, support from God, and direction from the Holy Spirit. You need to have a very strong relationship with the Lord for the Holy Spirit to direct you and guide you to the best way to deal with your children. When we discipline our children, they can grow up to be the light of the world and the salt to the earth.[23] Personally, I get upset when I see that our children are undisciplined and when I find that we are not putting forth more effort into raising them well, but rather, spoiling them and letting them live however they want. Of course, that is not correct.

---

23 Cf. Mt 5:13-16.

I | FOSTERING FRIENDSHIP BETWEEN SIBLINGS

1. Introduction
2. Principles for Fostering Friendship between Siblings
3. Problem Solving
    Stage 1: The Training Stage
    Stage 2: Becoming Problem Solvers
    Stage 3: Independent Problem Solvers

1. Introduction

Just as there are examples of problems between siblings in the Bible, there are also good examples, such as Peter and Andrew. Many of us think that Peter met our Lord Jesus Christ before Andrew did. However, the truth is that Andrew met the Lord Jesus Christ before Peter. Andrew was one of the disciples of John the Baptist, so he had the chance to meet the Lord Jesus Christ before Peter. When Andrew saw the Lord Jesus, he went to Peter. This shows the love between the brothers. "Again, the next day, John stood with two of his disciples" (Jn 1:35). (One of them was Andrew.) "And looking at Jesus as He walked, he said, 'Behold the Lamb of God!' The two disciples heard him speak, and they followed Jesus. Then Jesus turned, and seeing them following, said to them, 'What do you seek?' They said to Him, 'Rabbi' (which is to say, when translated, Teacher), 'where are You staying?'" (Jn 1:36-38). Where are you staying means, "Lord, we want to live with You." We will follow You. "He said to them, 'Come and see'" (Jn 1:39). "Come and see where I live, and live with Me," means "*You* will be My disciples, My followers." "They came and saw where He was staying, and remained with Him that day (now it was about the tenth hour)" (Jn 1:39). Andrew and the second disciple were definitely affected by the beauty and teachings of the Lord Jesus Christ. Note what Andrew did following this encounter with the Lord: "One of the two who heard John speak, and followed Him, was Andrew, Simon Peter's brother. He first found his own brother Simon, and said to him, "We have found the Messiah" (which is translated, the Christ)" (Jn 1:40-41). He told him that they found the Christ, the desire of all the nations, the hope for all generations. "And he brought him to Jesus. Now when Jesus looked at him, He said, "You are Simon the son of Jonah. You shall be called Cephas" (which is translated, A Stone)" (Jn 1:42).

The story of Andrew and Peter is wonderful. When my child reads the Bible and becomes filled from within his mind and heart, does he then go and get his brother with excitement and ask him to read with him? Does he tell him, "I went to a hymns lesson today and learned a beautiful hymn—I want you to come with me to this hymns lesson next time." Like Andrew had with Peter, how can I encourage the spirit of love between the children, such that they encourage each other to grow spiritually and mature together?

Additionally, although there were problems between Joseph and his brothers, when you read about how they wished to kill him in Genesis 37, his brother Reuben wanted to save him from their hands (Gen 37:21–22). He said, "cast him into this pit" (Gen 37:22) and he had a plan that, if they threw him into the well, afterward he could get him out and save him, instead of them killing him. However, Joseph was sold to the Ishmaelites.

I always tell our children, "Your best friend is your brother or sister." Rather than the children searching for a best friend and attempting to make friends elsewhere, I try to encourage them to see that their best friend is their brother or sister.

2. Principles for Fostering Friendship between Siblings

a. Teach Them to Be Responsible for One Another

Teach your children to encourage and help each other. When I see my brother doing something incorrectly, I should not say (as Cain said), "I do not know. *Am* I my brother's keeper?" (Gen 4:9). I must go and help him, encourage him, and cooperate with him.

b. Teach Them to Respect and Love One Another

Instill in them that the younger must respect the older and that the older should sympathize with and have compassion on the younger.

c. Teach Them to Pray for One Another

When you stand up to pray together, teach them to pray for each other. For example, when one has an exam, teach the rest of his siblings to stand up and pray for his sake. If one is sick, teach his siblings to pray for his sake. This will develop a bond of love between them.

d. Teach Them to Forgive One Another

If they hurt or upset each other, teach them how to apologize to one another. Apologizing is very important. It is one of the ways of accepting responsibility. Teach them to also ask for forgiveness from each other, and to say, "Forgive me for what I did to you." In turn, the other should not say, "No, I will not forgive you. I cannot forget what you did to me." Rather, he must forgive him and be able to say something like, "This issue is over. We all make mistakes and we love each other." Then, they can hug each other and end the situation.

e. Teach Them to Enjoy One Another's Company

Specify time for entertainment and playing, where they can all play together. Perhaps, all of you as a family may play and enjoy time together, filled with fun and laughter. Usually, these periods of time create pleasant memories when the entire family sits together laughing or playing or having entertainment time together. This deepens love among the family members.

f. Teach Them to Protect One Another

Do not encourage your children to tattle on each other. For example, one of your children comes to you and says, "Daddy, did you see what my brother did?" Do not encourage him by listening to this, as this is not a good habit for him to develop. Of course, from the beginning, do not ask him to give a report about his brother; refrain from asking questions such as, "What did your brother do?" By asking such questions, you encourage the child to think that tattling is okay to do, which it is not a good thing. This holds true unless there was something that threatens someone's safety. If that is the case, then his motive for telling you is not that he wants to *get* his brother into trouble, but rather he wants to tell you in order to *save* his brother or someone from trouble. Can you see the difference? Sometimes children tell on each other because they want their sibling to get into trouble with the parent(s). Never encourage this. Explain to him that if there is a situation where his brother is exposed to danger, it is okay to tell the parent(s) because it is out of love for his brother, and to save him from danger.

g. Teach Them to Honor One Another

Rather than tattling on one another, encourage your children to tell you about the positive things which their siblings do. If your son did something good, his sibling(s) should tell you, "Dad, my brother did this good thing today." Rather than just not telling on his brother, or worse, telling you about something bad his sibling did to put him in trouble, have him tell you about the positives. Say something like, "Listen, while we are out, I want you to notice the good things that your brother is doing, and learn from them, and tell me what you have learned from your brother." This way, you are directing his attention to the positive things his brother is doing, rather than concentrating on the negative things. You are diverting his focus. Instead of his focus being concentrated on the negative things, you direct him to have a positive outlook, which sees the good things his brother is doing.

Similarly if, for example, the parents are going out and leaving the children at home, it is a chance to encourage the siblings to take care of one another in a positive manner, by caring for one another, seeing what the others need, and helping each other. Give them some positive advice so that you are instilling the spirit of love and cooperation deep within them.

h. Beware of Favoritism

Rebecca's love for Jacob, as well as Jacob's love for Joseph, caused problems between the favored children and their siblings. This is why you need to be aware of favoritism. How?

- First: Do not compare children. Sometimes parents compare, but do not do this. You would immediately create jealously, or perhaps, even hatred among them.

- Second: Do not form a closer relationship with one more than the others. Do not make one child to be known as, "Dad's beloved child." This is not right. Do not make one child closer to you than his siblings.

- Third: Do not criticize one child severely and hurt his feelings in front of his siblings. It is better to take him aside and talk to him one-on-one in private.

- Fourth: Do not distinguish one certain child receiving all your praise. If you are going to praise, praise all of them. Look for the good qualities in each child and try to praise them for it.

- Fifth: Do not to give all your attention or all the opportunities to a specific child. Specifically, do not differentiate between the boys and the girls. For example, do not give all the good opportunities to the male children and treat the girls differently or not as favorably; this is not right. Similarly, do not ignore one child by giving all the others more care and attention than him. Sometimes people use this method in discipline by totally ignoring one child. This is very hurtful for the child's soul and psyche. The purpose of discipline is not how you can hurt the child; the purpose is how to help him improve. This is the target. When you ignore one, you can cause him to begin to hate his siblings for no reason, and not because his siblings did something bad to him, but rather, because of your harsh treatment with him, or by ignoring him, or because you treat all of his other siblings better than him.

i. Encourage Cooperation

When a family comes together and engages in activities, this brings the siblings closer to one another. It would be very nice if there were family activities for the entire family. A time for group prayer, Bible study, a time to go out or travel together, or get involved in a service together. A spirit of cooperation, often, develops when the all the family is involved together in a specific activity. Rather than the children fighting with each other, they would learn how to cooperate with one another. Each person would discover the talents of the other, and how to supplement the other's talents. This creates a spirit of love and cooperation as well as a spirit of fellowship among the family members.

j. Welcome A New Sibling

Many times when a new child is born, he takes all the parents' attention and the older children become neglected. Children frequently suffer during this period of time, and sometimes, some of them develop psychological problems. You may find that with the birth of a new child, one of the older children reverts back to involuntary urination or bed-wetting. The reason for this may be due to all the attention being given to the newborn baby while the older child is being neglected. This is why you should try to involve your children with the new family member. This new addition to the family is not just a guest. Involve them from the time of the pregnancy. For example, have your older child go out and buy things for the baby. By involving the older children in welcoming the new child, you give them attention and care and they do not feel left out.

k. Overcome Jealousy

If you find that there is some jealousy between children, you need to handle this with wisdom so that you are not increasing the jealousy. Teach them to be sensitive to one another's feelings. Teach them what St. Paul says: "Therefore, if food makes my brother stumble, I will never again eat meat" (1 Cor 8:13). Teach the child how to be sensitive to his sibling's feelings, avoiding what bothers his siblings, and never to say, "What do I have to do with this? It is not my business. Am I going to sacrifice my freedom and what I want for my brother?" Yes, of course, he sacrifices, because love is about sacrifice.

1. Manage Age Differences

One of the repeated complaints among children is that the older children are not able to tolerate their younger siblings. Perhaps the older child has a friend visiting and they are playing together. The younger child feels lonely and he begins to annoy the older child and his friend and ruins their time. They cannot sit together or play together or enjoy their time. The older child, then, begins to shout and insult his younger brother, and tell his parents to take him away, etc. How should you react to a situation such like this? If the younger child is at an age where he can understand, try to explain to him that this is a special time for his older brother and his friend, and offer him other attractive options that can occupy him during this time. If he is at a very young age and cannot understand, try the method of, "redirecting," to attract his attention to something else that will occupy him and keep him away from the two older children. Simultaneously, encourage the older child to deal with his younger brother with love. For example, he could pat him on the back and give him a hug and tell him that he will play with him, or that they will do something specific together, or go out together after his friend leaves. In this manner, you encourage them to spend time together. Yet, be aware of the problematic idea of "bribing." The older brother should not bribe his brother just for that time, but instead, have a genuine desire to spend time with his younger brother, and to play together and love one another. Thus, when it comes time for the older child to ask the younger child to leave him for a certain period of time, the younger child, since he loves his older brother, would stay away during that period, and leave them [the older brother and his friend] together in peace.

3. Problem Solving

What if the children caused a problem and fought together? How should you react if there is a conflict between siblings? There are three stages when it comes to solving problems or fights between siblings.

Stage 1: The Training Stage

In the first stage, you train them on how to solve the problem. "Problem solving" is a skill and a talent which can be learned through training and practice. You set the rule: Fighting at home is unacceptable. Insulting, hitting, or yelling at one another is unacceptable. Thus, the children will know that in the structure of the home, once there is a rule, there are also consequences for breaking it and rewards for abiding by it. When a fight takes place, if we are still in the first stage, perhaps, it would be better to separate them from each other and listen to each one separately in order to understand the situation and find out the truth. If you talked to them at the same time, they may distract each other, fight, and raise their voices, and this would not be the right atmosphere. Therefore, separate them from one another, sit with one child at a time, and ask each one of them what happened.

Since you are in the training stage, while the child is explaining to you what happened, make sure that he tells you facts without describing his brother in an inappropriate manner. As soon as he starts to say, "But my brother is selfish," or "he is greedy," etc., tell him, "It is not acceptable to speak about your brother like this. I want you to tell me what happened, without talking about your brother or describing him in this inappropriate manner." Ask him to tell you the facts (e.g., he was playing with a certain toy and his brother came in and pulled the toy out of his hands, so it fell and broke). This way, he is telling you just the facts, without describing or analyzing the situation.

Listen to the first child and then listen to the second child. Most likely, there is a pattern—a repeated type of interaction that occurs between them that triggers a fight. For example, one child constantly vexes his brother. Help your child to discover that pattern. Say something like, "Last time when you fought with your brother, what exactly did you do? How about when you had a fight with your sister; what do you think the similarities are between those previous two quarrels and this one?" Now, you want him to think and to see his own mistake. You are talking to him about his mistake and asking him to tell you about the similarities between the situations, which led to the quarrel and the problem. Afterward, teach him through questions and generating conclusions, how to solve the problem and how he could apologize for the mistake he made. He may attempt to get rid of those negative mannerisms or that character flaw.

Teach him how to overcome these points and to deal positively with his brother.

If this child were the victim, a good question to ask him would be, "If your brother repeated this same behavior with you again, what could you do differently to avoid a fight between you and him? What are alternative reactions if your brother insulted you again?" Here, you are training him and teaching him so that next time he can react differently—better. We usually have the same reactions to situations: "If he insults me, I will insult him. If he hits me, I will hit him. If he pushes me, I will push him." Tell your child, "As a child of God, what do you think the other reaction could be? What else could I do, so that rather than causing this insult to end up in a big fight, the insult would just end and not go any further? What are other reactions I could have?"

After listening to both of them and finding out who was at fault (perhaps, both of them were at fault), discipline all those at fault, each one according to the mistake. Tell each one, "This was the mistake you made and this is the discipline." Each person receives his discipline according to his mistake.

After sitting together and explaining to them the discipline, there is forgiveness as well as reconciliation. Ask them to apologize to each other, embrace each other, and forgive each other. Keep in mind that *forgiveness does not cancel or negate punishment and discipline*. This is a biblical concept. When David committed a mistake, he said, "I have sinned against the Lord." Nevertheless, Nathan said to David, "The Lord also has put away your sin" (2 Sam 12:13). There was forgiveness here, but there was also punishment. Nathan also told David, "However, because by this deed you have greatly provoked the enemies of the Lord, your son who is born to you shall surely die" (2 Sam 12:14). In addition to this, there were other consequences that the Lord specified to David as well (2 Sam 12:10-12). Thus, despite the fact that there was forgiveness, there was also discipline. Why is discipline important? Why do I say that forgiveness does not revoke the punishment? The purpose of discipline is improvement. I do not want my son to fall into this same mistake a second and third time. I want to help him eliminate this flaw in his character. Despite having said that you must discipline all those at fault, and each one according to his fault, teach them how to show love, by embracing each other, forgiving each other, and apologizing to each other. Thus, the problem has been resolved.

This is the training stage; and as you read, the parents are the ones who oversee the resolution of the problem between the siblings.

Stage 2: Becoming Problem Solvers

In the following stage, after you have begun to train them, and they have grown up a little bit and become more mature, you have them solve their own problems with one another without getting involved. Yet, this stage would still be under your supervision. There is a difference between involvement and supervision. In the first stage, the parent was very involved, listened to both children for the facts, found out the truth, and at the conclusion, decided on the discipline. In the second stage, the parent merely supervises without interfering, as I will explain.

The purpose of the strategy at this stage is that you want to lead your child to become spiritually mature and to have a mature personality, so that he is able to solve his own problems. This will help him so that in the future, he does not resort to calling the priest for help every time he has a fight with his wife and expect him to come and solve the problem. He must learn how to solve his problems independently. Sometimes, people call the priest for trivial matters. Do you know why? When they were young, no one taught them how to solve their problems amongst themselves. Thus, you find that as soon as he gets into a fight with his wife, the *first* thing he thinks of doing is to call the priest for help and to ask him to come immediately. You are an adult; solve your own problems.

Children must be trained to solve their problems. Therefore, in the second stage, you teach them to first be calm, and then, say, "Look, you have now grown up; you do not need Dad to tell you what you need to do. I want you both to go to your room together, pray, reproach each other gently, and then, reach an agreement together on how to solve the matter. Then, come out and tell me what happened." You could also give them some instructions on how to gently reproach each other. You may tell them, for example, that the purpose of reproaching is not to hurt my brother's feelings, but the purpose is reconciliation. The second point you could tell them is for each one to apologize for his mistakes, and then, to ask for forgiveness. The third point is to talk about situations and facts, without analyzing the situation. Thus, you teach them how to gently reprove one another in the right manner, so that when they sit together and reprove one another, they come out reconciled, and not with a second quarrel.

Nevertheless, do not move them to this stage unless you are assured that you have adequately trained them. The first stage may take months or a year or two years while you are training them on how to solve problems with each other. When you are confident that they have learned and can apply the principles of the first stage, move them to the second stage in which your role is supervision.

After they sit together and gently reproach one another, they come out and tell you what they agreed on and what the solution is. As you listen to the solution, pay attention, lest one of your children, who, perhaps, has a stronger personality, has imposed his opinion on the other. For example, he may have threatened his sibling that if he told their father something, he would hit him. Be sure that matters were resolved in a right manner, fairly and reasonably for both children. Do not say to yourself that it is enough that they are reconciled; so, it is over. No. If one child pressured the other, this would eventually lead to a problem. You do not need this to happen. Thus, keep your eyes open and look at what is happening.

If you feel comfortable about their agreed solution to which they both contributed, praise them. If you are uncomfortable, you may say, "You did a good job by sitting together," praising the effort even though they did not reach the desired result. Then, you may add, "But, I notice the following…! What is your opinion?" Explain and modify the solution through some questions that lead to something that will be fair and reasonable for both of them.

This second stage may also take months, a year, or two years until they reach the third and final stage.

Stage 3: Independent Problem Solvers

By the time children reach the third stage, there is more certainty about their abilities to reach fair and practical solutions in the second stage. This means that every time they propose their solutions, you are reassured (i.e., several times they offered good solutions). Now, they would be ready for the third stage in which they would have more freedom. I want you to create mature and responsible personalities in them, so that even if they were to have a problem, they would know how to solve this problem by themselves. In the third stage, do not ask them to report back to you about the solution. Say, "You have grown up and become adults. You may sit together and solve your problems together. I do not wish to hear anything about this matter. However, if you need my advice at any time, I am here for you. If you need my help at any time, I am here." Therefore, you are not completely separating yourself from them, because this gives them assurance that if they need advice or counseling, you are there and may help as needed. There is also no objection to follow up with them from time to time, and ask, "How are things going? Are things going well? What happened with this situation?" There is no harm in asking and following up, but not with every problem or situation that occurs.

In this way, you will have instilled in them a mature personality by which they are able to deal with problems they may encounter in life, or even problems in which they put themselves. In the future, when your child is in trouble at school or at work, or when he gets married and there is a problem between him and his wife, he will know how to deal with it by himself and solve it. He does not need to always go to someone to complain and have that person get involved and solve it for him.

J | CONFLICT BETWEEN SIBLINGS

1. Three Biblical Examples of Reasons for Conflict
2. Five Factors Affecting Conflict between Siblings
3. Four Causes of Conflict between Siblings
4. Twelve Tips to Reduce Tension and Conflict

In this lecture, I would like to speak about a subject that concerns many families: the conflict occurring between siblings at home. Many of us complain that our children fight with each other. Perhaps they do not fight with us, but they fight with each other. Some parents think that it is normal, and do not care if their children fight. They think that if the children fight, they will make up and everything will be fixed by itself. These parents take a negative stand and do not do anything, which is not right. Parents must help their children befriend one other, enjoy their time at home, and create nice memories, so that tomorrow, when they leave the house, when someone goes to live near work or gets married, there remain nice memories between them as siblings.

When we look at the Holy Bible, we find three vivid examples of conflict between siblings at home.

1. Three Biblical Examples of Reasons for Conflict

a. Jealousy and Envy: Cain and Abel

The first example is Cain and Abel and how conflict occurred between them. When Cain realized that God accepted Abel's sacrifice and rejected his, instead of repenting and offering an acceptable sacrifice before God, he was angered by his brother and killed him. This reveals to us that the reason for this conflict was Cain's jealousy. When he saw that Abel was better than himself, he hated him, as our teacher St. John says, "And why did he murder him? Because his works were evil and his brother's righteous" (1 Jn 3:12). Once he saw that his brother's deeds were good, he hated him and killed him. Of course, I do not know what role Adam and Eve had; the Bible does not mention what they did to prevent this problem from occurring.

b. Deception: Jacob and Esau

The second example in the Holy Bible is the conflict between Jacob and Esau. Perhaps, the reason for this conflict was Rebekah's love for Jacob and the father's love for Esau, (and how the mother encouraged her son to deceive his father in order to take the blessing and take the birthright of the firstborn instead of Esau).[24] Jacob successfully took the blessing by

---

24 Cf. Gen 25.

deception. He had previously taken the birthright when Esau returned from the field, tired and weary, and Jacob had made lentils and Esau wanted to eat of the lentils. Thus, Jacob took advantage of this situation and took the birthright. When Jacob took the birthright and the blessing, this caused a struggle or competition between them, and Esau was so angry with him that he wanted to kill him. Thus, Jacob was compelled to flee from his father's house and live with his uncle Laban for a long time (perhaps more than fourteen years), until he returned and they were reconciled. However, perhaps, true healing never occurred.

The first example reveals to us that the reason behind the conflict between the two was envy and jealousy. One saw the other as better than himself; so, he envied him and wanted to kill him, and he actually did kill him. In the second example, the reason for the conflict was deception and trickery. By deception and encouragement from his mother, Jacob took the blessing that Esau was supposed to take from his father. This also reveals to us that there was no communication between Isaac and Rebekah. If there had been communication between them, this would not have happened.

c. Favoritism: Joseph and His Brothers

As a third example, let us discuss Joseph and his brothers. Of course, the reason behind the conflict between Joseph and his brothers was the love of their father Jacob for Joseph and how he favored him above his brothers.[25] Perhaps, this was because Joseph was the son of Rachel, who was the beloved one of Jacob. He was also the next to youngest son and Jacob loved and spoiled him. This love and distinction sparked the jealousy of his brothers. They also wanted to kill him because of the multicolored coat that their father brought for him, and because of his dreams, which he had revealed to his father, mother, and brethren. This further caused envy and jealousy in their hearts, so they wanted to be rid of Joseph.

Thus, in the third example, we see that the reason for the conflict was the father favoring Joseph, the son of the beloved Rachel, above his brothers.

---

25 Cf. Gen 37.

d. Other Examples

Of course, there are other examples, such as the Prodigal Son and his brother (this one is a parable; all the others mentioned are real examples), Mary and Martha, and Ishmael and Isaac. Although Ishmael was the son of the maidservant and Isaac the son of the freewoman (the wife), conflict occurred between the two boys. Perhaps, there were many reasons for this conflict. Ishmael felt that he was the son of the maidservant while Isaac was the son of the freewoman, which may have given him a sense of inferiority, leading him to hit and attack Isaac. Also, Ishmael was physically strong, so he started beating Isaac. Perhaps, a third reason is that when Sarah started treating Hagar harshly, Ishmael wanted to take revenge for his mother, and therefore, started attacking Isaac. Finally, Sarah decided that Hagar and her son should leave the house to avoid these conflicts. Of course, there is a prophetic reason behind this, as St. Paul explains in Galatians 4; this is why God told Abraham to let Ishmael leave with Hagar, "for the son of the bondwoman shall not be heir with the son of the freewoman" (Gal 4:30).

Likewise, conflict may be caused by other reasons. Take, for example, the conflict that occurred between Moses, Aaron, and Miriam. When Moses married an Ethiopian woman, Aaron and Miriam were upset with Moses for this and spoke about him, but God defended Moses and told them, "If there is a prophet among you, I, the Lord, make Myself known to him in a vision; I speak to him in a dream. Not so with My servant Moses; He is faithful in all My house. I speak with him face to face" (Num 12:6-8), and at that time Miriam was struck with leprosy because she spoke against Moses.

From the beginning, since the time of Adam and Eve, there have been conflicts between siblings. If we study the examples in the Bible, we can learn a lot about sibling relationships. Sibling conflicts may be minor arguments, or they may be major arguments that reach the point of murder, like what happened with Cain and Abel, or perhaps the intent of murder, as happened with Esau. These conflicts not only happen when children are young and living at home, but they might continue with the children even after they grow up, are married, and have their own families and homes. We have often heard of siblings fighting over inheritance, for example. When the father passes away, the siblings fight each other for the inheritance. Conflicts also may occur if siblings are partners in a company.

e. Stressors Contributing to Conflict

When people live in the same house together, twenty-four hours a day, every day, it places stress on the relationship. Conflicts or differences are expected as we see with sibling conflicts. Notice engaged couples before they get married. Once they get married and live together, they begin to have conflicts with one another. As I said, living together under the same roof for a long time can increase conflicts between them. Even if best friends rent an apartment together and live together, they may have some conflicts with each other.

Conflict between siblings is expected, and yet, its presence places pressure on the parents as they try to see how they will deal with it. All parents want to see their children living in love, because when they live together in love, this relationship will continue throughout their lives. Parents also do not want conflicts in the home because this also can cause problems between the parents: The father might accuse the mother of being negligent in raising the children (which might result in them arguing), or the mother might accuse the father of being busy and not paying enough attention to the children (and so a fight might break out between them).

f. Benefits of Conflict

Allow me to pose a question: Is there any good that can come out of conflict between siblings? God's love always enables Him to bring "out of the eater ... something to eat, and out of the strong ... something sweet" (Judg 14:14). Thus, God is able bring about something good even from conflicts that occur between siblings.

g. Learning to Deal with Others

From conflicts, a person can learn how to walk in life, and how when engaged in a struggle, to reconcile with the other person, since typically when children fight, they reconcile. This is an opportunity to learn how to reconcile my relationships with others, to learn how to apologize for my faults, and to learn how to fix my weaknesses.

This is what God wanted to do with Cain, but Cain refused to learn. God told Cain to look at himself instead of killing his brother. He said to him, "If you do well, will you not be accepted? And if you do not do well, sin lies at the door. And its desire is for you, but you should rule over it" (Gen 4:7). God wanted Cain to understand this important message: "If you improve your condition and admit your mistakes, I will lift away My anger from you and accept your sacrifice and love you. However, if you insist on your anger, envy, and desire for revenge on your brother, sin is longing for you, but you are able to control it. So, do not say that you have an excuse to kill your brother."

h. Removing the Thorns

A monastery is a closed community. Monastics live together twenty-four hours a day, and it is anticipated that conflicts or differences would occur amongst them, because we are all humans. One of the fathers in the monastery always used to say, "If the monk comes to the monastery and wants to live the life of isolation from the beginning, and not experience the conflicts of the community with his brothers the monks, he will grow old having the thorns within him." What are the thorns? The thorns are our weaknesses. How does one recognize these weaknesses? One notices them in conflict within the community. From this person, for example, I realize that I do not have tolerance, do not have humility, do not have obedience, or do not have forgiveness. Thus, I find the thorns within me and struggle to pluck them out and purify my life. This will only appear through conflict with others in the community. If I resort to isolation from the beginning of my monastic life, this can make a person sit in his cell, but because he does not grow through conflicts with others, he will grow old in the monastery and the thorns will still dwell within him. This is why the community life is very important, because it purifies a person from his weaknesses. The same applies in the house with siblings, where they help you realize your weaknesses and shortcomings, and where you are nurtured and mature.

i. Monitoring the Ego

From these conflicts, there are lessons for each person to learn: 1) How to reconcile; 2) How to tolerate; 3) How to forgive, 4) How to deal with others. Also, good training at home can help a person acquire many talents for socializing by drawing from relationships with siblings. This is an opportunity to be freed from egotism, because one learns to give-and-take at home. Parents need to encourage children to give-and-take. There is a nice saying in the Paradise of the Fathers: "A brother asked an Elder,

'Is it good for me to live without giving or receiving?' The elder answered him and said, 'If you do not give then you have cast off love [mercy] and if you do not receive then have cast off humility,'[26] because giving is a sign of love and taking is a sign of humility. The arrogant person thinks that he is above receiving from another person. An egocentric person does not like to take from others; his honor would be disturbed. Through this, we can teach our children how to give-and-take, as the expression goes, "Life is give-and-take." In the family, through the conflicts that occur between siblings, there is an opportunity to teach our children many lessons.

As I told you, sometimes, even in history, we read about siblings who fought with each other over kingdoms. For one brother to take the kingdom from his brother, he went to war against him. Just as there are examples of conflicts between children, there are also very good examples of siblings who communicate very well together. Take, for example, Maximus and Dometius and how they lived in love together and encouraged each other on the spiritual path.

If we analyze the reasons for conflicts between siblings, this can help parents understand how to reduce these conflicts and reap lessons to help their children live together in love.

2. Five Factors Affecting Conflict between Siblings

a. Relationship between the Parents

First, the relationship between parents themselves can be reflected on the children. If you study the story of Jacob and Esau, you will find that there was no communication between their parents, Isaac and Rebecca. Rebecca knew that Jacob should receive the blessing and that Esau should serve his brother. She knew this throughout her pregnancy.[27] She heard Isaac asking Esau to go hunting and prepare a meal, to bless him.[28] For some reason, she avoided transparent communication with Isaac and did not remind him of the promise of God that Jacob should receive the blessing, not Esau. Instead, she planned with her son Jacob to trick his father and to receive the blessing. So, it is clear, here, that there was no communication

---

26 Found in the Arabic version of Paradise of the Fathers, page 433.
27 Cf. Gen 25:22–26.
28 Cf. Gen 27

between the parents. This actually affected the relationship between Jacob and Esau, and made Jacob escape and run from Esau, who was extremely angry. Esau even wanted to kill Jacob. Therefore, the relationship between parents can also affect the relationship between siblings.

b. Relationship between the Parents and Their Children

Moreover, the relationship between parents and their children can affect the relationship between siblings. For example, Jacob favored his son Joseph. Because he favored him, he created jealousy in the hearts of his brothers. Not only that, but Jacob encouraged tattling. We read in the Book of Genesis that when Joseph was young, he used to go and tell his father about the wrongdoings of his brothers, and Jacob encouraged this behavior. Of course, this created tension between Joseph and his brothers.

c. Birth Order

The third factor influencing sibling conflict is the birth order of the children. Much research has been conducted which shows common attributes in the oldest children, common attributes in the middle children, and common attributes in the youngest children. Birth order is a factor in sibling conflict. Though current literature and research is still somewhat inconclusive, some suggest that first-borns tend to be higher achievers, middle children tend to be compromisers and more mellow than the other positions, and youngest children tend to be more creative, manipulative, charmers, and get away with more than the older siblings.[29]

d. Age Difference

The age difference between children is another factor affecting the relationship between them and also the cause of possible conflict between them. Children who are born one year apart differ from those who are born two years apart, and so on. If children are born in close proximity to each other, this increases the competitive spirit and jealousy between them, but if there is a greater difference in time between them, the older child fosters a sense of responsibility toward the younger child. An older child, sometimes, feels like the younger child is his own child, and his expectations differ from the expectations of two children who are close in age.

---

29 https://www.psychologytoday.com/blog/fulfillment-any-age/201305/is-birth-order-destiny
https://www.huffingtonpost.com/2015/05/13/birth-order-personality_n_7206252.html

e. Gender of Siblings

Research reveals that gender is a factor that influences sibling conflict. For example, boys typically fight with each other more frequently than girls fight with each other. Girls and boys use different methods of fighting. Boys may fight with each other in a physical manner, while girls may tend to tease each other. If the siblings are both genders, the conflict between them usually differs than if they are the same gender.

Factors that affect conflict include: 1) The relationship between the parents themselves; 2) The relationship between the parents and their children; 3) The birth order of the children; 4) The chronological difference in age between siblings; 5) The gender of the children.

f. Research Results

Research has shown (of course, this research was not done on Christians only, and most of the statistics that I will mention involve research conducted outside Egypt) that 80% of siblings were able to reconcile their differences and live in peace and love, even if there was conflict between them when they were younger. Of the 20% that were not able to resolve or heal from their conflicts to restore the relationships, 10% either had apathetic relationships with each other, meaning no attachment or care for each other, or just civil relationships with each other. The remaining 10% continued to have enmity with each other, to the point of revenge or dealings in court. Of course, one hopes that if research were conducted on the children of God, the percentages would be different. We expect and hope that the results would indicate that 100% of siblings were able to love each other and reconcile their differences. This is for biological siblings, as well as for spiritual siblings.

3. Four Causes of Conflict between Siblings

a. Competition

The first factor in conflict between siblings is competition, which may begin as early as with the arrival of the second child. Usually, with the birth of the second child, the older child might develop a type of jealousy, because as firstborn, he had all of the parents' attention. Moreover, the grandparents, aunts and uncles all lavish a firstborn child with attention. With the birth of the second child, this new child shares this attention, which causes a type of envy and jealousy for the older child. This is often demonstrated by older the child developing a negative attitude or behaving strangely when the second child is born. Adjustment to the new baby is easier if the first child has relationships outside the home. This can happen if there is a difference of more years between the two children. For example, if the first child is six years old and then a new baby is born, this 6-year-old has relationships outside the home, so he will welcome the new baby. For younger children, if they start going to daycare or a preschool program and interact with other children, the adjustment to the new baby becomes much easier. I am not saying this as a recommendation that you have to follow; I am just pointing out the research.

The firstborn child may take his anger out on his parents, especially the mother, because in his mind, the mother is the one who brought this other child home. This anger might be expressed by screaming, hitting his mother, being stubborn, or disobeying her. If she carries the younger child, then the older child wants to be carried, seeking the same attention that is being given to the newborn baby. This reveals to us that young children like to have the full attention of their parents, not wanting anyone to share in this love. This brings us to conclude that at such a young age, conflict between siblings is mainly due to the children's desire to receive the full attention of the parents. This is why preparing for the birth of the second child is very important. Parents need to begin preparing the older child during the pregnancy to understand and accept the arrival of another child.

Moreover, after the birth of the second child, the challenge for parents is how to convey to their children that they are equally loved, that each one is very special, and that both children take the same amount of love and attention. The more successful the parents are at relaying this message, the more relieved the children become and the easier the adjustment will be. When parents emphasize that each child is significant and special to them in a unique way, and that they appreciate each one's unique qualities, this decreases the competition and struggle between the children.

Competition increases, not only with the birth of the second child, but if the parents constantly compare the children. For example, they may compare their academic achievements, behaviors, or attitudes, or make one of them feel more loved than the other. When a child feels that a sibling is more distinguished or spoiled by the parent, or that the two are being compared to each other, this breeds a sense of resentment and rejection of that sibling. This is what occurred in the story of Joseph where they not only rejected him, but also wanted to kill and get rid of him completely.[30] They actually sold him as a slave in order to get rid of him.

Competition may also begin without the intervention of the parents, like in the story of Abel and Cain. Cain started to feel like he was in competition with his brother when God did not accept his offering, but accepted Abel's. Note that this is not favoritism. Favoritism means preferring one child for subjective reasons. However, if your son has accomplished something and you are rewarding him for this achievement, this is not considered favoritism, especially if you are fair in rewarding the achievements of all your children. Therefore, we cannot say that God was biased, or favored Abel more than Cain.

Cain disobeyed God and was angry when God accepted Abel and dealt with Abel better than with him.[31] If you analyze Cain's behavior, you find that it reflects a desire to get away with his mistakes. This is immature and, irresponsible behavior: "I want to do whatever is wrong and I do not want anybody to tell me that it is wrong. I refuse to bear the consequences of my wrong behavior." God gave Cain very wise advice, and told him, "Why are you angry? Why has your countenance fallen? The solution is very easy. If you correct yourself, there will be acceptance. I will accept you. But, if you insist on your rebellious behavior, be watchful. There is a sin lying in wait for you, and her desire is for you—the desire of sin is for you. But you can control this and overcome the sin." The Lord is telling him, "Instead of fighting with Abel and feeling that you are competing with him, just correct yourself, offer a proper offering, and it will be accepted." Unfortunately, Cain did not listen to God's advice, but rather, and was led by his own anger and ended up killing his brother Abel.

Thus, competition can happen because of the way parents treat their children, as in comparing them to each other, or because of irresponsibility or immaturity, or because of jealousy, like with the arrival of the second child.

---

30 Cf. Gen 37.
31 Cf. Genesis 4.

b. Displaced Anger

The second cause of conflict between siblings is displaced anger, which is easier to direct toward a sibling than toward others. For example, if a child was bullied by others at school, and was unable to do anything about it, he may come home very angry because of the difficulty he is facing. Wanting to express his anger, his younger sibling becomes a safe target. Also, since they are always together, if the child tries to control this anger, at some point, it will be released on the person with whom the child is continually living. Siblings are easy targets because they are together all the time. We should understand that, sometimes, the conflict between siblings is an expression or release of anger acquired from another situation (occurring, perhaps, completely outside the home, for example, at school or with friends), but expressed through sibling conflict.

When parents notice that one child is picking fights with his siblings for no clear reason, they should consider that maybe something is going on outside the house. If the child is angry, the parents should talk to him, and say, "My dear son, what is wrong with you? Is everything okay? Is everything okay at school? Is everything okay with you friends?" When you ask him such questions, maybe he will start to tell you what is wrong, especially if he feels safe to speak to his parents, if he is not afraid. Many parents in this situation try to punish the angry child because he is arguing or fighting with his brother, but punishment, here, will make him angrier and will not solve the problem. However, if you ask him if there is anything wrong, he may tell you about what is happening. You may be able to help him, and this will ease the situation.

c. Favoritism

Parents may contribute to tension, arguments, or fighting between siblings when they favor one child more than the others. I gave you the example of Jacob and how he dealt with Joseph, and how this caused a lot of tension between the siblings. Sometimes, parents may be unaware that they are favoring one child over the other. In their conscience, they believe that they are not favoring one. Some parents may use favoritism or comparison as a means of encouraging their child to be better (not realizing that they are partial), and in their heart they say that they love all their children equally. I want to clarify that what is inside your heart is not important; rather, what your child *feels* is more important. If your child feels that you do not love him, or that you love his sibling more than him, you need to see how you can change these feelings, even if you do love your children equally. This feeling must have a cause or underlying reason. As long as the child feels unloved or that the others are more loved, this feeling alone will keep the child in constant conflict with his siblings. Do not be satisfied in saying that God knows that you love them all equally. See what you need to do to change the perception of the child that feels that you do not love him or that you love his siblings more. The remedy is in changing this perception.

This concept also applies to priests. If the congregation feels that the priest is partial to certain members or groups in the congregation, this causes jealousy between them. This is why in the vow that priests take on the day of their ordination, they say, "I will not have a distinct preferred group from the congregation." The spiritual father should make each of his children feel special and loved. The more successful the priest is in doing so, the more that love prevails between the congregants, and they become as one family. If the congregation begins to feel that the priest has a distinct group, this causes problems between the congregants. What occurs in the church is analogous to what happens in the family.

Here, I want to differentiate between rewarding good behavior and favoritism. Rewarding good behavior is right and teaches the children that good behavior will be rewarded and bad behavior or a bad attitude should be punished. Rewarding good behavior is something objective but favoritism is completely subjective. "I like this son more than the rest of my children. I favor him." It is something in me, not something out there; it is something subjective. This causes a lot of tension.

In the story of Mary and Martha, the Lord did not favor Mary over Martha; Martha was doing something wrong. As John Chrysostom said, Martha was serving at the wrong time. There is time for service and there is time to sit with the Lord. What Martha did wrong was not that she was serving, because we need service, but that she was serving at the wrong time. That is why when she started to complain to the Lord, the language she used was aggressive. She attacked the Lord— "Do You not care?" And she attacked Mary, her sister. But how did the Lord address the tension between Mary and Martha? He brought Martha's attention to the worry and anxiety in which she was living, and that now, it is the time to sit with the Lord and learn from Him. He explained that her worries and anxieties should not replace the time in which she should sit at the feet of the Lord with Mary and learn from Him. So, here, the Lord was disciplining wrong behavior, as He did with Cain and Abel. There was no favoritism here. He was rewarding Mary's good behavior and rebuking Martha's wrong behavior.

d. Boredom and Seeking Attention

The fourth reason is boredom or seeking attention. Sometimes, when children have free time, not knowing what to do with it, they argue; arguing gives them something to do together. It is their way to fight boredom. Moreover, it will actually be more fun for them when Mom and Dad join this fight, because now, everybody is busy. This is why keeping your children busy and trying to focus their attention on sports or exercises fills their time and makes them avoid conflict with each other. Parents should relax when they see their children fighting, because it is expected, and in many situations, it is normal. Parents need to skillfully judge when to intervene and when to refrain from intervening. Fighting can be a tool to get the attention of the parents. Many times, when children act out, they are doing so just because they want to attract their parents' attention. If the parents take sides, this might encourage the children to prolong the argument, because they feel that the parents are neither equal nor fair in their treatment.

There are also other reasons that we can mention, such as, hatred, envy, or the concept of "win or lose." Winning gives the child a sense of delight and victory, but the parents need to watch out for these causes, in order to decrease conflict between the siblings.

4. Twelve Tips to Reduce Tension and Conflict

I will give you twelve small tips to help in reducing tension and conflict between siblings, or to benefit from the conflict and build the personality of the child.

a. Do Not Encourage Tattletales

Do not encourage your children to tattle on each other. Some children like to tattle on the others in order to draw closer to the parents. Once the parent comes home, the child comes to give a full report of everything that happened. Sometimes, the parents lend an ear to these words. This causes the other children to be upset, feeling that someone is telling on them. If this results in punishment, it especially increases the hatred between the siblings. For this reason, we need to teach our children when to speak and when to remain silent. As parents, do not sit there and listen to everything your children say. Teach your children the difference between good telling and bad telling. Of course, there are major circumstances that deserve attention. For example, if one child places his life in danger, or endangers the life of a sibling, and a child comes to tell out of concern, then we should listen because the child is coming out of love, not out of malice. Otherwise, we should not encourage tattling. Our children should not be rewarded for telling on their siblings.

What applies to the family also applies to the larger family—the church. As servants, or priests in the church, we should not encourage people to be our informers; this is inappropriate. If someone comes to inform me, I should look to the purpose behind the action. Is this person coming to complain, to get the other person in trouble, or is this person coming out of concern for the other? I would be encouraging wrongful behavior and sin if the person who brings me information succeeds in turning me against someone else.

Parents need to teach their children that it is not good to tattle on others, and to tell only if they see that a sibling is in danger. If they love their siblings and want to rescue them, but do not know how, then they should come out of concern. Otherwise, if they are coming to tell on them, to get them in trouble, or to show off that they are better than them, we should not listen to this. You need to teach your children this, so they do not grow up having this habit of transferring information or gossiping. This builds neither the family nor the community.

b. Encourage Unity

Actively encourage bonding between your children. Try to create an atmosphere in which everyone wins, not where one wins while the other loses. For example, ask the older sibling to read the Holy Bible with or for the younger sibling, and then, bring to the attention of the younger sibling how the older sibling loves him, and to the older sibling how the younger sibling respects him. Here, you are creating a win-win situation in an activity where they are working together and creating a bond of love with each other.

You might, for example, have the siblings organize their sibling's birthday party. For example, tell them that their brother's birthday is in a week, and ask them how they would like to celebrate it. Allow them to plan it. Do not take over as parents, but rather allow the children, no matter how young, to participate in the preparations. This will increase the love and bonding between them. In preparing the party, they will feel important, and simultaneously, the birthday child will rejoice and feel love for his siblings who arranged for his party. Encourage them to give gifts to each other on occasions (feasts, birthdays, graduation, etc.), no matter how small or symbolic, even if it is a picture on which they write a nice note to encourage each other.

Instead of comparing between them, use words that increase the loving bonds between them. For example, tell the boy that his sister loves him very much, or bring to the younger boy's notice of how his older brother was helping him in his studies. These words encourage them to see the positive points in each other. Also, intentionally make sure the children hear you speaking about how others love each other. For example, if their aunt is coming to visit, you may speak with her about how her children love each other and help each other, while your children are listening. This way, you are giving them an indirect message that this is a praiseworthy action. Children want the praise and approval of the parents during the early years. If they know that this is something that pleases the parents, they will do it. You may also let one of your children overhear you talking to his siblings about the good things he does for his siblings. So, while you are speaking to your son about how good his brother is to him, make sure the other son overhears that you are speaking well about him to his brother. This will actually foster the bonding between the two children.

c. Keep Them Occupied

Keep your children continually busy with positive, edifying activities. Be creative in keeping them busy. I do not mean turning on the TV and having them watch cartoons twenty-four hours a day. Rather, teach them life talents, alongside spiritual activities in the church (such as hymns classes, competitions, St. Mark's Festival, etc.). There is no objection to teaching your children other skills like music, sports, or swimming. These are all good skills for the children to learn. This way, they will not have free time that makes them fight with one another.

You might buy them games that make them think and also cooperate with each other. There are games where two play, and in the end, one wins and the other loses, but there are other games where they work together, and at the end, both win, having accomplished the goal, perhaps, building something together, gaining a sense of accomplishment or victory, and cooperation. Games that involve a winner and a loser, especially if there is tension between siblings, will increase conflict, envy, or jealousy between them.

d. Give Individual Attention

Spend time with each child individually, just as you spend time with all the children together. You may have activities for all the children together, but you need to have time to spend with each child individually. This special time makes the child feel important to the parent, and as I said, much of the conflict is due to competing for the parents' attention. If you are able spend time with each child, individually, even if it is only for minutes each day, this would be very good. For example, you might call the first child to you and ask what he learned in school, how he spent his day, and what he plans on doing that night. Next, call the second child to you and ask the same questions. Spend five minutes or more, if needed, with each child. This special time with each child makes the child feel that he/she is the center of attention to the parent. As in service, we emphasize the importance of individual work as much as group work, the same applies to the family. It is very important for each child to feel that the parents are spending special quality time with him/her on a regular basis (not only on special occasions).

The mistake we make is that we do not spend individual time with our children, except when there is a problem. When a parent says, "I need to talk to you," the child immediately understands that there is a problem; there has been a complaint. This causes uneasiness. Even during the time you spend with the child, he will be on edge, knowing that he is in trouble. We do not want our children to immediately think, "What did I do?" when the parents ask to speak with them. If you spend time with the child consistently, then even when there is an issue to be discussed, the child will not be disturbed, but rather assured.

There is no objection, if you are going shopping, for example, to take one child one time, another child at another time, etc. When you take each one individually for an errand, this makes the child feel that you are giving him/her attention. Do not always focus on the same child with the same parent; for example, for the father to always take the son and the mother to always take the daughter. Alternate the parent/child combination, so there is continual communication with both parents.

This will keep the children from struggling for your attention, as we have mentioned that, at times, children bicker to gain the attention of their parents. If they are already gaining the time and attention of the parents, they do not need to compete for this attention. Individual conversations with the parents mature the personality and nourish the emotional needs, while giving the children a sense of appreciation.

e. Allow Older Children to Act Their Age

Allow an older child to enjoy life as a child, not as a mature person while still in childhood. Many times, the older child, even if only five or seven years old, is placed in a responsibility greater than his age, being told, "You are the older child. Take care of your siblings." This happens to the point that when there is conflict between the older and the younger child, and the younger child is in the wrong, sometimes, we blame the older child, saying things like, "You are the older one; you should not have done this. So, what if your little brother hits you? Grow up. Are you not the older one?" When we place too much responsibility on a child who is still six or seven years old, we are placing on him a greater burden than he can handle. This creates anger and resentment in the child's heart toward the parents and the siblings. If there is conflict between two siblings, do not always give the victory to the younger sibling (because he is younger), but examine who is at fault and speak with that one. Do not place more responsibility on the older child above what he can bear. If this is a child, expect mistakes from him, because he is still a child.

[For more on this concept, see Part I, I.]

f. Teach Them to Resolve Their Own Conflicts

Teach children to resolve their own conflicts. This is an opportunity for you to instill and build in them skills of communication and reconciliation. Teaching children how to resolve issues involves three stages. In the first stage, the parent intervenes directly and reconciles them.

In the second stage, the parent intervenes *indirectly*. First, the parent speaks with the older child individually and instructs the child on what he should have done. Next, the parent brings the second child and does likewise. Finally, the parent sends them to discuss it and reconcile with each other, and return to the parent, after having resolved the issue, to report what they have done. In the third stage, when conflict arises between them, the parent pretends not to notice, keeps silent, and leaves them to reconcile their differences.

Besides helping them learn how to resolve their differences, pretending not to notice has another benefit. If they are fighting to get the parent's attention and the parent gives them attention, they have a gained their intention. Subsequently, each time they want the parent's attention, they will fight. But, if they fight to get the parent's attention, and the parent ignores them, they will understand that this method is not successful. Parents need to teach their children how to gain attention in appropriate ways, or parents may give them attention without them having to fight for it.

If both children come to complain, have them sit down together (as described in the third stage) and reconcile their differences. Tell them, "You are siblings who love each other, and I am sure that you can reach an agreement together." Here, you are teaching them problem solving, which will help them later in life. Never take the side of one over the other.

g. Avoid Labeling Your Children

Avoid giving your children labels, especially if they are negative labels. For example, you might call one child the "blabbermouth" of the family, and this nickname might spread among the siblings, cousins, and relatives. You might call a child the "worrywart" of the family. Children tend to see each other through these nicknames. They might tease each other with these nicknames, and thus, cause tension between them. Oftentimes, when we jokingly give nicknames to the children, the children take this seriously, which makes them look down upon themselves, leading to low self-esteem. Additionally, giving children nicknames is a way of comparing them, and this has potential to cause tension and jealousy between them.

h. Praise Good Behavior

Praise and reward good behavior, including the bonding behaviors between the siblings. If they argue with each other, and then reconcile, make sure they realize that you noticed that they reconciled and that you are happy with this development. This way, they will learn that reconciliation will get their parents' positive attention. Again, as I told you, children especially want their parents' approval and are willing to do anything to please them. The more you praise the good behaviors that further bring them together, the less sibling conflict there will be.

i. Do Not Pay Attention to Every Conflict

Do not give attention to every action or conflict that occurs between the children. In the Psalms, we say to our Lord, "If You, Lord, should mark iniquities, O Lord, who could stand? But there is forgiveness with You" (Ps. 130:3-4). God is not standing there with a rifle, watching our every action. Overprotective parents do not allow any mistakes, and there is an inquisition over the slightest hint of a mistake, although the issue could have passed. The danger of discussing every single situation is that it imprints each situation in the parent's mind and in the child's mind, possibly causing sensitivity between them, although, if it were allowed to pass, it would have been more easily forgotten. A person might turn a blind eye to some behaviors, as the expression goes (this expression is a bit extreme): "If you do not see blood, do not get involved." The point is not to make a big deal over every issue. Many times little children fight, but to them, this fight is fun, just something to keep them busy, or only a means to gain a parent's attention.

Ignoring some behaviors is also considered a discipline technique because you are refusing to reward bad behavior with attention. Even if you punish the bad behavior, attention is still given. If the child is acting out to get your attention, and you provide it, even if through punishment, the child wins. On the other hand, by ignoring this attention seeking, inappropriate behavior, you are sending a message that you refuse to give attention to negative behavior.

j. Do Not Compare

Do not compare strengths or achievements between the children and respect their abilities. Each child has his or her own abilities and capabilities. One child might excel in school, while another might not be able to excel in the same way. It is unfair to compare between them. You have to understand that children are at different ages and each child has a different intellectual, creative, athletic, etc., make-up. Their levels of intelligence differ and each one has distinct talents. They differ in their strengths and weaknesses. You cannot compare them, saying, "Your brothers did not do this. Why are you doing this?" Or "Why are you not getting good grades like your sister?" Every time you compare them to each other, you are creating sensitivity between them. Treat each one as an individual who has unique abilities, capabilities, talents, and weaknesses.

k. Listen to Both Sides

If you intervene in a conflict, you need to first listen to both sides. Do not make any decisions while only listening to one side. Children always need to feel that their parents are just. Make every effort to understand and to find out what went wrong before accusing, disciplining, or punishing. If the children begin to feel that their parents are taking sides, this is not a good sign. It increases the potential conflict between the children. Furthermore, do not give one child some liberties while withholding freedom from the other. Be evenhanded in the rules and disciplines established in the household. In placing rules and guidelines for the family, be fair in applying them to everyone, especially between boys and girls. Oftentimes, parents give excessive freedom to the boys, but greatly restrict the freedom of the girls. Be fair.

When you hear of a conflict between two children, do not think too much about who is at fault and who is not at fault. If there is a conflict between two people, typically they are both at fault. Rather, focus on how to bring peace between them. Many times, I tell people, "You could act as a judge, or you could act as a reconciler." A judge's objective is to find out who is right and who is wrong, while a reconciler does not focus so much on who is right and who is wrong, but rather, on how to bring peace between the two people. Sometimes, when children feel that a parent is acting as a judge, each one becomes a prosecutor and a defense attorney, accusing the other sibling and defending himself/herself. If the parents are looking to reconcile, looking for peace, rather than focusing on pointing the finger, the children will cease to accuse each other and focus on how to reconcile. Do not be a judge; be a peacemaker.

l. Build Individuality

As much as I have encouraged fostering teamwork between siblings in order to strengthen their bond and unity, it is also imperative for each one to have his personal time and space. All of us need some place to spend personal time, even our children. Just as we want to increase the bonds between them, we also want to stress the individuality of each person, and each person's time, activities, and personality, to dismiss the idea of one child being the leader and the others, followers. Each should have his/her own individual maturing personality. Teach each one how to spend time alone and how to have personal space to spend time alone reading, playing, or listening to something. Just as there are joint games, tools, and possessions that teach them how to cooperate, there is no objection to having personal possessions. This gives a sense of individuality. We need to nurture both the sense of individuality as well as the sense of unity.

In conclusion, we spoke about how sibling conflict is expected and ancient (it has existed since the days of Adam and Eve). We mentioned benefits one may reap from conflict. We also discussed some factors that increase conflict, some causes of conflict, and some advice for decreasing conflict. Parents certainly have a very important role in helping their children avoid sibling conflict through raising them in the fear of God, fostering bonding and love and all these Christian qualities—forgiveness, patience, endurance, and acceptance. I will conclude with the following verse: "Now the fruit of righteousness is sown in peace by those who make peace" (Jas 3:18). For our children to be righteous, they need to be planted in an atmosphere—a house—full of reverence, where the parents are peacemakers between the children and themselves. In this way, our children will be righteous.

Glory be to God forever. Amen.

K | CHILDHOOD: NEEDS AND DEVELOPMENT (HOMILY TO SERVANTS)

1. Internalization and Identification
2. Children Seek Approval
3. How Children Learn to Respect Authority
4. Helping Our Children Gain Experience
5. Correcting Our Children

It is important to understand the needs and development of children, as this will help us to serve them.

When we were born, we did not have any power or experience. We were totally dependent on others, and "others," refers to our parents; Children completely depend on their parents.

1. Internalization and Identification

Children start to develop experience and learn how to handle their lives through two important processes: (1) Internalization, (2) Identification. Internalization is when the children internalize the values of their parents. Identification is when they identify with the parents and imitate them. The first important value that a child should internalize is love. If the child feels that he is loved, and that his parents and the church care about him, this will make the difference that I previously discussed for building a good relationship in childhood. It is critical for the latter stage when the child becomes an adolescent and goes to the church with questions, or has some doubts. How can we build this good relationship? In childhood, it is love. If the children internalize that their church loves them, their priest loves them, their Sunday school servants love them, and their parents love them, they will accept the boundaries and rules that are set for them.

Identification will start at about the age of four, but sometimes as late as the age of six. Usually, the son identifies himself with his father and the daughter identifies herself with her mother. They have found that if this process of identification does not go well, for example, if there is a big conflict between the son and his father or a big gap between the daughter and her mother, this may be the cause of homosexual tendencies later in their lives. Failure to identify with the same gender and feel loved and supported by the same-gender parent—the son with his father and the daughter with her mother—could be the source of homosexual tendencies later in life.

2. Children Seek Approval

Children want to feel the approval of the authority figures in their lives. They want to know that their parents, the church, and Sunday school servants approve of them. This approval is very important so that children will not feel inferior or develop a guilt complex. That is why encouragement and the use of positive reinforcement are very important. I remember very well when one of the youths told me that he did not believe in God. I asked him why. He told me, "God is always angry and disappointed with me. Whatever I try to do, I am wrong. He is never pleased. So, I do not want to deal with Him. I want Him to stay away from me. I do not want to deal with this angry God all the time." When he was a child, whenever he did anything, he would hear: "God will be disappointed with you; God is not happy with you; God is mad at you." He heard this over and over and over. He never felt approved by this God. This God is always angry. I am trying my best, but He is never pleased. Thus, he resolved in his mind that he did not believe in Him. It is very important to encourage and show approval to our children at this age.

3. How Children Learn to Respect Authority

As important as it is to internalize love, it is equally important to internalize power and authority. If his parents and the church show love and care, while simultaneously show authority in a good way, the child will learn how to respect authority. However, if authority is used to abuse its power over the children or to discipline them harshly, the children will reject authority and will rebel against every authority, whether it is that of the church, of God, the government, or the parents. If the parents and the church show no authority (if they are very passive), the child will be confused about authority, because he never understood what authority means. How will the child learn about authority if he feels that he is equal in authority and power to his Sunday school servants, parents, or the church? There are two extremes: Either no authority at all or the abuse of authority. Neither extreme is helpful for children. The child should internalize a positive type of authority. He should internalize that there is authority, but it is there to protect him; this authority is working for him, not against him. That is why St. Paul teaches us, "Do not provoke your children to wrath, lest they become failures."[32]

4. Helping Our Children Gain Experience

We need to train our children in how to gain experience in their lives. This is done through giving them small tasks and training them in how to

---

32 Cf. Col 3:21.

excel in these tasks. Encouraging them when they accomplish a task will help them develop self-confidence and self-motivation. They will develop healthy ambition and be able to take risks without fear.

5. Correcting Our Children

Another important attribute that children need to internalize during childhood is correction. They should know that correction is very important and is working for them, not against them. That is why the apostle Paul said to Timothy regarding the Scripture, that it is profitable for correction.[33] Love and acceptance do not conflict with the concept of correction and discipline. Yes, harsh correction will make the child develop fear of failure. That is why he will never try to take a risk, but will stay on the safe side. However, if the correction is administered gently and kindly, the child will be able to take risks and will try new things to develop his life experience without any fear of failure.

---

33 Cf. 2 Tim 3:16.

Part II

ADOLESCENCE

A | ADOLESCENCE

1. Introduction
2. Three Stages of Adolescence
3. Rebellion
4. Parents' Reactions
5. Uncertainty
6. Spiritual Changes during Adolescence
7. Biological Changes
8. Mental Changes
9. Psychological Changes
10. Social Changes
11. Common Characteristics of Adolescence

1. Introduction

Adolescence is one of the most challenging ages. We, as parents and Sunday school servants, find it difficult to understand and deal with adolescents. Perhaps, even the adolescents themselves, sometimes, do not understand why they are doing the things they are doing. This is because adolescence is a time of transition from childhood into adulthood, and therefore, the youth want to prove themselves. Furthermore, there is internal tension, between being, acting, and behaving like a child. On the one hand, he still also has the emotions of a child, and on the other hand, he is merging into adult emotions. This tension does not only occur with the adolescent, but there are also the expectations of society, family, and the church. Others, often, want him to behave as a mature adult. He is rebuked, belittled, or ridiculed when he behaves like a child. This is why there is a lot of anger during this stage of adolescence.

Conflicts, almost always, start and/or increase during adolescence, which we call the rebellious stage. Conflicts, usually, occur during adolescence due to our lack of understanding about what is happening with our children at this stage. If we understand what is taking place with them and what they are experiencing, most of these conflicts will decrease or disappear altogether. Moreover, when the youth, themselves, understand this phase and all the changes that occur during this time, whether physical, psychological, emotional, biological, social, and spiritual, it will help them to understand themselves better.

In this lecture, one of the key points we will discuss is how to accept and deal with our children when they are wrong. In fact, accepting our children is much easier than accepting our spouses! This is because God planted a natural and unconditional love in us toward our children. No matter what our children do, when we are reconciled with them, we let go of any hurt. Our hearts become so tender, making forgiveness and reconciliation easy.

At this age, adolescents are seeking love, compassion, acceptance, and understanding more than anything else. These are the things that keep the children from drifting away. There is a difference between accepting the person and accepting his wrongdoings. I am referring to accepting the individual, not his wrong behavior.

2. Three Stages of Adolescence

As you know, a large percentage of a child's personality is formed and developed during the first eight years of life. However, the final shape of personalities is actually formed during the years of adolescence. This means that at the end of adolescence, one's personality has taken its final shape and form. For this reason, this stage is the most important and dangerous stage in life.

The period of adolescence is divided into three stages:

1) The First Stage—Pre-teen Stage (from ten to twelve years of age). During this time, we see the first signs of rebellion. The children start to rebel against their parents or any kind of authority. This rebellion, or what is perceived as rebellion, will be discussed in the next section. Also, boys and girls start to see each other differently; the two genders become aware of each other.

2) The Second Stage (from age thirteen to sixteen). This is a stage of turbulence and great emotions in the life of adolescents. It is the most serious and dangerous stage in children's lives. During this period, the youth are confused between being children (dependent) and being adults (independent). There are also many other changes, such as physical and biological changes, feelings of attraction to the opposite gender, discovering one's own identity and gender, and understanding themselves.

3) The Third Stage (late adolescence—from age seventeen to twenty). When teens have successfully passed through the previous two stages, at this third stage, they will adapt to the culture and society in the right way and the final form of their personalities will be shaped.

The transition from one stage to another must go smoothly. The child must move from one stage to the other without lingering or getting stuck in one stage for a long period of time. For example, it is not acceptable that someone lives in the second stage of adolescence when he is twenty, twenty-five, or thirty years old. This can happen if the parents do not facilitate the smooth transition between the three stages of adolescence.

3. Rebellion

The period of adolescence is considered an age of rebellion and lack of acceptance of all the surrounding circumstances. However, we need to correctly understand what we perceive as rebellion from the adolescent. In reality, it is not rebellion, but growing into maturity and independence. At every stage of our lives, starting from life in the womb, there is some sort of rebellion. The fetus lives in the womb for nine months, during which time, it gets used to its surroundings and life in the womb. The first thing the child faces when he is born is new surroundings that are completely different than when in the womb. He feels separated from his mother, with whom he felt connected while in her womb. That is why he reacts by screaming, which does not subside until the mother takes the child in her arms. This crying is a sort of rebellion, as if the child is saying that he did not want to be born or be separated in that manner. When his mother holds and hugs him, he feels secure because he feels reconnected to his mother, as when he was in the womb, and that is why he calms down.

Little by little, the child gets accustomed to being held by the father and the relatives, etc. Then, the child starts to become familiarized to his new surroundings and the fact that he and the mother are actually two entities, not one.

The child continues in this stage until he starts walking and running, when he begins to feel that he does not need to be carried in order to move around. The child runs from here to there and the mother runs after him. The child starts to have a taste of freedom, a sense of independence, and thinks that he can live totally independently. Soon, he realizes that he is not independent and that he needs his mother and father, and so he reconnects with them again, but in a different way than he had done previously. Now, he recognizes there are set boundaries between him and his parents. He realizes that he is an individual who is different from his father and mother. He may do some activities by himself, like sleep alone in his own room, but he still feels a lot of dependence on his parents. In this stage of childhood, we all enjoy our children because they are obedient and pleasant. They need us and always return to us.

When the child moves from childhood into the age of adolescence, he again seeks independence and freedom. Because of this, he starts to rebel. He wants to assert himself and defy any authority that might prevent him from enjoying his independence, his sense of self, and the feeling that he has his own opinions and autonomy. In reality, this is a very crucial stage, which facilitates reaching the stage of maturity. For many people who suffer from low self-esteem, the root of their problem can be traced back to not being able to prove themselves during adolescence. A lack of self-confidence is due to the fact that during adolescence, youth feel that they are not trustworthy, and therefore, do not develop self-confidence.

Parents become the very first authority against whom the child rebels because they are the ones to whom the child has listened and obeyed in the first ten to twelve years of his life. When the child disobeys his parents, this gives him the sense that he has become an independent person, with his own word and opinion. Unfortunately, when parents see their adolescent wanting to be independent from them, they perceive this as rebellion, or that their child is becoming bad, disobedient, turning against God, or drifting away from spirituality. However, this is not the case. The child is growing. He is not only aware, but wants to prove that he and his parents are distinctly separate being. If we understand this concept, we will know how to deal much better with our adolescents.

4. Parents' Reactions

When, as parents, we understand the changes our children are experiencing, our role transforms into how to facilitate their transition from one stage (childhood—immaturity) to the other (adulthood—maturity). If we insist that the children must be obedient and compliant to us at all times, and that we should be the ones making all the decisions, this will hinder the children's maturity and growth. Instead of smoothly facilitating this transition into adulthood, many times, parents suppress their children's growth. They want them to be dependent on them and they want to control them, as in the first ten years of their lives. That is one reason that major conflicts and tensions occur between parents and their children during this period. The second reason for the tension and conflict could be because the children want to have their independence, without realizing that they still need their parents. The correct term is actually *interdependence*, which means that they still need their parents, besides having their own boundaries and life, and their parents also depend on them (perhaps, emotionally, physically, sometimes financially, etc.). Many people do not fully understand the real meaning of interdependence—perhaps, until they reach maturity, after the age twenty-one.

When parents increase their power and control over the children to rein in their rebellion, the children may become more rebellious, not less. Instead of this approach, we should teach children how to make reasonable decisions during this stage. We should give children options and explain each possibility, the pros and cons for each choice, and the potential consequences of each path. Then, we should let them make their own decisions and allow them to bear the consequences of these decisions. They want to be free and assert their personalities. We should not control them. Control increases rebellion, and adolescents may become angry, threaten to leave the house at the age of eighteen, or fight with their parents, etc. They may even call the police on their parents. This is the outcome of many years of suppression and total control of the child.

If, at this stage, the parents continue to force the child into being submissive, to give in to his parents demands, and to continuously obey, a second outcome may occur, which is that the child will submit to this control, and as a result, develop a weak personality. Even as an adult, he will not be able to form an opinion. Anyone would be able to tell him what to do. These children can end up being prey in society, because they cannot say "no" to anything, even to the bad influence of others around them. They may fall into sin, not because they are bad, but because they cannot say, "no." They were taught that saying, "no," is wrong, and that, "good children do not say no." Thus, they do not have enough courage to say, "no," even when someone is asking them to do something they know is wrong.

5. Uncertainty

This stage is also characterized by uncertainty or indecisiveness; there is always a great deal of hesitancy. Let us not get too concerned about the children's indecision, because it is normal at this age. It is due to the fact that adolescents want to be mature and childish, simultaneously. They want to be responsible while still living carelessly. Also, they want to be joyful, but with all the changes that are happening, they are depressed and unhappy for no given reason. We, often, hear teens saying, "I am upset, but I do not know why!" Their emotions are changing. The hormonal changes in their bodies cause them to go from happiness to sadness without any reason. The child also might be full of optimism or pessimism without any logical reason. In spirituality, adolescents go back and forth between being very religious to being unreligious. Sometimes they are calm and obedient and sometimes rebellious and disrespectful. This uncertainty and indecision is a feature of the transition from childhood to adulthood. [It is important to point out that the erratic emotional changes in adolescents should be within reason, and not overly or grossly exaggerated, to make sure that there are no underlying psychological disorders, or any external, influencing factors, such as bullying at school, medical issues, etc.].

6. Spiritual Changes that Occur during Adolescence

Several changes occur during adolescence. We will begin with the spiritual changes.

a. The Need to Understand Principles

In the first eight to ten years of their lives, Bible stories and the saints' biographies are entertaining and pleasant. During adolescence, these narratives alone become insufficient and are no longer fulfilling because adolescents want to understand principles. They need more explanation and they want to understand "why." The adolescent wants to know why David did what he did, why St. Anthony lived like he lived, why St. Demiana chose what she chose, and how they all succeeded in having a great relationship with God, etc. When they start asking why, some might perceive this as argumentative, which is another incorrect perception. They are not arguing; they want to understand, because their perception is increasing. They are growing into maturity.

b. How to Form a Personal Relationship with God

That is why this is the best time to teach our youth how to have a relationship with God, and how God is not an idea, but rather, God is a reality—a real Being, because we deal with Him: "That which was from the beginning, which we have heard, which we have seen with our eyes, which we have looked upon, and our hands have handled, concerning the Word of life" (1 Jn 1:1). This is the beginning of learning how to have a relationship with God. You should teach your children how to experience having a relationship with God. It is highly recommended to teach children to make time for prayer, to read the Holy Bible, and to apply God's word in their lives.

c. The Dangers of Sin

This stage requires that parents describe and explain the concept of sin, its dangers, its evils, and how it can destroy peoples' lives. We should teach adolescents and expound on how to make the right decisions and choices, because many of their choices could have serious consequences. We can use the story of Adam and Eve to emphasize this point: Because Adam and Eve made the wrong choices—they sinned—and the consequence was death and expulsion from Paradise. It is very important to discuss and explain sin because there are a lot of temptations and experiences of warfare during this age. If teenagers begin any bad habits during this period, unfortunately, it may take years to correct. This is why we need to protect our youth from developing such harmful habits, such as smoking, substance abuse, and engaging sexual immorality, by explaining to them the destructive effects of sin and how sin can injure and leave long lasting scars in their lives that can take years to heal.

If from the beginning, you explain that sin is very evil, you are protecting them. At the same time, you present to them Christ, who, through having a personal relationship with Him, gives happiness, joy, and fulfillment, versus sin, which leads to death and destruction. Invite them to choose. The earlier our teaching is Christ-focused, the better off we all are. We need to start these lessons as early as ten years of age, or based on the child's level of maturity and acceptance. I strongly recommended encouraging children to commit to the Holy Mystery of Confession starting at the age of ten, in order to begin to develop a strong relationship with their father of confession, to learn that there is sin, and to know that there is an alternative through a loving relationship with God.

d. Discussing Choices

At this stage, parents must use the word, "choice," and should always teach their adolescents to choose and be responsible for their choices and its consequences. We can tell the youth that they have two choices, the way with God, which leads to life, and the way of sin, which leads to death. "Which one will you follow? It is your choice." For example, at the age of twelve, a child may tell his parents that he no longer wants to serve as a chanter deacon during liturgy. This will probably upset the parents. However, parents must understand that it is not that the child does not want to serve any more; rather, the child just wants to exercise his right of saying, "no." He just wants space to make his own decisions. In this case, we must give them this space, but guide them to make the right decision. In this example, tell that child that he has the right not to serve as a deacon; nonetheless, let him think about the pros and cons of serving and of not serving, and discuss them. At the end, assure him that it is his decision, but explain all the blessings and pros for serving that he will lose if he chooses not to serve. Always focus on the point that it is their choice so that they do not feel that we are forcing decisions on them.

In many instances, parents drag their teenage children to sit with me, thinking that in thirty minutes, I will change the child and convert him or her into the submissive angel they want him or her to be. Youth come to my office against their will, and I see how upset some of them are. I tell them that they do not have to continue and may leave. In many instances, the children leave. Since they felt that their free will was respected and they had the choice, a lot of them come back. In this case, the meeting with them is more productive. We must respect the youth's wishes and assure them that we are not denying them their right to be independent. In turn, this will alleviate a lot of the confrontations parents may experience with their children at this age. It will give the adolescents a sense of security that their parents are not trying to take away their independence. The confrontations mainly arise due to insecurities the teenagers feel because they want to be independent from their parents.

e. Making Space for Personal Prayer

Also in this stage, if you are used to praying together as a family, children between ten and twelve years of age will start saying that they no longer want to pray with the family and that they prefer to pray by themselves. Many parents get very worried when faced with these statements. They worry about why their child refuses to pray with them. They also start thinking that maybe the child will not actually pray, will not pray properly, or will just recite the Lord's Prayer quickly and that will be it. Again, this is another way for the preteens to reassert their personality. They are indirectly saying that they are independent, have their own personality, and do not have to pray with the family.

When this happens, how are you going to react and respond? Are you going to tell the child, "No! Do not pray by yourself because we pray as a family?" Are you going to tell the child to go ahead and pray alone? In fact, we should tell the child how happy we are that he wants to have a personal relationship with God. Parents should take this opportunity to teach their children how important it is to have a personal relationship with God. Make sure to show them that they made the right decision when they decided to have a personal relationship with God. Please do not scold them and force them to pray with the family. Rather, introduce them to a new concept, namely that, although praying by yourself and developing a personal relationship with God is important and a correct decision, and all of us should have time for personal prayer, there is also a special blessing bestowed on the family when they pray together. This is as Christ told us, "For where two or three are gathered together in My name, I am there in the midst of them" (Mt 18:20). Therefore, it is important to pray, not only individually, but also as a family to receive God's promised blessing.

Moreover, God has promised that if two agree on any request from God, He will respond and fulfill their request; "Again I say to you that if two of you agree on earth concerning anything that they ask, it will be done for them by My Father in heaven" (Mt 18:19). So, praying together has another blessing because if we, as a family, request something from God while praying together, He has promised to give it to us.

After these explanations, parents should pose these questions to their child: "What do you think? Is it better to pray as a family, or individually, or both—as a family and individually?" Most probably, when you react this way, they will respond by choosing the option of praying as a family *and* individually. You did not say, "No. We will continue to pray as a family." When you oppose adolescents, you lead them to stubbornness and opposition toward you. It is much better to encourage the children by saying, "It is a blessing that you want to pray by yourself, and to build a personal relationship with Christ; however, there is a special blessing in praying as a family. So, what do you think?" When parents ask the question, "What do you think?" it gives youth the feeling of maturity. Therefore, most probably, they will agree with you because they want to prove to you that they are in fact mature and able to make the right choices.

f. Forming Healthy Relationships with the Believers—the Body of Christ

Here, you can also introduce another concept, the importance of going to church, because all of us are members of one body [Jesus Christ] and we are connected together. Teach your teenagers how to develop a healthy relationship with the body of Christ—the other believers, their peers in Sunday school, the priest [Abouna, Father], other adults, and Sunday school servants. It is very good to do this during this time because they will have a sense of satisfaction when they have healthy relationships with others. With this satisfaction and self-actualization, they will grow with self-confidence and positive self-esteem, not with pride or arrogance. Through these healthy relationships, they will gradually mature. Our souls are relational souls. Our souls grow through relationships. This is why God said regarding Adam that it is not good for him to be alone.[34] The more we are engaged in healthy relationships, the more we grow into maturity in a healthy way.

g. Addressing Guilt

Finally, if they start to develop bad habits, they may also develop a disproportionate sense of guilt, and this creates enmity between the person and himself. He does not accept himself because of all the bad habits he is doing. This is not good for an adolescent's maturity. Thus, you need to teach them about God's forgiveness and God's love and acceptance. You need to present to them the image of Christ who accepted the sinful women and forgave her sins and healed her from her wounds. Do not present the image of the Pharisee who judged the women and did not accept her. Many times, we present the image of the Pharisee and the judgmental attitude that contributes to increased guilt. This will not help in a teen's growth toward maturity. On the contrary, you need to present the image of the Lord Jesus Christ who came to our world and died on the cross for one reason—to forgive our sins. God *knows* that we will commit sin and God *knows* that we are sinful. That is why He came to forgive our sins and to heal us from all our iniquities and trespasses.

These are the spiritual changes adolescents face. It start by just listening to stories and progresses to developing a personal relationship with the Lord Jesus, to learning about sin and its dangers, to seeing how to make good spiritual decisions in their lives.

---

34 Cf. Gen 2:18.

7. Biological Changes

Biological changes usually occur at an earlier age for girls than for boys. These changes typically occur at the age of ten, eleven, or twelve for girls and at the age of twelve or thirteen for boys. It is wrong to compare the physical growth of boys and girls at this age. We have to understand that boys and girls grow and mature differently.

a. Muscular Growth and Bone Growth

In this stage, muscular growth is slower than bone growth, so some boys are not well coordinated in their movements or sometimes things fall from their hands. If we make negative or harsh comments about their coordination or physically losing grip, this may really hurt them. They are at the stage where they are building and developing their personality, and harsh comments can hurt them deeply and make them suffer from the unfairness of the remarks. Negative comments embarrass the adolescent, especially if they were made in front of other people. They feel that their personality is mocked and shaken. Therefore, parents must be very careful about the remarks they make about their children, especially in front of other people and, in particular, in front of the opposite sex. Self-image is very important to boys and girls at this age. It is important and well recommended not to mock the children at this age, and especially in front of the other sex.

b. Changes in Appearance and Self-Acceptance

Young children usually look innocent and have angelic faces. Once they start to grow in adolescence, even their faces start to change. Sometimes, children notice the changes in their looks and they often cannot accept their appearances and themselves. Again, negative and/or harsh comments, or mocking by parents and siblings about how they look can be damaging to one's personality and can hamper self-acceptance. This is what leads to low self-esteem and a poor self-image, because the child cannot accept himself. We have to be very careful about the comments we say to them. We need to encourage them and state positive comments to help them accept themselves and develop a positive self-image of themselves in this stage. Accepting oneself is very important during adolescence. If we do not accept who the adolescent is during this time, the person may continue all his life not accepting who he is.

Both boys and girls at this age tend to change their appearances frequently for self-acceptance. They change their hair length or style. Boys sometimes shave; sometimes grow a beard, etc. It is okay to notice all these changes they are making to their appearances while trying to find something acceptable to them. Keep in mind that this is normal behavior at this age.

Be careful about making negative comments about being a girl or being female. This hurts self-perception because it leads them to not accept their gender. Some girls say, "I wish I was a male so that I would be more accepted by my family and society." This is especially true in a culture that discriminates between males and females. Therefore, we need to be very careful with any comments we make because one comment can create a barrier against self-acceptance. The Lord said, "love your neighbor as yourself" (Mt 19:19), which implies that we need to love ourselves, and we need to accept ourselves. If I do not accept myself, if I am not at peace with myself, or if I am not reconciled with myself, this can hinder my growth progress and maturity.

Also, a boy's voice starts to change because of the growth of his trachea. If we start making fun of how his voice is changing—for example, if he is a deacon and parents or siblings make fun of the way he sings a hymn—even as a joke, this will make him lose his self-confidence. Therefore, next time he is singing, he might get very self-conscious about his voice and become unable to sing, or he may make mistakes. In this stage, children are very sensitive and they take every comment very seriously.

Children also sometimes try to extract a word of acknowledgement or praise from their parents because it is important to them and their self-esteem. For example, a son, who is a deacon, tells his father that he served at the altar in the sanctuary today. Then, the father answers and says simply, "Yes, I know!" That is all he says. That is not what the son is expecting. He wanted acknowledgement of his accomplishment and a compliment on what he has done, be it a nice hymn, reading, or anything else that he perceives as an accomplishment. These compliments are very important for the children's self-esteem. However, some parents think that they are protecting their children from falling into the sin of pride! First, parents need to build a child's self-esteem, self-image, and self-confidence, then, worry about pride. Negative comments at this age carry the great risk of causing a future lack of self-worth when children grow up.

c. Eating Habits

Moreover, in this stage the body grows very quickly and children start to eat more than usual. Please be careful not to mock or make fun of them, especially girls. Also, avoid telling girls to watch what they eat to maintain their weight and figure because they can develop eating disorders in this stage. Teens become torn between the biological and physiological needs of their bodies and the need to maintain an image based on what they have been told. However, we must advise and teach healthy eating habits, such as how many meals they should eat per day, how to choose healthy food, and how to avoid indulgence in junk food, etc. Again, we guide, lead, and teach without negative comments. Avoid all negative comments because they can lead to eating disorders, especially for some girls.

I remember when I was in middle school in Egypt, we learned about the "balanced diet." This was a very important lesson for adolescents, which indirectly taught us what a balanced diet is. It explained that eating a well-balanced meal was sufficient in supplying the body with its needs, without the accumulation of excess fat.

d. Blood Circulation

Many parents also complain that their children become very lazy. In fact, they are more than likely not lazy, but their circulation cannot keep up with their rapid physical growth. This means that there is not enough blood to nourish the growing body. That is why physical activities and exercise are very important in this age, because they stimulate the circulatory system to produce enough blood to nourish the growing body. This might be a remedy for what we think is laziness, which, actually, may be the inability of the circulatory system to meet the needs of the growing body.

Therefore, health education and knowledge are very important for our children in this stage. We should explain to them the physiological and physical changes that are happening in their bodies, whether they are boys or girls. Moreover, we must explain the role of sports and exercise in growth and how they will overcome what feels like laziness. Also, we should emphasize the importance of a healthy diet and nutrition. All these are very important topics that parents should discuss with their children in this stage.

8. Mental Changes

Another form of change and growth in this stage is mental growth: growth in the mind and the ability to think. That is why teenagers need discussions and persuasion. Parents, usually, complain and wonder why their adolescent children are always asking, "why," or want to discuss every topic. This is simply because the child is also growing intellectually.

The first six years are called the stage of "what." From age seven to age twelve is called "how." From age twelve to age eighteen is called "why."

The first six years is the stage of "what" behavioral concepts or principles parents should plant, even without teaching the child how to practice them. For example, in the first six years, the child should know that there are things called, "prayer, fasting, confession, communion," etc., without knowing how we fast or how we pray. When the family stands up to pray, the child will do the same. If the child moves here and there during prayers, it is okay. During this age, parents are just planting the concepts and principles they want to instill.

In the stage of "how," from ages six to twelve, children learn how to pray, how to fast, how to read the Bible, as well as any other behavioral principles. The third stage, the stage of "why," is from ages twelve to eighteen. It is the stage of discussion. Parents need to explain why we pray, why we fast, and why all these traditions are important.

9. Psychological Changes

a. Effects of Hormonal Changes

We must understand that the hormonal changes of the body during the period of adolescence have psychological effects on both boys and girls. Androgen, the male hormone, can lead boys to be aggressive. For girls, progesterone may cause water retention, leading to a bad temper and or increased sensitivity. Therefore, parents must understand that these psychological changes have underlying biological reasons.

During this time, parents must show their adolescents that they understand what is going on in the youth's body and psyche. They should surround them with love and compassion and not add to, or increase, their anxiety. Comfort them and give them confidence. Explain these changes to them and tell them that these changes are all normal and that all adolescents go through this uncomfortable phase. Help them understand that once the hormones in their bodies start to reach a balance, everything will go back to normal. Discussion and explanation will make it easy for them to accept themselves and not perceive themselves as weird or different.

b. Anxiety

Adolescents suffer from anxiety during this stage because of all these changes. Anxiety may occur in relation to school, homework, the future, being accepted or loved by friends, etc. They are always anxious about something! This can sometimes lead teenagers to wear strange outfits, or want to have a tattoo, or to have certain body piercing. The main reason for thinking about or doing these things is because they want to fit in with the crowd, because they are seeking acceptance by their friends. They want to conform to the society around them.

When youth tell their parents that they want a tattoo or a piercing, these statements can come as a shock to parents! However, parents should control their tempers and reactions, and try to discuss these issues with their children. Calm and reasonable conversation that is full of love and compassion may convince the teens that these changes are unnecessary for them to be accepted by their friends, whereas yelling and asserting your power and control over them may cause your children to have a negative reaction and rebel.

Teaching adolescents how to put their confidence in God will take care of all of anxieties during this stage,. You need to teach them that for everything, there is a divine element and a human element. Once they do their part, God is faithful to do His part for them so they will be successful. Also, give them examples from the Scripture, such as the three young saintly men, Daniel, or Joseph, and how, when these people did their part faithfully and honestly, God accomplished the divine element and did His part with them, and they became successful in everything they did.

c. Lack of Confidence

Another psychological change during this stage is shyness and a lack of confidence. The question, "What do people think of me?" and especially what the other gender thinks is very important at this age. They are very self-conscious about this issue, which may lead to shyness and lack of self-confidence. As parents, we should respond to *all* their questions so that they do not get wrong answers from outside sources.

d. Authority

In general, but particularly at this age, parents should not get into a power struggle with their children. Do not try to assert your word and opinion against the child's because if the child succeeds in asserting his word and starts to challenge you, you will lose your authority over him. On the other hand, if you manage to challenge the child and assert your word, you might feel that you have won, but in fact, you have just broken the child's self-image.

Do not keep challenging your children by saying things like, "I said so," or "Let us see who has the last word." It does not work this way, *even* if the child is challenging you. Everything can be solved by discussion and conversation. Of course, discussions and conversation take a long, long time and a lot of energy. Sometimes, especially after long days at work, parents may not have the patience or energy for these discussions. However, this is the right way to deal with children at this age. You must spend time and energy with them, discuss and negotiate with them. The alternative is that you might lose them. Aggression and asserting power might give quick resolutions, but in the long run, you are destroying the child's personality. Then, you hear adolescents saying, "I will deal with this until I am 18 years old and that will be it. I will leave home!" I have noticed that the most dangerous year that youth face is freshman year in college. Children who were oppressed by their parents, and especially those who go to school away from home, experience a sudden burst of freedom, and sometimes get in a lot of trouble by trying everything in front of them. That is why we believe that if the child survives freshman year without major problems, he will be okay for the rest of his life. However, a great deal of children get into trouble and get lost during their freshman year; for example, they lose scholarships, or they learn and acquire bad habits and bad behavior.

The more love, compassion, and understanding we have toward children, the more we will have the ability to talk with them, teach them, and convince them of our ways. Of course, not every discussion will end with agreement. When everything else has been tried and has failed, we can assert our opinion and say, "no," to whatever there is a disagreement. However, "no," should be the last resort and, of course, it is wrong if the parents always say, "no." When the child faces a critical situation and the only answer is, "no," so be it. However, make sure to minimize the frequency of this response. When parents say, "no," it should be the last resort after having tried to talk and discuss and convince. Then, the parents should tell the child that they would make the decision against the child's wishes, because they have his best interest in mind. Moreover, they should tell their teenager that they understand that he is upset and unhappy now, but in the long run, he will understand and appreciate his parent's decision. All this should be conducted with love and compassion, while avoiding power struggles.

Furthermore, because self-image is very important during this period, if there is any discipline that needs to be done, it is better to do it in private and not in front of everyone. If you discipline an adolescent in front of everyone, this will destroy his self-image. It is better to have a conversation between you and him alone. Conversely, when there is a reward to be given, it is better that this be done in public. This will help them to have a good self-image.

10. Social Changes

a. Decision-Making

Teenagers want to be independent, but they do not know how to make decisions. Sometimes parents make the decisions for their children. It makes the parents very happy that their thirteen, fourteen, or sixteen-year-old child comes to them to ask for their opinion and does what they suggest. They feel their child is very obedient, not knowing that making decisions for their children hinders their maturity.

Making decisions for youth is wrong, even if the child asks you. Rather parents should teach their children the process of decision-making. For example, a teenager asks his parents which university he should attend. If the parent chooses one particular university and the child agrees, the parent will feel happy because the child is obedient. However, by doing that, the parent does not teach the child how to make decisions or how to choose appropriately. It is much better if the parent starts by asking, "What are the choices in front of you?" Let them think of what they have. Suggest that the child list all the choices in front of him. Then, ask the child to list all the pros and cons for each choice. Start by discussing each choice, with all the pros and cons. Parents can add their input, for example, regarding scholarships, tuition, school ranking, etc. The parents' role, here, is to guide the child. Then, the parent should ask the child, "Now, what do you think?" If you have trained the child the correct way, he will most likely make the right decision. Here, the parent is training the child how to make an important decision in his life, which is much better than making the decision for him. Teach your children how to make decisions in their lives.

Another example is if a daughter tells her mother, "I am going to church. Which dress should I wear?" If the mother answers by choosing an outfit, as small an issue as this might seem, the mother is not helping her daughter to mature. Instead, the mother can answer by telling her daughter to think and choose something that is appropriate for church. This is teaching!

Sometimes, teenagers ask for advice. The parents give it, but the adolescent does the opposite! This upsets the parents, and they think or say, "Why did you ask me?" The answer is that they want to assert that they have an independent personality. This is not rebelling against the parents; rather, it is an assertion of having an independent personality.

In many instances regarding dealing with adolescents, the best thing to do is to turn a blind eye; but do not turn a blind eye all the time!

b. Arguments

Adolescents are, often, convinced of something, but they want to argue for argument's sake. They keep arguing to prove that they have a different opinion. If the discussion has turned into an argument, the parent should tell the child, "Since we cannot reach a decision now and each one of us is repeating his point of view, what do you think? Let us each think about what we discussed and consider each other's opinion and revisit the topic some other time." This way the parents are correctly putting boundaries and ending useless arguments and discussions that do not edify. Do not let the discussion take hours, because sometimes children in this age keep arguing until the parent loses his temper or becomes totally exhausted.

c. Freedom

Let them earn their freedom. When the adolescents use their freedom successfully, parents should reward them by giving them more freedom and responsibility. If they succeed, give them even more freedom and more responsibility.

d. Contracts

Using contracts is a good idea. For example, if the teenager wants to buy a cell phone, video games, or any of the devices they like, parents should make a contract with their child before purchasing anything. If a parent buys a certain device and the child ends up spending hours using it, wasting his time, when the parents say, "Do not spend so much time using the device," it is too late, because the child has already become accustomed to spending such a long time with this device.

Before parents buy a cell phone for their child, tell him, "We need to agree on some things." Then, they should ask him some questions. Do not list your requirements; rather, get the adolescent to answer your questions. For example, "Do you think Dad and Mom have the right to look at your cell phone?" Since the child wants to get the phone, he will likely answer, "yes." By doing so, the parents got one point in their favor, and the child, himself, said it! Then, parents should ask, "How are you going to use the phone?" The child will answer with all the correct answers, in order to get the phone, which is okay and good. However, if you buy the phone *first*, none of these agreements will take place.

During my visits with families, some parents complain that their child spends seven or ten hours a day playing video games. When I talk with the child, I suggest that ten minutes a day is sufficient; that shocks the child. Then I ask him, "What do you think?" He thinks and answers that maybe one hour a day. Of course, from the beginning I wanted to reach one hour a day, but if I suggested it in the beginning, he might have bargained and reached three hours a day. The art of bargaining is to give an impractical and shocking number first. Also, when the child goes from ten hours to one hour during the bargaining process, do not agree on the hour right away, although that is what is in your mind. Rather, bargain some more. Let him feel that for you to reach one hour will take some effort for you. Say, "No, one hour is too long; half an hour is more than enough." Let him work to obtain this hour; thus, he will not request a change the following week.

Contracts are very important before you buy anything. Before you buy a car, make a contract; otherwise, you will find that once the child gets the car, he is always out and comes back home at three in the morning. Then, you take the keys away and he argues, and it becomes a problem. So, a contract is important, especially if it is written and signed by the parent and child. I am serious about this. A signed contract asserts the importance of the issue and that he will be held accountable.

e. Social Systems

It is important for the adolescents to know that they are part of a complete social system, and can say, "I am part of a system." The importance of understanding that the adolescent is part of a system is that he will recognize that all of his decisions, actions, and thoughts will be tied with this social system. The social system affects me and I affect it. Therefore, I have to be mindful of the traditions of this system. I have to respects other people's opinions, even if I disagree with them. I have to be an unselfish listener, and not think of my own comfort only. If the child learns this early on in life, later when he gets married, he will not be selfish and think only of his own comfort. On the other hand, if the child was not taught these things at a young age and only thought about what gives him comfort, when he gets married, that will be the way he thinks, and will, ultimately, behave accordingly.

f. Sexual Desires

Sexual desires increase during this stage. Sometimes, the adolescents suffer from disturbances in their spiritual life because of their sexual desires. Unfortunately, due to the lack of sexual education for the youth provided by the majority of parents, as well as by the church, most of their knowledge comes from wrong sources.

Sexual desires at this age lead to psychological burdens; the children become very sensitive, and they completely dislike criticism and scolding. Sometimes, sinful thoughts attack them and this is the time when they might fall and acquire bad habits or get involved in inappropriate relationships, such as dating.

When I discuss the topic of dating with adolescents, I start by telling them, "Let us define dating in order to answer if it is right or wrong." When I ask them, "What is dating?" Their answers are usually "church-appropriate" responses. They provide the answer that you want to hear. When they give you the answer you want to hear, your response would be, "If you do it the way you are defining it, and follow some rules, it is okay." However, teenagers will never say what they really feel because they know that it would not be approved.

In meetings with adolescents, when I ask about the definition of dating, sometimes if one of them gives the ideal response, the rest disagree with him, stating that this is not the reality. So, the teenagers know and correct each other. Once, at one of the youth conventions, His Eminence Metropolitan Serapion[35] told the children, "The reason the clergy always get questions about dating is not because you do not know the answer; rather, it is because you are waiting to hear a different answer. If we asked any of you to give a lecture about dating, you would do it better than us. So, you are just hoping to hear a different answer!" Thus, allow them to answer and discuss these things.

Furthermore, encouraging the adolescent to practice the Mystery [Sacrament] of Confession without fear or shame is very important. As fathers of confession, we should not show disgust to anything the adolescent says. When an adolescent comes to confess about something, first he says very little, and then, looks at the priest's face to see what it will convey. If Abouna's [the priest father] face changes, he will cut the confession short. It is recommended, that when the adolescents say something that could warrant a reaction, to respond by saying, "When I was your age, I had similar warfare." Personally, I use this technique when I get confessions like that. This way, the adolescent does not feel that he is abnormal or strange. When he hears that Abouna or Sayedna [His Grace, the bishop] faced the same warfare, he will feel comforted, and it is a fact that we have all experienced these types of warfare; we are not lying. It is normal and natural that adolescents face these struggles. The way we deal with these challenges is what is different between this person and that person. The goal is to make adolescents understand that temptations and warfare are normal. He is not strange. He is not an evil person if he confessed that he is in love with a girl at school. How we deal with the

---

[35] Metropolitan of the Diocese of Los Angeles, Southern California, and Hawaii

situation is what makes the difference. If the parent responds by being upset and says, "What do you mean you are in love? We do not accept that," etc., the child will not continue to tell you what is happening and will not risk telling you anything else in the future. We have to understand our children and encourage them to discuss everything with us without fear or shame.

g. Role Models

Adolescents like heroism. That is why they like to put up pictures of their role models, such as singers, movie stars, athletes, etc. Also, some boys like to put up pictures of cars. Occasionally, I see in homes that children have all these large posters of music artists and athletes, and then, this very small picture of the Lord Jesus Christ, which their mothers probably stuck on their wall. Here, we should direct their attention to role models from the Church, such as the saints, characters from the Bible, and people with leadership and heroic characteristics from everyday life. It is very important to teach them the right concept of power and heroism. Therefore, sharing the biographies of saints, stories of biblical characters, and the leadership qualities of current leaders will satisfy the adolescent's interest in heroism.

11. Common Characteristics of Adolescence

I will conclude with some common characteristics of this age:

- **Frequent change of mind.** That is because of their uncertainty and is evidenced in the frequent change in friends. Today, this person is his friend, and tomorrow a different person is his friend.
- **Sensitivity.** That is why we should be very careful about our remarks and comments to them.
- **Fear of and anxiety about society.** This occurs when society pressures them to act as adults and mature persons, while they still act as children.
- **Desire to love and be loved.**
- **Anger, stubbornness, and rebellion.** We should accept them with complete love. They need to experience changes. We should give them enough self-confidence. Sometimes, the best treatment for stubbornness is to close your eyes.

- **Discussion until a solution accepted by both parents and child is reached.**
- **Some of their childish attitudes still exist.** Do not scold a youth by saying, "You have a mustache and you still act like a baby!" This is normal. They keep going back and forth between childhood and adulthood.
- **Good role models.** This is important for their love of heroism. When the parents are good role models, this will satisfy their need of finding a good role model for themselves.
- **Adolescents love those who make promises and fulfill them.** If you promise, you must fulfill. If you want your children to open up to you, you must be trustworthy. If you promise and do not deliver, you will lose their trust and they will not share anything with you.
- **Do not sit on a high tower when you talk to them.** Do not say, "When I was your age, I never did that." Or, "Why is this generation acting like that?" Even if you were an angel when you were a child, please assume the role of a human being in order to win your child. Therefore, we must befriend our children and talk with them and share with them.

  Exposing or publicizing their secrets is a problem. For example, if a girl shares some secrets with a servant and the servant shares them with someone else, this will make the girl lose her trust in the servant and in the church, etc.
- **The adolescent prefers advice and suggestions, not orders and preaching.**
- **Their physical energy should be used properly.** Sports, trips, activities, and humanitarian activities are very important.
- **Idle time.** If we help them fill their time and decrease the amount of idle time, their minds will not wander into sin. Try to help them fill their time with learning music, participating in sports, joining church clubs, helping the poor, serving at a food bank, or volunteering at homeless shelters, etc.

B | PROBLEMS WE ENCOUNTER WITH OUR CHILDREN DURING ADOLESCENCE

1. Anger
2. Seeking Attention
3. Clothes and Appearance
4. Career Choice
5. Homosexuality
6. Guilt
7. Inferiority
8. Lying
9. Cursing

During the age of adolescence, many problems arise. I will discuss nine problems or challenges that our youth face at this age, as well as how parents can deal with them.

1. Anger

The first problem we encounter with adolescents during at age stage is irritability. Often they are easily angered and argumentative. Sometimes, this irritability, anger, and tendency to argue do not only occur in the house, but also in school; some youth may cause trouble with their teachers or peers. These problems may also show up in church, at youth conventions, etc. Note that if this irritability is not addressed and corrected during adolescence, it can potentially continue throughout an adolescent's whole life.

The youth who habitually fights with others enters into a vicious cycle. Often, these youth lack self-confidence and security, and thus, make up for this deficiency by aggression. A person who has self-confidence does not need to prove himself by raising his voice or by fighting. No one likes an angry, screaming person. Therefore, when he gets irritated with others, people begin to dislike him. This creates feelings of rejection and being unloved, which further increases his feelings of insecurity and lack of inner peace, setting in motion the process again.

Why does this become a major problem during adolescence? Why does irritability appear during adolescence? The first possible reason is that the adolescent may feel a lack of acceptance, self-rejection, or rejection from others. There is a sense of inner anger, which manifests itself as irritability. He is rejected, others do not accept him, and so he tries to make up for it.

Another reason lending to irritability during this period is an increasing need for compassion and love. If a youth has not been satisfied with compassion and love during childhood, when he enters adolescence and still does not feel compassion and love, irritability increases. He is upset with his parents because they are not providing him with the compassion and love that he craves, which manifests as anger and irritability.

The nonexistence or lack of discipline at home can increase irritability. Perhaps, the whole house uses this method of interaction; the father yells, the mother yells, and when the children yell, the response is also by yelling. We do not teach our children manners. We should teach them how to speak in a low voice, and how to ask for what they want in a nice way. The nonexistence or lack of discipline leads a youth who finds that he is growing up and growing taller to become, sorry for the expression, a bully. He starts to raise his voice and no one is able to stand up to him.

Moreover, a lack of spiritual growth can lead to increased irritability. The person who is raised in church knows very well that "the wrath of man does not produce the righteousness of God" (Jas 1:20). The person who is maturing within the church never turns to anger and irritability.

There are several methods we can use to deal with an adolescent's anger. First, allow him to express what upsets him in a courteous way. When the child begins speaking in an angry way, we can address his anger by saying, "There is something bothering you. Tell me what is upsetting you, but in a different way." Assure him that you will listen to him but he must speak in a calm manner and not in an angry tone. If the reason for his anger is the nonexistence or lack of discipline, we need to institute appropriate measures of discipline. These should not be destructive, but rather constructive, and encourage anger management. Moreover, and most importantly, is the acceptance of the Lord Jesus Christ in one's life as the forgiver of one's sins. When I feel that God loves me and has forgiven my sins, I will be able to forgive others; as Christ has forgiven me, I forgive others. Many times, we cannot forgive others because we cannot understand God's love for us and His forgiveness. When youth are satisfied with God and filled with the Holy Spirit, they will bear the fruit of the Spirit in their lives, including longsuffering, kindness, and meekness. They would be meek people. God said, "learn from Me, for I am gentle and lowly in heart" (Mt 11:29), and it is said about the Lord Jesus Christ that "He will not cry out, nor raise His voice, nor cause His voice to be heard in the street. A bruised reed He will not break, and smoking flax He will not quench" (Is 42:2-3).

The earlier parents start, the better. As soon as I find my child starting to get angry, I should act. I should not ignore the issue. As a father or a mother, I should talk to him about the situation and encourage him to overcome his anger through a strong relationship with God and by teaching him how to express himself in a nice way. Moreover, I should punishment or discipline when necessary.

2. Seeking Attention

The second problem at this age is excessive attention seeking. Some people want everyone to pay attention to them. We can recognize if this is a problem for a youth if we notice that he jokes excessively, beyond what is appropriate, or excessively creates an atmosphere of laughter. The opposite is also true; this person may become overly annoying or bothersome to others around him.

When this behavior is excessive, whether the laughter and jokes or the annoying and bothersome behavior, the goal most likely is attention seeking. He uses this behavior because he wants others to give him attention. It is, usually, considered a problem only if he is annoying and upsetting others, but if he is joking, we say that he is funny. However, in reality, the person who jokes a lot, especially when he cannot differentiate when it is appropriate to do so, is seeking attention. The Book of Ecclesiastes says there is "a time to weep, and a time to laugh" (Ecc 3:4). Even though it is inappropriate and excessive, this person makes jokes during a spiritual meeting or during the homily. When joking goes beyond its limits, it is reflective of and makes one aware of an attempt to seek attention. This is an ego problem.

There is also a third type of attention seeking, which is trying to please others. The silent child who wants to seek attention does so by trying to please others and gaining their admiration and praise. He will grow up to be what we call a "man pleaser," which means he is solely concerned about pleasing those around him, even at the cost of truth and the commandments of God. Thus, the person who is able to express his opinion may do so by being funny or by annoying others, while the one who does not know how to express his opinion may seek attention by being a people-pleaser, even at the expense of the commandments. This is what made St. Paul say, "For if I still pleased men, I would not be a bondservant of Christ" (Gal 1:10).

There are several reasons why a child attempts to seek attention. One possible reason is that they do not receive appropriate attention at home, school, or church, etc. To make up for this lack, they become annoying or excessively humorous in order to attract the attention of others. The child who tries to please others does this in order for people to praise him. He needs their compassion and words of praise. By doing for people anything they want, it is as if he is begging for praise and personal attention.

A third reason is that perhaps when the child was young, his parents excessively put him on display for others. They would say such things as, "See how much he has memorized. Look at what he did. Look at what he did at school," etc. When this is done excessively, the child gets used to hearing praise and his ego being fed. When he grows up, if he does not find the same attention he is accustomed to receiving from his childhood, he tries to find ways to seek excessive attention from others.

With this in mind, we should be moderate in giving our younger children praise and admiration, no matter how talented they are. Perhaps, we think that because he is still young, giving him all that praise will not affect him. However, when this child grows and reaches adolescence, his ego will have gotten used to praise during the first nine or ten years of his life. When he does not receive this same attention as a teenager, he will hunger for it.

In order to remedy this, we first need to find the underlying reason, whether it is because of excessive praise from childhood, a lack of praise and attention in childhood, or an inability to express his opinion, which leads to people-pleasing behavior.

Starting from when our children are young, we should practice giving them appropriate attention, meaning that when the action is good, praise and encourage it in an appropriate amount. When we feel that the child is starting to joke excessively or to be annoying, we should ignore it, making it clear that this behavior will not warrant him any attention, thereby, encouraging him to change his behavior. If every time he jokes, we respond by giving him attention, laughing, and agreeing with him, we reinforce the behavior; it reassures him that this is a successful way to gain attention.

We can differentiate between the funny boy and the boy who wants to attract attention by noticing the appropriateness of the time for humor. The one who is trying to attract attention loses discernment in differentiating between the time for laughter and the time for being serious. For example, they joke around even if a serious topic is being discussed; they do not consider the importance of the discussion. The loss of discernment is a sign of being extreme. Of course, we can talk to him and tell him that this behavior is wrong, and that there is time for everything under the sun. We can explain that things done at the wrong time are not correct. There is an Egyptian proverb that says, "Laughter without a reason is bad manners," meaning that it is considered rude when someone laughs when it is not an appropriate time or place for laughter. Therefore, we must help children develop self-confidence.

3. Clothes and Appearance

The third problem that many of us may face with our adolescents is making the right choice for clothes and appearance. We find that many youth try to express their individual personalities either by wearing certain inappropriate clothing or through certain hairstyles. By inappropriate clothing, I mean two things; first, clothes can be inappropriate for the place. For example, a boy may come to church in shorts or sports clothing, showing a lack of discernment for what is appropriate for church and outside of church. On the other hand, inappropriate could refer to what is not appropriate for us as Christians, in general, as the children of God. Unacceptable clothing includes when youth, and perhaps, especially the girls, wear very tight, revealing, or sheer clothing. These three things are unacceptable.

There are several reasons why adolescents begin wearing inappropriate clothing or styling their hair outlandishly. For example, boys may grow their hair, cut it a certain way, or grow their beards—something would be wrong about his appearance. Girls may apply too much makeup or use makeup that is unsuitable for their age. One of the reasons may be that they want to bring attention to the fact that they have grown up. This reveals a lack of self-confidence; they are resorting to appearance to get the attention of others. Inappropriate clothing or appearance could also be a sign of rebellion and anger against the parents. The teenager intentionally goes out wearing inappropriate clothes to shame his or her parents, take revenge on them, or express anger toward them.

Sometimes, girls may wear inappropriate fashions because they feel insecure about their looks, appearance, attractiveness, or femininity. They turn to excessive makeup or clothing to attract attention. This is a lack of self-confidence. Another possible reason is a lack of balanced direction at home from the father and mother regarding their teenager's clothing and appearance. This guidance should start from childhood and continue until adolescence. We should instill in our children the importance of going out in sensible clothes that are both acceptable to their peer group as well as to their identity as Christians.

Another reason could be pressure from society, which we call, "peer pressure." A girl sees that all of her friends dress like this; the boy sees that all his friends at school have this haircut. Also, during this period, their role model could be a soccer player, athlete, or singer, and our children are truly very much affected by these role models. This is, yet another sign of lack of confidence. Perhaps, the fashion trend at the time is to shave one's head, so you find that all our boys are shaving their heads. Then, one athlete grows his beard, and you find all our teen boys growing their beards. Then, a singer or an actor shaves his head on the sides and grows his hair on top, and all our children do the same. It is as if our children have no personalities; they blindly copy what they see. For them, this athlete, singer, or actor is a role model. However, if I have self-confidence and principles, I do not change my mind depending on what they decide is fashionable. Sometimes, the peer pressure they face at school or the jokes from their friends make them want to follow the norms of the modern culture, void of Christian values or principles.

The last reason, which is also the first reason, is, of course, not observing spiritual and biblical principles. Perhaps this point is missing in the parents. If the mother wears inappropriate clothing or uses excessive makeup, we cannot blame the girl who is copying her mother in these actions. We can address this by giving them a nice compliment for attention; a brief and honest comment may bring positive results. If the underlying reason is rebellion, children will not respond to being ordered to change. They are doing this because they want to defy you. Therefore, the solution is not to talk about clothes, but to deal with the challenge of rebellion. If we do so, the clothing dilemma will be resolved. Thus, if we deal with the spiritual problem, the clothing issue will be solved.

In the book, *Release of the Spirit* by His Holiness Pope Shenouda III of thrice-blessed memory, he talks about a certain youth that he visited when His Holiness was still a Sunday school servant. When he went to visit this youth, he found that he had grown out his hair. Back then, it was considered improper for a boy to grow his hair. Now, it is fashion. The youth had long hair and he met H.H. while smoking cigarettes. Pope Shenouda says that he did not talk to him about his long hair or the smoking. He did not address these things because, in this situation, the long hair and the cigarettes were an outward sign of an internal sickness. If I remedy the internal sickness, the external appearance would be fixed, as the Lord Jesus Christ said, "first cleanse the inside of the cup and dish, that the outside of them may be clean also" (Mt 23:26). H.H. dealt with the inner life of this person, and the life of this youth changed by the grace of God. He was able to build a good relationship with God, without Pope Shenouda talking to him about the cigarettes or the long hair. The appearance of this youth changed because he accepted the Lord Christ into his life.

4. Career Choice

The fourth problem that youth face during this age is the challenge of choosing their career. As parents, we have a role in this decision process. During this period, youth start to seriously think about what career they should choose for themselves. Unfortunately, there are many currents that influence the youth, the challenges of adolescence, the start of college, and spending a year or two taking general courses without deciding on a major. This is a sign of confusion. There is no clear vision for life. Other youth start college and keep changing their majors. Their vision for life is also not clear. A third group only wants to fulfill their parents' agenda because of the pressure they put on them. The parents want their children to be doctors, lawyers, or engineers, and the child does so just because his parents want it. Sometimes, parents pressure their children to do what is unsuitable to their child's interest and intellectual abilities. Sometimes, the opposite occurs: A person's intellectual abilities, interest, and values may allow him to go to a more competitive university, but because he is rebelling against his parents, he refuses to do so. He would rather go to a mediocre college as a way to take revenge on or to punish his parents.

Furthermore, I have found that many youth cannot differentiate between a hobby and a career. For example, someone has a talent, perhaps in music or sports, and even though he would not find a job in this field when he graduates, he wants to go to a college that is suitable for this talent or hobby. He does not think about if he is going to find a job after graduation or not, or if this is going to provide him with a career in which he can eventually support himself and a family in the future or not. I often tell the youth that they should differentiate between a hobby and the future. I explain that when I am planning for my future, I should choose a career that would provide me with work opportunities upon graduation, enabling me to have a household and provide for my family and myself.

Sometimes, the pressures of adolescence, its many challenges, and the deviations that may occur might make a person careless about choosing a clear career for himself. Years may go by without choosing a clear career. It is our role and responsibility, as parents and servants, to help our children start forming a vision during this time. However, helping does not mean telling them the majors they should choose, but rather, trying to guide them in discovering the most suitable career. And again, it should be a *career* that will provide this aspiring young adult with a future, and a not a hobby.

Some things to consider when helping our children include their intellectual and personal abilities, grades, and GPA [grade point average], personality, and any physical or learning disabilities. Someone who has physical weakness, for example, may need to avoid certain careers. We should also consider what the main interests in life are for the college bound student. We can seek professional advice from people in the career he is considering and read together about different opportunities in these professions. Perhaps, they could look for an opportunity to work, volunteer, or shadow a professional in a facility in their career of interest, for example, in a bank, hospital, or school, etc., even for a few hours. All these things can help our children choose a suitable career according to their interests, abilities, and values.

5. Homosexuality

The fifth problem parents may encounter is their child disclosing—and yes, this happens—that he or she is homosexual. We should not ignore this possibility, because it exists. We pray that God protects us, and we hope that we can deal with this issue in a correct way, but we do not want to be blind. Sometimes, when a parent hears this statement of disclosure, it feels like a catastrophe. They do not know what to do if they hear their son or daughter say he or she is homosexual, or if they discover this in a different manner. The children may reveal it to the parents if they are able to talk to them. However, if they do not talk to them, and the parents find out another way, it is catastrophe for them. This is a lengthy topic, but I will try to explain succinctly the causes and how to manage a situation in which a child reveals homosexual orientation.

Sometimes, when children are growing up, there could be a weakness in the balance of their sexual behavior. This may lead some of them to feel attracted toward a person of the same gender. It may start as an attraction, but unfortunately, Western societies emphasize that homosexuality is not a sexual abnormality or deviance,[36] but, rather it is just another way of life. Here, with the presence of even a small attraction, the youth starts to quickly believe that this is what he or she is.

Another reason is the loss of balance between the father and the mother in dealing with their children. For example, there may be a family in which the mother is over-controlling and the father has a weak personality. In a family like this, the son will see, in the personality of the mother, that she is the leader of the home. In other words, she is the dominant figure of the household. Subconsciously, the son will avoid the opposite sex because he sees his mother, who represents the opposite gender, as strong, controlling, and depriving the father of his authority. Thus, the boy will steer away from and become afraid of the opposite sex. This may cause him to be attracted to a person of the same gender.

Also, if the father has a weak personality, whether or not the mother is controlling, the boy can lose respect for his father because he cannot control the house and because of his weak personality. He starts trying to find a male figure in his life to replace the father and this may cause him to be attracted to a person of the same gender. We found that in many cases of homosexuality, especially in boys, there are problems between the child and the same gender parent, meaning, there is either a problem between the boy and his father, or between the girl and her mother. This sometimes causes them to search for another male or female figure, respectively, in their lives.

If there is an excessive attraction between the mother and her son, this may lead the boy to feel that he will never find a woman like his mother in the whole world. This makes him turn to the same gender just to satisfy his sexual need. However, he is not attracted to the opposite sex, rather, in his mind, he will not find anyone like his mother.

Unfortunately, many people today talk about homosexuality as something normal, and some are even bold enough to say that the Holy Bible has nothing in it that condemns it. However, by reading the Epistle of St. Paul to the Romans, we see the contrary, "For this reason, God gave

---

36 Homosexuality was removed from the DSM [Diagnostic and Statistical Manual of Mental Disorders] in 1974

them up to vile passions. For even their women exchanged the natural use for what is against nature. Likewise also the men, leaving the natural use of the woman, burned in their lust for one another, men with men committing what is shameful, and receiving in themselves the penalty of their error which was due" (Rom 1:26-27). In the same chapter, the apostle says, "For the wrath of God is revealed from heaven against all ungodliness and unrighteousness of men" (Rom 1:18). These verses are clearly about homosexuality.

If we look at these verses carefully, we see that God differentiates between the natural use and that which is against nature. The verse is clear, "exchanged the natural use for what is against nature," nullifies the argument that this is natural. The verse also demonstrates that homosexuality could occur in the two genders, males with males and females with females. The third point is the use of the phrase, "vile passions," which means that these emotions have controlled that person to the point that he is in bondage to these emotions and has reached the lowest points. His thinking has become so distorted and he is not aware, but is rather defending this thinking. Vile passions do not refer to something simply vile, but to the extreme low points of vileness.

The next point is when St. Paul says that the "women exchanged the natural use" and "likewise also the men". The usage of the word, "exchanged," indicates that homosexuality is a *willful, voluntary* action and not an action forced on the person, in spite of his will.

The fifth point in this verse is that this sexual conduct is described as lust and not love: "burned in their lust for one another". This is a lust—a satisfaction of lust, and not love. This action is also described as a "shameful" act when it says, "committing what is shameful". This means that a person has put in his heart to rebel, not just against natural rules, but also against God's rules and commandments. The last point is that when he says, "the wrath of God is revealed from heaven," it shows that this unnatural action is strictly punished by God. Sometimes, punishment can occur on two levels. The earthly punishment is that many of the unnatural sexual activities lead to sexual diseases, such as AIDS. On the other hand, if they do not repent, this could deprive them of the kingdom of heaven.

I would like to clarify that there is a big difference between someone who is striving and someone who is neither striving nor trying at all.

If a person has fallen under the sin of homosexuality, but is striving to overcome it and knows that this is a sin, God accepts him, even if this person dies while he is striving. We all strive against sins. Who among us is going to go to heaven having conquered *all* his sins? There is a crown given for striving and a crown given for conquering. The danger lies within the person who tries to defend this sin, justify it, or deny that it is a transgression; rather, he declares that it is a natural thing and not rebellion against God's commandments. This is the person that needs our concerns. However, if a person is suffering from homosexuality, and knows it is wrong and a sin, but is striving and offering repentance, even if God permits and takes his life before he conquers this sin, he is accepted in front of God as long as he remained striving.

If my child tells me that he has this problem or if I discovered that he has this problem, what should I do? First of all, although it is very hard for any one of us to hear such a problem, we must deal with it calmly, trusting in God's love. If I do not deal with it calmly, I could lose my son or daughter. God came for the sinners and He dealt with all of them calmly. They brought the woman who was caught committing adultery to the Lord Christ and He dealt with her calmly. He dealt with the sinful woman and the sick man at the pool of Bethesda calmly. I must also be calm, and my example should be the Lord Jesus Christ. We read in the Bible that, "God demonstrates His own love toward us, in that while we were still sinners, Christ died for us" (Rom 5:8).

As clergy—Father Confessor, father, mother, or servant, if a child is telling us this is a *problem*, the first thing we must do is show appreciation for the child's demonstrated courage to eliminate the problem and to talk to us about it. Also, we should be sensitive when we talk to this child and show love, as Christ showed love to the woman caught in sin, even though they say that this woman was not repentant since they caught her in the sinful act. The Lord would always say, "go in peace," but He did not tell this woman to "go in peace," because, as the Bible says, "'There is no peace,' says the Lord, 'for the wicked'" (Is 48:22), and she had not, yet, repented. Christ would, usually, say, "Your sins are forgiven," but He did not say this to her, either. She was not repentant at this moment, but the Lord still showed her love and told her, "Neither do I condemn you," and "sin no more" (Jn 8:11). Thus, we need to offer unconditional love to the person, for Christ loves him, her, me, you, all of us, and died on the cross for us while we are sinners.

I should also completely understand all the aspects of the problem, the underlying reasons, and the dynamics at home. Are there prevalent dynamics at home such as I described earlier—a fractured relationship between the son and the father or between the mother and the daughter? Is there a relationship that contains attraction between the son and his mother, a father with a weak personality, or a controlling mother? Was the child subjected to some kind of sexual abuse at school at a young age? I should try to understand all aspects of this problem. Of course, I should also seek help from professionals in our church that specialize in this field. Thank God, we have man specialists in this area in our church communities. With God's grace, they were able to succeed with many cases.

For the person striving against this sin, you should confirm that God loves him or her. Many times, because we want to lead them to repentance, we talk about God's wrath. However, as I previously said, we need to differentiate between the one who is striving and the one who is defending the sin, finding excuses for it, and saying it is not a sin. For the person striving, I should confirm God's love for him. This is the teaching of the Bible: Christ is the "friend of tax collectors and sinners" (Mt 11:19). I must give him hope that this problem has a solution, and in many cases, people were able to change their behavior and direction. I should encourage the person to build a strong relationship with God, because as God said, "without Me you can do nothing" (Jn 15:5). If he was subjected to sexual abuse or any other hardships when he was young, the specialists may also help regarding this issue. Of course, this is a big topic, but I have discussed what relates to us as parents, servants, or clergy, what we should do if we hear something like this—and not as specialists.

6. Guilt

The sixth problem our children may encounter during adolescence is the feeling of guilt. Sometimes this feeling of guilt is validated and sometimes it is imagined. Validated, because I did something wrong or I am living in a wrong way. At this age, a lot of our children may fall into sins of sexual immorality, such as impure glances, bad thoughts, visiting indecent websites, or even having sexual encounters with others. As a result of these thoughts and actions, the child may have extreme guilt, view himself as a sinner, and believe that God does not accept him. He may stop going to church. The child would not admit that he is a sinner and cannot go to church; instead, he would come up with many excuses of why he is not going to church. Another way teenagers deal with these behaviors is to justify them: "Everyone else does the same; everyone dates," etc. They try to become desensitized to sin. In this case, the child goes to church, takes Communion, serves as a deacon, and continues to live in sin, because he perceives that his thoughts and actions are normal behavior. Thus, they either develop an enormous sense of guilt or they normalize the sin.

Another reason for guilt is the fact that, especially in high school, youth are making a lot of decisions concerning their future—colleges, majors, placement tests, service hours, etc. This adds a lot of stress in their lives, especially if they are unsuccessful, which could lead to guilt; and guilt is not a good feeling. That is why God freed us from this feeling in repentance through the Mystery of Confession. The three things Adam experienced as a result of falling in sin are fear, guilt, and shame: Fear, when he hid from God after he heard His voice; shame, when he covered himself with leaves; guilt, as a result of committing the sin and being driven out of the Garden of Eden. Cain also conveyed this feeling of guilt when he said to the Lord, "My punishment is greater than I can bear" (Gen 4:13). In repentance and returning to God, there is a true liberation from the feeling of guilt. Those who have experienced true repentance and prayer, and then, Confession, say that they feel that a huge weight was lifted off their shoulders. That is the feeling of guilt that comes with sin, from which one is completely freed in the Mystery of Confession.

We should teach our youth at this age that guilt is a result of sin. Nonetheless, because of God's love for us and His compassion upon us, He freed us from this sensation through His blood. Confession is a gift to us from our Holy Father. If you have a spot cleaner, you will not worry about stains, because you know they can come off. It is the same with repentance, Confession, and Communion; they comprise the strongest formula against the feeling of guilt. Christ's blood cleanses us from all sin. "If we confess our sins, He is faithful and just to forgive us our sins and to cleanse us from all unrighteousness" (1 Jn 1:9). Explain to the child that the church offers us this beautiful gift. Because God loves us, He offers us this gift, and made it that as long as we confess our sins, we are forgiven and freed from the guilt produced by these trespasses: "I said, I will confess my transgressions to the Lord, and You forgave me the iniquity of my sin" (Ps 32:5). I am freed from sin and my sick soul is healed. In this case, I present Christ and the Church as our redeemer and liberator from sin, where at this time of their young lives, a lot of youth feel that Christ and the Church are contrary to their freedom and desires. However, we present to them the opposite: Christ gives us true freedom, happiness, and peace.

Imagined guilt may be due to having a strict conscience, when a person judges himself for things that God does not judge him. Maybe this tight conscience is due to a feeling of inferiority, or it develops as a result of others always wanting him to constantly live in an ideal state and not at a practical level. It creates in the person continuous self-blame, inner blame, and inner instability. They may complain about physical pain, fatigue, headaches, etc. Moreover, adolescents want to be perceived in a certain way by others and there is a gap between who they really are and the perfect image they want others to perceive. The perception others have of them is important to them. If they do not reach that goal of presenting a positive image to others and there is a big discrepancy between the ideal person they want to present and the real person they feel like they failed. Subsequently, they are consumed with feeling guilty, bad, and sinful. If they reach this point, they may not care about their image anymore and express negative behaviors without caring for what others around them may think, because they already feel that they failed. They may not express feelings of guilt, but rather, talk about despair: "There is no use. There is no purpose in life," etc.

People who have feelings of guilt can also punish themselves by not eating certain foods or by wearing certain clothes. They punish themselves because they feel guilty. They may continually blame themselves, become excessively critical of others, or always expect blame or rebuke from others. On the other hand, they may participate in excessive acts of service or helping others to compensate for, reduce, or eliminate feelings of guilt.

Imagined guilt may also be due to the constant and unnecessary criticism of their actions by the parents. Due to their lack of understanding, parents may blame them for a lot of things that are not deserving of blame.

Thus, the reasons for guilt could be internal or external. As parents, when we want to remedy this, we need to know if this feeling of guilt is true or imaginary. If it is true, then repentance, returning to God, and accepting God's forgiveness are the cure. "Create in me a clean heart, O God, and renew a steadfast spirit within me" (Ps 51:10). If it is imaginary, building up the personality, self-confidence, and understanding of who I am to God are very important. Accepting the love of God, His forgiveness, and being at peace with myself are the solutions for the feelings of guilt.

7. Inferiority

The seventh problem is the feeling of inferiority. Sometimes, with the growth that occurs during this period, many youth may feel inadequate or unaccepted by others, causing them to feel inferior. This feeling of inferiority has several signs. As mentioned earlier, youth may try to excessively attract attention to themselves. They may also be shy. There is an acceptable shyness and an excessive shyness. With excessive shyness, they cannot talk to anyone. If they talk to someone one-on-one, they get confused. This could be an internal feeling of insecurity or inferiority.

Feelings of inferiority could also appear in being closed-minded and accepting nothing less than perfection, to cover up the inner feelings of inferiority. It could also appear in controlling others, since controlling people are always suffering from feelings of insecurity and inferiority. It may make the person an introvert, because he cannot face others; he feels less than the others so he becomes a recluse. Sometimes, continuous criticism by others over trivial matters could lead to this. Furthermore, it could also be due to confusion between the meaning of humility and inferiority. Humility is to say that I am nothing, but "I can do all things through Christ who strengthens me" (Phil 4:14). However, feelings of inferiority *only* say, "I am nothing. I am less than everyone else." Inferiority does not boast, "I can do all things through Christ who strengthens me." Of course, another reason for feelings of inferiority is if someone truly suffers from a physical problem or lower intelligence, which can make him feel inferior to others.

The majority of the time, this feeling begins in childhood, especially if the boy or girl did not find love, acceptance, and encouragement, from the parents, or if they were frequently reprimanded, or if they were chastised for trivial reasons. We say in our prayers, "If You, Lord, should mark iniquities, O Lord, who could stand?" (Ps 130:3). If God is not marking our iniquities, we should not be marking the iniquities and mistakes of our children.

Moreover, making fun of children in front of others causes them to lose self-confidence. Therefore, we need to be careful not to make fun of our children in front of others. Making fun of youth as they are getting older shakes their self-confidence and makes them feel inferior. In addition, comparison between siblings, cousins, relatives, or friends can make a person feel inferior to others. Furthermore, inferiority can develop if we always make the children doubt their abilities, for example, if a child tries to do something and we say, "No, you cannot do it. I will do it for you." We should not make decisions for our children and stifle chances for them to do things on their own. All these are reasons that can cause feelings of inferiority.

The cure is that we must give our children repeated experiences that fills them with confidence. This year, our high school and college youth will organize their own conventions in our diocese. I am expecting the priests, servants, and parents to encourage their children. If we do not encourage the youth, and these conventions are unsuccessful, this could have a negative effect on them. This is a chance for us, as clergy, servants, and parents to encourage our youth and to instill confidence in them as they are organizing their conventions for the first time.

A group of servants from the Youth Bishopric in Egypt shared the following story with me about the first time they organized a convention, many years ago, under the auspices of His Grace Bishop Moussa.[37] They said that the retreat was not as successful as they had imagined. Bishop Moussa held a meeting with them after the convention. The servants told me that they went to this meeting, expecting that His Grace would rebuke them because the convention was unsuccessful. However, His Grace praised them for a successful retreat. He encouraged them by telling them that what they had done was wonderful and that it was the first time for them to organize such a convention. He mentioned things that were really successful about the convention and this encouraged them to arrange more conventions in the following years. Now, the Youth Bishopric conventions are held from Alexandria to Aswan, and are very fruitful. If H.G. Bishop Moussa had not encouraged them after the first convention, perhaps these conventions would have ceased. In these situations, we have a responsibility to encourage our children and give them opportunities for gaining self-confidence because this will encourage them more and more. If anyone is suffering from feelings of inferiority, this approach will make them overcome these issues.

---

37 H.G. Bishop Moussa, General Bishop of the Coptic Youth Bishopric

As I previously mentioned, do not criticize everything your children do. Do not mock them, even in jest, in front of others, and do not keep track of their mistakes. There are some things of which we should let go and turn a blind eye to. For example, if adults are talking and a youth has an opinion, do not put down his opinion. Listen to him, even if his opinion to you is nonsense. You need to understand that for his age, it is good that he thought about and shared his ideas or perspectives. We should listen to him and encourage him. The earlier we remedy the feelings of inferiority, the easier it is to cure. Treatment becomes more challenging if inferiority remains within a child for a long period of time without being addressed.

8. Lying

The eighth problem is lying. Some children begin to lie around the age of ten to twelve. People have discovered that there are nine types of lies our children tell during this age. The first type is what we call, "imaginary or fantasy lies." Sometimes a child tells imaginary stories in order to attract the attention of others. The second type is called, "traditional lies." The child copies his parents, family members, or other adults when they lie or change information, even if just a little bit of it. His family lies, so he lies.

The third type is called, "lies of exaggeration." The person exaggerates the truth; for example, he tells a story and exaggerates the details. The fourth type is called, "social lies." This is when we teach our children to lie. The child answers the phone, but parents tell him to say [a lie]— "Dad is not home." In this situation, the parent is teaching the child to lie, and in the mind of the child, it normalizes giving wrong information. "Dad told me to say he is not home."

We call the fifth type, 'defensive lies," in which a person lies to avoid punishment. This is the most common type in adolescence. Many children, for example, when asked if they did something wrong, would say that they did not, in order to avoid punishment. This can happen with adults, too. If the police stop someone for speeding, the first thing that comes to mind is what to say to the officer to avoid getting a ticket. Be sure to teach your children not to lie. If we encourage our children to say the truth, even if it is incomplete, it will help the children feel secure and at ease; thus, they may refrain from lying to defend themselves. A good example of this in the Bible is the Samaritan woman. When the Lord Christ asked her to go call her husband, she answered and said, "I have no husband" (Jn 4:17). In reality her answer was not very honest. Her answer was incomplete; it was not indicative of her previous marriages or her current relationship. However, Christ accepted her answer and kindly confronted her with the truth. Initially, the Samaritan woman was defending herself. She was getting water from the well at midday; most people get water early in the day or at sunset when temperatures are cooler. However, she was trying to avoid encounters with people when she ran into Jesus at the well. This is why she confronted the Lord Jesus, "You are a Jew and I am a Samaritan; why are you talking to me?" Jesus spoke to her gently and told her about the living water and that whoever drinks from it shall not thirst. He then asked her about her husband and when she answered—with partial truth, He commended her reply and made her feel at ease. He then addressed the complete truth about the five previous men to whom she was married and about the man with whom she was currently living who was not her husband. When the woman felt at peace, she put her guard down and was no longer defensive. We need to give this same assurance to our children so that they can freely talk with us about anything at any time; that will free them from defensive lying.

The sixth type is lies of compensation. For example, if a father expects high grades from his child in school, and the child did not get this high grade, he may forge the report card to meet his family's expectations. He gives wrong information to leave a good impression with the parents, the Sunday school servant, the teacher, or the friend.

We call the seventh type, "lies of enmity." For example, a boy might be upset with his parents because they criticize him a lot. So, to get away from responsibilities at home, he will feign sickness. Though he is not really ill, he lies to upset his father or mother. The eighth type, we call, "lies of revenge." The child says bad things about himself that he did not do in order to shame his parents. He may also make up lies about them. He wants to take revenge on them for their bad treatment of him.

The last type is called, "pathological lying." This is when a person lies continuously. This might begin in childhood and can continue into adolescence, and perhaps, throughout life. It may be due to emotional imbalance within the child that increases during puberty. This is also a sign that the teenager does not accept himself and that is why he turns to lying in order to change his image. St. Augustine faced this type of sin. He constantly lied, to the point that when he was with his friends and they were sharing stories of evil things they had done, he would not have anything to share, so he would make up stories to be able to fit in with the crowd. Children may do the same and lie about things like having a girlfriend and things they had done so that they feel accepted, and thus, fit with others in their social group. This lie could remain with them and their friends would ask them about what they had told them, and thus, the lie would continue to grow.

Regarding treating pathological lying, perhaps professional help would be needed to help with this problem. We may need to build a healthy relationship between the adolescent and his parents to help us extinguish these patterns of lying.

If I find out that my child is telling lies, I must discover the reason behind it. I should explain to him that lying is a sin that can prevent me from entering the kingdom of heaven, as it says in Ephesians 4:25, "Therefore, putting away lying, 'Let each one of you speak truth with his neighbor.'" If I know that my child is lying, I should think about how to remedy this behavior and not about how to punish it and correct his behavior. When I encourage honesty (he tells the truth and I encourage him), this could be a way to remedy the problem of lying. Parents should also show the child the difference between their love for him and their hatred for his lying. They should explain that they love him but hate the lies. Moreover, do not ask questions that make your children lie. If you know that your child behaved inappropriately when he went to his friend's house and you ask him to tell you what happened when he was with his friend, he may react by lying and say that nothing happened. This question leads him to lie. However, if you tell him, "I heard that, yesterday, some wrong things happened when you were at your friend's house. I hope that you will tell me the truth so we can remedy this together," you are communicating to him that your goal is to correct and not to penalize him.

In most of our dealings with our children, we tend to use one of the following three methods: 1) Interrogation, to prove the son or daughter guilty, 2) Interview, for information gathering regarding specific situations, or 3) Kind dialogue, to illustrate empathy and understanding. The purpose of the third type is seeking a solution or a positive outcome. Good parenting is more concerned with helping the children, rather than proving them guilty or collecting information. Ask yourselves, which method are you using to deal with your children? Will this method protect them and bring them to shore safely?

9. Cursing

The last problem we encounter with youth at this age is the issue of cursing. During this period, youth may become accustomed to cursing, although the Holy Bible says, "Let no corrupt word proceed out of your mouth, but what is good for necessary edification, that it may impart grace to the hearers" (Eph 4:29).

The reasons for cursing are many. It could be imitation of the adults at home; if they curse, the children will curse. Sometimes, parents laugh when little children say curse words,. Here, you are encouraging my children to curse, and when they grow up and become adolescents, they will continue to do so. Sometimes, a parent may tell his young child, "Curse at your uncle," and then, everyone laughs; but in reality, you are teaching him something wrong that will continue with him.

Cursing could also be an expression of anger inside the person, which could continue with him throughout his life. If and when he gets married and has a family, he could curse certain members of his family; but, in reality, the cursing is directed toward someone else. Another example is a girl whose father dealt harshly with her gets married, and then her husband begins to do the same things as her father used to do. Her husband's actions remind her of her father, and she may start cursing her husband and using harsh words against him, because there is anger inside her, and she is projecting her anger toward her father but onto her husband. Subconsciously, she wants to direct these curse words to her father, but she is directing them to her husband who reminds her of her father's personality.

There are different ways to remedy cursing. First, the family itself should be a good example; they should take to heart the verse that says, "Let no corrupt word proceed out of your mouth" (Eph 4:29). Moreover, if the adolescent is angry with someone and is holding a grudge against him or her leading to cursing, we can teach him how to forgive and love others, and how to accept forgiveness from Christ so we can forgive others.

If you remember nothing from what has been discussed, remember that a strong relationship between the adolescent and God is the answer to many of our problems. In reality, it is the answer to all of the problems. Without any doubt, the problems that occur during adolescence are bigger than the nine problems discussed. This is a critical age and needs our full attention. It is also necessary that we give our children time, whether it is for discussing sexual education or for dealing with the nine problems mentioned that are common to our children. Therefore, we will be able to bring up prosperous children for the society and for the Church, in accordance with the effort that we put into raising them. This period with our children, although challenging, can also be the most beautiful stage in their lives if we learn how to deal with them in a positive manner. It is the happiest time for the parents to see their children as they mature into young adults, making their own places in society. I hope we can learn to deal with our children in a healthy and constructive way.

C | Sexual Education for Adolescents

1. Spiritual Formation Requires Effort
2. Sexual Education
3. Fulfilling the Needs of Our Children

Sexuality is a holy gift given to humanity by God. Through this gift, God continues the world. God made the sexual relationship to be for marriage; outside of marriage, it destroys. Once again, outside of marriage, it destroys. Furthermore, having sexual relationships at a young age will affect marital life in one's future. I would like to address what our role is, as fathers and mothers, in the sexual education of our sons and daughters. I will cover the subject from all angles.

1. Spiritual Formation Requires Effort

We all know that starting at age of twelve or thirteen, some changes occur in children's bodies. These changes make them more aware of their sexuality. At this point, teenagers may differ in the way they deal with their sexual energy. Some teenagers may start to drift away and go astray, while others may experience sexual repression. Some teenagers may live in hypocrisy, and some may live a holy life. Parents play an extremely big role in their children's sexual education.

Some parents think that raising our children is limited to taking them to Vespers on Saturday, the Divine Liturgy on Sunday, and Sunday school. They may think that this is sufficient for raising their children properly. Listening to parents whose children go astray, we, often, hear, "I brought him with me to church every Sunday and he took Communion." Indeed, the parents brought him with them, but did they make sure he was in church or did the child spend the time standing outside? In the parents' minds, they think that bringing their children to church and letting them partake of Holy Communion will automatically make them saints.

By all means, coming to church is very important. However, if the child spends three to four hours at church but spends the rest of the week with the parents at home, who is going to teach your children to have pure thoughts? Who will teach the children good behavior? Who will teach the children how to speak properly, other than you? It is you, as parents, who teach your children all these things. Who will teach your children to think purely, and to behave and speak properly, other than you? Only you as parents can do these things, through guiding your children and setting a good example. It must be your guidance and your example.

2. Sexual Education

a. Understanding Sexuality from a Teenager's Perspective

The understanding of sex that a teenager forms stays with him throughout his life. The teenager usually gets this understanding from the home. However, if at home, healthy sexual awareness and education is not provided, the child will form his understanding from what he hears on the streets. The understanding that the teenager forms about sexuality will reflect not only on his sexual life, but also, in his social, physical, and spiritual life, because sexuality influences one's feelings. All of this will be affected by what you instill in your children and what you teach them—but what do you really teach them? Unfortunately, fathers who encourage their sons to have sexual relationships *hurt* their sons. I was having a conversation with one father who told me, "When my sons grow up, I will let them have as many relationships as they want so that when they get married, they will have experience." This was his conviction and he felt very strongly about this. I told him, "You will destroy your sons this way. With this wrong conviction, you will destroy your sons!"

Furthermore, the differentiation in treatment between boys and girls makes our children form a wrong understanding about the opposite sex. For example, there are fathers who let their sons do whatever they want, and at the same time, put a lot of restrictions on their daughters. I do not mean to imply that girls do whatever they want, but the differentiation itself will make the boys look at the differences between the genders in a wrong way—not in the way that God created us.

b. Instilling a Correct Awareness in Our Children

Therefore, the parents' role is to instill a correct awareness in their children. To achieve this and provide them with a correct awareness, we must have the correct awareness and the right information. Thank God, there are now many resources by which to gain knowledge, enlighten ourselves, and learn sound information about sexual education, to enable us to raise our children well and to talk with them in the right way. Mothers can talk to their daughters and fathers can talk to their sons about their bodies, how to deal with their changing bodies in the proper way, sexual development, appropriate hygiene, and about how to deal with the opposite gender. As I mentioned earlier, the three dimensions are pure thoughts, good behavior, and proper speech.

The parents who let their children get their knowledge from friends, the street, or the Internet and social media—or do not provide any information at all to their children—actually, leave their teenagers in a state of confusion. Believe me, you could have prevented a lot of mistakes if you, as parents, would have spoken to your teenagers in all honesty, prayed with them, and encouraged them.

You must raise your child with sexual education that has the fear of the Lord. The Psalm says, "Unless the Lord builds the house, those who build it labor in vain" (Ps 127:1). So, your children's upbringing must have the fear of God. These children are a gift from God. The same Psalm says, "Children are an inheritance from the Lord" (Ps 127:3). Thus, God gave you children to raise them for Him, and to present them as chaste boys and chaste girls.

c. Having Discussions with Your Adolescent

Sometimes, parents refuse to discuss sexual matters with their children. This is probably because they feel they are inadequately prepared to address this subject, or they do not know how to answer their children. This is especially true when young children ask embarrassing questions and their parents feel that they do not know what to say. The result is that they completely ignore the subject. This sometimes makes the parents treat their children as if they were younger than their age. In a way, they deny that their children have grown older and have started to understand sexual matters. The parents resolve to treat their teenagers as if they are still seven, eight, or nine years old, when they are already twelve, thirteen, or fourteen. The fear of talking to your children is unhealthy. If they ask you a question to which you do not know the answer, there is nothing wrong with telling them, "Give me a day or two, and I will be able to answer you." If you do not know how to find the answer, you can go to someone that you trust and can help you. Ask God for wisdom in how to discuss sexual matters with your children in a wholesome and chaste manner, and to instill in them correct and healthy principles. Being afraid and avoiding discussing sexual matters with your children is more harmful than it is beneficial.

When teenagers begin to feel attracted to the opposite gender, they may approach you about dating. This may frighten some parents and cause them to completely shut down the idea without any regard to the adolescent's emotions. In some instances, parents may portray the child's feelings as a sin and as something against Egyptian culture and religion. Rather, parents should acknowledge that it is normal to have feelings for the opposite sex (not that it is normal to have a boyfriend/girlfriend), but, in fact, it is something good that God instilled in us to continue His creation, and to fulfill this gift though the Mystery of Matrimony. When youth come to confess about any sexual or physical sins, I assure them that these feelings are not a sin and that they are actually holy; the key is how we respond to these feelings so one may not fall into sin.

There is a correct way to deal with these feelings, and an incorrect way to deal with them, which would lead the youth into sin. If a boy says he is in love with a girl at school, I will say, "These feelings are normal, but let us talk some more about it. I want you to not only love this girl, but every girl in your school." I would explain that there is a difference between love, which requires sacrifice, and lust, which is the desire for something. One may desire an apple, and after he eats it, he may have enjoyed it, but the apple is gone. Gradually, explain to the youth that if one truly loves someone, he has to care for the other person's feelings, protect her, and choose the right time: "To everything there is a season, a time for every purpose under heaven" (Ecc 3:1). Explain to your children how to deal with these feelings in the right way.

Dialogue and understanding what the adolescent is feeling and experiencing is very important in dealing with them at this age. I urge you not to condemn their feelings and turn them away. You are telling them that they are wrong and sinful, when, in fact, they *have* internal feelings that they are trying to resolve. Who has never felt attracted to someone of the opposite sex? When confronted with such a situation, you must make your child feel normal. It is not strange to have feelings for and be attracted to the opposite gender. Help them accept themselves, and teach them how to handle their feelings and how to react to them.

3. Fulfilling the Needs of Our Children

Sexual education is not only about lectures and setting an example, but it is also about satisfying the inner thirst of our children. Our children need tenderness and love. This need increases during adolescence. Your role as a parent is to satisfy the child's need for love and tenderness. If a parent cannot fulfill that need, the children will try to find it outside the home. There must be mutual trust, sympathy, care, and love. Of course, parents need to be firm when needed, but at the same time, it cannot be that the only things the adolescent experiences from Mom and Dad are orders, firmness, and severity. Adolescents also need to experience their parents' true love, which will gratify this need.

In God's dealings with people, even with the sinful ones, He always satisfies their psychological needs. For example, in the miracle of the bleeding woman who came from behind and touched the hem of His garment (Mt 9:20), the Lord Christ told her a very important thing. She was already cured; He could have said, "Thank God that you are healed." However, He told her, "Be of good cheer *daughter*; your faith has made you well" (Mt 9:22). This word, "daughter," is a psychological treatment. This woman felt like an outcast; she felt that she was defiled. People rejected her. All her life, no one came close to her because, according to the Old Testament, a bleeding woman was impure. Thus, when the Lord Jesus Christ called her "daughter," it immediately gave her the sense of acceptance, love, and gratification. As parents, we all must give our children this feeling of love.

In case your son or daughter misbehaves, and talks back to you, your role is to keep the balance between guidance and discipline without losing love. The goal is to present the Lord to the children, Jesus the Forgiver, the Healer, and the Triumphant, who rose from the dead. The Lord Christ is able to forgive you, heal you, give you victory, and renew your youth like the eagle. Our children hesitate to talk to us because they do not know what our reactions will be. Because they fear our reactions, they may refuse to talk to us at all about important matters.

D | ADOLESCENCE: NEEDS AND DEVELOPMENT (HOMILY TO SERVANTS)

1. Relationships with Adolescents
2. When Adolescents Choose Friends
3. When Adolescents Try to Discover Their Gifts and Abilities
4. Preparing the Adolescent for Life as an Adult
5. When Adolescents Deal with the Opposite Gender and Learn about Sexuality
6. When Adolescents Question Principles and Values
7. Serving Adolescents
8. Understanding Maturity

Understanding the needs and development of youth is essential in order to know how to serve them. If you read Galatians 4:1–5, you will find that St. Paul speaks about the stage of childhood as slavery. This is because, even from the legal point of view, the child does not own his life. He cannot make decisions for himself, so, in that regard, he is not different from a servant or a slave. When a child reaches the age of twelve, he wants to break free from this captivity. He does not want to be in bondage anymore. He desires to be mature. In order to express this maturity, he becomes rebellious. He wants to deal with adults as equals. This is why we should expect some sort of rebellion when we deal with teenagers. The purpose of this rebellion is in order for the teenager to claim his freedom and begin his life as an adult.

1. Relationships with Adolescents

This desired freedom also explains why most of the time spent in adolescence is like a storm. During this time, the teenager goes back and forth between childhood and maturity. Sometimes he behaves like a child and sometimes like an adult. Therefore, we should not think that he is already an adult, treat him as such, or expect him to behave as one.

Rebellion is very clear when it comes to responding to authority and making decisions. At this age, the adolescent does not want to be under authority. He wants to make his own decisions. This is why the relationship with a teenager should change from control to influence. What do I mean by this? When I deal with a little child, the relationship with him is one of control. I direct and control what he does. Children accept this control and submit to it. But, once the child becomes a teenager, he does not accept control anymore. Since the main feature of this stage is rebellion, I cannot control him; rather, I have to influence him. If I build a good relationship with my children, influence will be easy. However, if I do not build a good relationship with them, influencing them will be difficult.

This is not to say that I must never exercise control, but control, now, should not be in the manner I exercise it with the little children. It should be in the form of explaining each choice and the consequences of each choice, so if they violate any of the rules, by their own choices, by their own freedom, they will suffer the consequences of their disobedience. Again, I am emphasizing that the adolescent at this age will not accept control. Many servants serving youth try to control the adolescent at this age. That is why friction or conflict arises between the adolescent and the Sunday school servant. Because of this, adolescents have stopped coming to church, serving as deacons, or participating in any church activities.

It is not only difficult to control the adolescent, but it is also *not good* to control the adolescent. This is because if we control them, we are killing their personalities. We are creating very weak personalities that will remain in the stage of childhood for a long time. God wants us to grow, and not to be dependent. If we attempt to control them and they accept it, we would be creating dependent personalities. Instead of trying to control the adolescent, we need to train ourselves, to control *ourselves*, and to control our reactions when the adolescent rebels against us. We need to understand rebellion as a stage in life and not in terms of, "they are bad." Sometimes, when we interpret their behavior as, "this son" or "this daughter is bad," it makes us not know how to deal with them in the right way. If we understand it is a natural step in their growth and development, we will be able to control our reactions and ourselves when they rebel.

This is, often, played out at youth events and conventions. When the youth start acting up, we see many servants lose control, yell, scream, and punish. Once I said to the servants at one of the conventions, "I do not want police officers; I want servants." There is a big difference between having a security team or a police officer, and having a servant. If I want to keep the structure and order in the convention, I could get a security team, and they will keep the order better than the servants. I want a servant—a servant who understands the needs of the adolescents at this age, and knows how to deal with them. The goal is not just to control them, but rather, to understand their needs and try to influence them positively. That is why I said that at this age, the adolescent is building his personality, and he is using this rebellion as a way to build his character. It is during this time that he learns how to use his intelligence, his abilities, and his gifts, to deal with the world around him.

The stage of adolescence is a golden opportunity for us as Sunday school servants. This is because when a teenager exercises rebellion, he first exercises rebellion against his parents, because during childhood that is where the main force of control is. That is why during the stage of adolescence teenagers are more likely to listen to external influences and resources than to their parents. They will allow external resources to influence them more than their parents. External resources could be the church, Sunday school servants, friends, or the media. External influences are actually more powerful at this age. This is a sign of the adolescents' independence from their parents. If we build a good relationship with our teenagers, our influence on them will be more than the influence of the media or the influence of their friends. However, if we do not have a good relationship with them, as adolescents rebel against their parents, they will rebel also against the Church. We see many young deacons who used to attend and serve until the age of thirteen or fourteen, and after this age, they stopped. He stops not because he became bad, but as a sign of rebellion: "I will make my own decisions. I will not serve because my parents tell me to serve. This is my decision. I am not going to serve as a deacon." Actually, we need to use the adolescents' tendency to lean toward external influences (more than their parents) through building good relationships with our teenagers. That way, they will allow the Church and the servants to influence them more than society.

2. When Adolescents Choose Friends

As a sign of independence, adolescents will start to form friendships. It is very important to teach them and to train them on how to make relationships and how to choose their friends, because the friends and relationships they make during this stage will serve as their support system for the rest of their lives. If they do not learn how to make good choices for wholesome relationships and to choose suitable friends, this will have a negative effect on them.

Moreover, if the adolescent is not weaned from his dependency on his parents at this age, he might continue to be dependent on them, maybe, until his thirties or forties. We have seen many examples of this situation. There are some adults who are above thirty or forty years of age, who have this unhealthy sort of relationship with their parents, and even after they marry, still take instructions on how to run their houses according to their parents' meddling. This is because the parents did not help them during adolescence to be weaned off of their dependency on them. If they discover this dependency later in their lives and try to wean themselves off of it, it will be a real challenge, because the ability to make relationships and choices at adolescence is greater than in the late thirties and forties. That is why we, as servants, and through our relationships with the adolescents and their parents, need to influence them to start to be weaned from their parents and to make good choices in choosing their friends and relationships with others.

3. When Adolescents Try to Discover Their Gifts and Abilities

An adolescent will begin to discover his gifts and abilities during this stage, and will also start to choose the activities that he likes to do. As I said, many times, they tend to go back and forth between childhood and adulthood, and therefore, they will need direction. One of the most common features among our youth is that if they are not directed, maybe after two or three years of college, they will not have chosen a major or decided on a career. Also, many people, perhaps after completing their undergraduate education, decide to completely switch their major or career. This means that they were not well trained to be independent and to make their own choices—good, thoughtful, reasonable choices.

As a sign of rebellion against his parents, an adolescent, at this age, may not want to make a clear choice, but at the same time, he does not understand what he wants. That is why he becomes and remains indecisive until a very late age in life. Many parents try to push their children in a certain direction. They tell them they want to see them become doctors, engineers, or lawyers. Maybe this is not the direction that the adolescent wants for himself. That is why conflict and tension may arise between the parents and their adolescent. The role of Sunday school servants can be as mediators of peace between the parents and the adolescent, by understanding the needs of the adolescent, and directing him to make sensible choices, not by telling him what he should choose, but by training him on how to research his options and make well-informed decisions.

Having meetings with the parents to explain why their children are doing what they are doing at this age is very essential. It is important to explain that this is not because the teenagers are bad, but rather, it is a very normal sign of growth and development. We should explain to the parents that it is better for them to lose the conflict with their children, rather than to lose the son or the daughter altogether. If parents train their adolescents on how to make choices, but at the end, a particular choice is different from the parents' preference, it is better for the parents to accept their child's decision and lose the battle, rather than lose the relationship with their child.

At this age, adolescents will make many choices. They expect their decisions and choices to be respected. That is why influence is very important at this stage. If I have a positive influence on the adolescent, he or she will listen to me and to my direction and guidance. Again, I want to emphasize that I am not telling the adolescent what to do, but I am training him or her on how to make right choices.

4. Preparing the Adolescent for Life as an Adult

One thing that will help the growth and development of the adolescent is to let him deal with the external world and to go outside the boundaries of the home. Working at this age, making money, learning how to manage time and finances, dealing with a boss and coworkers, and acquiring various practical and interpersonal skills from these experiences will improve and develop his personality. The question that servants should consistently ask themselves and be ready with an answer is, "How can I prepare my students, disciples, or children to live on their own and to make good choices when they are alone?" Very soon, the adolescent may go to college away from home and away from his church. It will be *very* challenging when these young adults move away for college if they does not learn during their adolescence how to make choices, how to live alone, and how to make the right decisions regarding important matters. In my experience, I have seen many youth drift away in the first year of college, and we lose them. The first year of college could be shocking because once he moves away from the comfort of his home and from his church, and has not learned in the years prior how to make right choices, he will most likely be influenced by all the negative effects of the world around him during the freshmen year. Unfortunately, many youth have lost their scholarships, failed in school, experimented with drugs and alcohol, attended many parties, and subsequently, ruined their lives in the first year of college. Therefore, starting very early, from age thirteen or fourteen, the beginning of adolescence, we need to train and teach them how to be independent, how to make their own choices, and how to make the right decisions.

If we understand their needs, their challenges, and what they are experiencing in their world, it will end a lot of the power struggles between adolescents and any figures of authority in their lives, whether parents, the church, Sunday school servants, or any other kind of authority.

5. When Adolescents Deal with the Opposite Gender and Learn about Sexuality

Another important matter for adolescents, or maybe earlier, is learning about the opposite gender and how to deal with the opposite sex. They will discover their bodies and the signs and symptoms of puberty. They will feel attracted toward the opposite gender. When the church, Sunday school servants, father of confession, or parents tell them that dating is wrong, they do not understand why it is important to control their emotions. What they need is validation; they need to hear that these feelings are normal. It is normal at this age to be attracted to the other gender. However, if they start to hear that it is wrong from Sunday school servants or their Fathers of Confessors, they will say, "Nobody understands me. I do not have control over my feelings. I feel attracted to this girl," or "I am attracted to this boy." Validating their feelings, showing them that you really do understand that it is a normal stage in their lives, and teaching them about sexuality—especially the Christian concept of sexuality, are very important during this age. If an adolescent does not learn about sexuality from the perspective of the Church, he will learn about it from his peers or the media. What the world teaches about sexuality has nothing at all to do with God's plan for sexuality!

When they learn that sexuality is God's precious gift to humanity, how to deal with it in the proper manner, and that when we deal with it in the correct way, it actually will lead to enjoying this gift to its maximum. Thus, when they hear external information, whether from friends or the media, it will not influence or affect them negatively. Therefore, it is imperative that the Sunday school curricula include lessons about sexuality for this stage. We must also provide our students spiritual and accurate advice and teach them to set boundaries that they need to follow, without suppressing their feelings or emotions. And again, this is a golden opportunity for the church and Sunday school servants because many parents become anxious about the sexuality of their children. The adolescents will not listen to their parents. However, if they have a good relationship with the Church and the Sunday school servants, these will be very instrumental and influential in teaching them about sexuality and training them in how to discipline themselves, control their passions, and set the appropriate boundaries in order to follow God's plan for sexuality.

6. When Adolescents Question Principles and Values

As a sign of rebellion, the adolescent may also question the principles and values that he learned from his parents. He may doubt whether what he learned from them is right or wrong. Here, in the land of immigration, the adolescent may also wonder whether what he learned is based on cultural expectations or not. That is why we hear many adolescents say to their parents, "Do not enforce your Egyptian culture on me. I am American (or I am Canadian), and you are Egyptian." This statement means that the adolescent is now questioning the values and the principles that were planted in him by his parents. Adolescents want to understand *why* they are doing what they learned to do, so that when they do it, they will do it based on their convictions and because they are sincerely persuaded that it is the right thing to do, not only because their parents told them to do it, nor because it is merely imposed on them by the culture. Again, the role of the Church will be very significant. If they trust the Church and the Sunday school servants, they will ask the servants or the priest about the values and the principles they learned at home. If they do not have this good relationship with the Church and the servants, they will go to their friends or their school or the Internet to check and find answers for these questions. I think you know very well what will happen to them if they seek answers to their questions regarding values and principles beyond the scope of the teachings of the Church and the home.

If they do not find compelling reasons for these good values and ethical principles, one of two things will happen. They will either become hypocrites, meaning that they will do things in front of the church or the parents to please them, but behind their backs, they would live another life; or they will explicitly show their rebellion and completely change into different people. If this happens, they will not listen to their parents or their church. This illustrates the caliber of developing good relationships with our children from childhood until they reach adolescence. The role of the church is vital, because the church is another authority, different from the authority of the parents. If the children respect the Church and her authority, and trust the church and the servants, they will take their questions and doubts to the church for answers. However, if they do not trust the church or the servants, they will go outside to find the answers to their questions and doubts.

If we have coached our youth on how to choose friends, and surrounded them with godly friends, then, even if they do not trust the church and their own parents, and if they go to their friends, their friends will give them the right answers (if they are godly). If they did not learn how to choose friends, then, when they go to their friends to find the answers, it will be a starting point for a period of great drifting from God and the church. The adolescent at this stage wants to form his own values and principles. He does not want to just follow blindly what he had been taught. He will ask until he is convinced. Thus, spending time with our adolescents is a chief priority. Being patient with them, listening to them, and answering their questions are also crucial.

7. Serving Adolescents

One-on-one visitation is very important during this stage. I want you, as Sunday school servants, to go to your adolescents (from ages twelve, thirteen, or fourteen) and spend time with them, and listen to their questions and doubts. Do not show that you are disgusted with their questions—how they dare ask such questions. Rather, understand that now, they want to form their own values and principles and to be convinced of them. Therefore, be patient and ready to respond to all their confusion and give them the support that they need. This is how they will go through this, sometimes, turbulent stage of adolescence, peacefully.

Spending time with our adolescents is so critical. I cannot emphasize enough the importance of visitation at this stage. I remember very well how, when I was an adolescent, my Sunday school servants came and spent time with me *every week*, for maybe 30 minutes to one hour, during which time we talked and had discussions. I went to them with all my questions and I found answers. These answers help the person to start forming his own opinions about many questions in life.

8. Understanding Maturity

Our role for our teenagers as they go through this stage in the formation of becoming mature youth, capable of accepting responsibility, is very significant. These youth will become our churches' future servants who will influence others and will share their experiences with future generations. A major sign that the adolescents are growing in the right direction is when we see that they are thinking correctly, and making right choices and wise decisions. They are able to disagree, but with respect. They can disagree with their parents, with us, as clergy, or with Sunday school servants, but without turning disagreement into conflict.

If youth are thinking correctly, making right choices and decisions, able to disagree and express their own opinions with respect to the others' opinions without turning disagreements into major conflicts, then, actually, we were able to serve them properly and help them pass through this stage in their lives peacefully.

Maturity is to move from being under the authority of parents to being under the direct authority of God. In childhood, the parents work as mediators between God and the child. It is similar to the Old Testament as when we were in our childhood stage with God. That is why we had mediators. The prophets and the priests were our mediators between God and us. However, in the New Testament, we have a direct relationship with God. In the same way, maturity for our adolescents means that they will move from the authority of the parents to the direct submission to God's authority. When he was a child, his parents corrected him, but as an adult, he is corrected by the voice of the Holy Spirit inside him, and the fear of God is inside him; he is under God's authority. It is like Joseph, when he said, "How then can I do this great wickedness, and sin against God?" (Gen 39:9). He is under the direct authority of God. Adolescents grow to be adults and are not children anymore. Thus, they will deal with others as equals in maturity.

E | Adolescence (Homily to Youth)

1. Growth in Adolescence
2. Sexuality
3. Masturbation
4. Ten Biblical Facts about Sexuality
5. Sexual Immorality

1. Growth in Adolescence

Adolescence is a very special age. I would like to start by giving you the example of our Lord Jesus Christ when He was twelve years old. What does the Bible say about Him? We read in Luke 2:52, "And Jesus increased in wisdom and stature, and in favor with God and men." If we analyze this verse, we find that "Jesus increased in wisdom," which means that during this phase, individuals begin to grow intellectually and become wiser. The Lord Jesus also increased in "stature," which refers to physical growth. There is both intellectual and physical growth. The phrase, "and in favor with God" is about spiritual growth; "and men" is about social interaction and social growth. Thus, this is a precious age in which a person experiences growth in at least these four dimensions: intellectually, physically, spiritually, and socially. The youth who pay attention to their growth in the right way—, a godly way, when they reach the age of maturity and pass the age of adolescence, will indeed be the salt of the earth and light to the world.[38]. Youth, who do not pay attention to their growth during this period, according to these four dimensions, may suffer from major problems that may last until the end of life. The Lord Jesus Christ is our example, as St. Peter told us, that He [Christ] left us "an example, that you should follow His steps" (1 Pet 2:21). Let us follow in the footsteps of our Lord Jesus Christ.

2. Sexuality

In this section, we will mainly address the adolescent's physical growth, and focus on one point within it, which is sexuality. In the beginning of adolescence, youth experience physical growth and many noticeable changes in their bodies. These changes are caused by hormones, which will also affect one's emotional status, social relationships, intellect, and also spiritual life. As individuals grow physically, they begin to recognize their sexuality. They will understand more about the differences between the two genders, and they will develop attraction to the opposite sex. This attraction is normal because of hormonal secretion. Attraction to the opposite gender is normal and expected. However, how you deal with this attraction is what will determine your spirituality and personality.

---

38 Cf. Matt 5:13-16.

Some people do not exercise self-control and respond to this attraction in a wrong way. They start to date and develop intimate relationships. They allow themselves to cross boundaries. They allow touches, hugs, kisses, etc. There is definitely a feeling of pleasure and gratification in all of these activities. Thus, they continue and reject any advice telling them that it is not the right time for these kinds of relationships to develop, and to wait until the right age to have a mature relationship. What will happen? More than 99% of relationships that begin at a young age end; they break up. When you break up with someone, it is damaging to your soul and to your emotions, not less than the damage of divorce between adults because, just as in a marriage, there is an emotional connection, so also, in dating, there is an emotional connection. What hurts people in divorce? It is the emotional separation, and the same happens when you breakup with a girlfriend or boyfriend. Furthermore, when one starts dating very early, his choices are based only on attraction. Because of the feeling of pleasure, one feels that this girl is the best person in the world, not knowing that he is saying this to himself just because of the attraction and because he just discovered his sexuality (and vice versa).

It is biblically and morally well known that any sexual relationship outside the boundary of marriage is wrong. While one develops these feelings toward the other person, one also develops a sense of guilt; he knows that he is doing something wrong. There will be two feelings inside the heart. There is the feeling that says to continue and pursue this relationship because it is gratifying, like Samson when he said, "she pleases me well" (Jud 14:3). At the same time, there is another feeling that says, "No. This is wrong. This is not right." In order to resolve this inner warfare between these two contradicting feelings (one saying to pursue it, the other saying to end it), different people resolve it in different ways. Some people resolve it in a godly manner and say, "No, I will consider all boys, or all girls, as my friends. I know it is too early to start a one-on-one relationship. I will focus on my studies and my relationship with God." This group will resolve it in the right way and they develop self-control.

The other group will completely suppress the voice of guilt or the voice of the Holy Spirit who is telling them that this is wrong. They will suppress this feeling or His voice. That is why St. Paul tells us, "Do not quench the Spirit" (1 Thess 5:19). In order to completely suppress the voice of the Holy Spirit, they will avoid going to church and to their spiritual father for confession. They will avoid going to Sunday school, or attending youth meetings, and meeting with their Sunday school servants. They do this because they know that in any of these spiritual activities, they will hear the voice that says, "This is not right." They do not want to hear this, so they will isolate themselves and continue in this wrong relationship. As mentioned earlier, in breaking up, they become emotionally and spiritually devastated. Furthermore, this behavior may lead to other forms of sin, like smoking, taking drugs, going to immoral places, or becoming addicted to pornographic sites, etc. Thus, they will drift from bad to worse.

We said that one group will resolve this attraction issue in a spiritual way and a second group will suppress the voice of the Holy Spirit within them. A third group will resolve it hypocritically, meaning that they will keep a godly image in front of their families and the church, but when there is a chance to do something wrong, they will do it. They will do it in secret when no one is watching them or suspects anything. They become hypocrites—preserving an exterior image of godliness, but from within, they are impure and ungodly. We need to know that the second group (the ones who are pursuing ungodly relationships and immorality with all its forms) and the third group (who are living in a hypocritical relationship) will suffer the most. St. Paul said, "Every sin that a man does is outside the body, but he who commits sexual immorality sins against his own body" (1 Cor 6:18). In 1 Cor 6:19, St. Paul is telling us, "Do you not know that your body is the temple of the Holy Spirit who is in you, whom you have from God, and you are not your own? For you were bought at a price" (1 Cor 6:19,20). Furthermore, there is a godly law that says that you will reap whatever you sow.[39] Therefore, if you sow godliness, you will reap godliness; and if you sow corruption, you will reap corruption.

It is very important during adolescence to understand one's sexuality, to make right decisions, to look at the other gender with purity, and to wait until it is the proper time to have a godly, intimate relationship within the boundaries of marriage, thereby developing self-control. Proverbs 3:7,8 says, "Fear the Lord and depart from evil. It will be health to your flesh, and strength to your bones." When a person fears God and stays away from evil, he will have health and prosperity.

---

39 Cf. Gal 6:7,8.

3. Masturbation

The third group that live in hypocrisy may, often, fall into the bad habit of masturbation. As mentioned earlier, this group wants to keep an external image. Therefore, falling into this sin will not expose them because this is something done in secret; but, at the same time, it provides the gratification they are seeking. Many adolescents start practicing this bad habit out of curiosity while discovering their bodies and their sexuality. Because of the pleasure that accompanies this habit, it, gradually, becomes addictive. Unfortunately, some youth use it as release for their stress and pressure—any type of pressure or stress. If they are pressured by their sexuality, they may use this self-gratification as an outlet to release sexual tension and bodily pressure. Also, it is addictive because, usually when practicing this habit, they allow their minds to imagine many ungodly things. With this imagination, the sexual desire becomes stronger and this pattern becomes more addictive.

What are the negative effects and consequences for the people who are practicing this habit? From a psychological perspective, it will make the person selfish because the focus is on pleasing oneself. The more one succumbs to this habit, the more selfish this person will become. When this person gets married, the focus in the intimate relationship in marriage may still be on oneself. He may completely ignore the feelings and emotions of the wife, which will cause serious problems between the couple. Because masturbation is usually accompanied with imagination, it will ruin the pure image of the other gender in one's mind. It will not help in developing pure and innocent relationships with the other gender. The more one imagines bad things while practicing this habit, the more he will perceive the other gender as just a body, not as a human being. Thus, it will be very challenging to have a pure and innocent relationship with the other gender. Masturbation can make one feel he is living in an imaginary world. They develop stories and fantasies in their mind so it will disconnect one from reality to an imaginary life.

From a spiritual point of view, it is sin. The Lord told us in the last of the Ten Commandments, do not lust after the wife of your friend.[40] The Lord Jesus Christ also told us in the well-known *Sermon on the*

---

40 Cf. Ex 20:1).

Mount, "Whoever looks at a woman to lust for her has already committed adultery with her in his heart" (Mt 5:28). It is a sin of sexual immorality.

Is there hope for someone who is enslaved to this bad habit, and perhaps, has been for a very long time? Absolutely. Yes, you can overcome it through the grace of God. I will give you some useful points to follow. If you apply these practical recommendations, you will be able to overcome this sin through the grace of God.

1. Do not rely on yourself or on your power to overcome this bad habit. You need to admit your weakness completely to God and ask Him to give you victory over this addiction. Confess your weakness to God with all sincerity. Tell Him, "God, I am unable to overcome this habit and I am totally weak. You are my only source of help, and I am humbling myself before You to give me power and strength to overcome this bad habit." Without prayer, you cannot overcome it. If one tries to do many exercises but does not pray about it, he will not overcome it.

2. Stay away *completely* from any source of temptation. You cannot listen to songs that make you sexually excited. You cannot watch movies that are sexually arousing, and say, "I will overcome this bad habit." No. You need to stay *completely* away from any source of evil and any source of temptation that can entice you to engage in this bad habit.

3. Be honest in your confessions. You need to say exactly what happens to your spiritual father. Do not just give him a hint and let him guess what you are implying. We learned that exposing our sins honestly would empower us over our transgressions. Hiding any sin will make it overwhelm you. I want you to confess this sin as soon as you fall into it. I will reveal to you a trick that Satan uses most of the time. When a person falls in this sin, Satan will tell him, "Now, you fell in sin; you will say it anyway to your spiritual father in confession; so, keep doing it until the next time you confess." Therefore, the person will keep doing it, but, here, is the trap. The more you do it, the more you become addicted to this habit. If you are honest and you confess it as soon as you fall into this sin, you will get this spiritual uplift from your Father Confessor and from the Mystery of Confession, and when you take Communion, you will have command to overcome this sin.

To summarize these points: Pray about it, stay completely away from any source of temptation, confess the sin immediately to your spiritual father as soon as you fall into it, and expose the sin completely. If you follow these recommendations, your body will gradually forget this addiction and you will be able to overcome this sin. The earlier you overcome this sin in your life, the better your spiritual, physical, and emotional health will be.

4. Ten Biblical Facts about Sexuality

I would like to remind you of ten biblical facts that will help you to understand your sexuality and God's plan for sexuality.

1. God is the Creator of all creatures, as we read in Genesis 1:1, "God created the heavens and the earth."

2. When God created man, He created him in His image and likeness (Gen 1:26). This means that through the grace of God, *you can* live a godly life. You have all the elements needed to live a godly life. In the resurrection of the Lord Christ, He gave us all we need to live a godly life. Thus, do not say it is impossible. No, it is possible in Jesus Christ.

3. God gave sexuality to humanity as a holy gift from Him to participate with Him in creation. God is the Creator, and He created us in His image after His likeness, and He gave sexuality to humans in order to be the tool by which God will create more people in the world. We participate with God. That is why sexuality is something holy and we should keep it holy. We can read about how God gave us sexuality to participate with Him in creation, that through sexuality, God will create more people in the world. In Genesis 1:28, He says, "multiply; fill the earth." God gave us this authority. Therefore, sexuality is a holy gift from God.

4. God created us and created our souls to grow in relationships, not to live lonely. Our souls grow in relationships. That is why God said, "*It is* not good that man should be alone; I will make him a helper comparable to him" (see Gen 2:18). God wants us to be in relationships, but not just any relationship—godly relationships. During the age of adolescence, we need to have

many friends from both genders, and we need to learn how to deal with one another in a pure, godly, and innocent way. When it is time for marriage, one will choose a godly person to continue and to enjoy the rest of their lives together.

5. When God created a helper fit for Adam, He created a *woman and not another man*. Some people say homosexuality is normal, when two boys or two girls have an intimate relationship. This is not normal. Our Creator, our Manufacturer, is God. When He created a helper for Adam, He created a female for him, not a male. God said about Adam, and about man, in general, "a man shall leave his father and mother and be joined to his wife, and they shall become one flesh" (Gen 2:24). He did not say to be joined with another man, but "to be joined to his wife."

6. God arranged for complete transparency between man and woman within the boundaries of marriage. As we read in Genesis 2:25, "they were both naked, the man and his wife, and were not ashamed." "Naked and not ashamed," means the ability to uncover all one's thoughts, all of one's feelings, and all of one's plans, to uncover everything with the other person, without the fear of being ashamed, without the fear of rejection. This is God's plan.

7. God created sexuality because He had a plan for it. God wants the relationship between the man and the woman in *marriage* to be full of love, affection, emotion, and intimacy. In Proverbs 5:18,19, there is a beautiful passage about how the relationship between husband and wife should be full of affection, love, emotion, and fellowship. This Proverb says, "Let your fountain be blessed, and rejoice with the wife of your youth. As a loving deer and a graceful doe, let her breasts satisfy you at all times; and always be enraptured with her love." Here, the Bible tells us that God wants the couple to have an intimate relationship that is full of the fear of God and full of all godliness. It is a holy relationship.

8. Any sexual relationship outside the boundaries of marriage is a sin. That is why God told us, "whoever looks at a women to lust for her has already committed adultery with her in his heart" (Mt 5:28). Just a lustful look is considered adultery.

9. Your sexual energy should be used to glorify God within marriage. You should not waste it and you should not destroy it in any sexual immorality. God gave you this blessing, this holy gift—the gift of sexuality, to glorify Him by participating with Him in procreation.

10. Finally, from the beginning, Satan has wanted to ruin this holy gift of sexuality. He wants to destroy this gift in you by installing in your mind and in your heart bad, corrupt ideas about sexuality, and encourages you to practice many sexual immoral things, whether it is pornography, masturbation, unchaste touches with a person of the opposite sex, or homosexuality. Satan wants to destroy what God created. We are currently living in an age where Satan is doing all he can in order to destroy this beautiful and holy gift of sexuality. Do not be deceived. Satan will be using you to attack God. When Satan plays with your mind to fall into any sexual immorality, he is using you to destroy God's plan, but he will never be able to do this. It is your choice to be one of God's soldiers or, unfortunately, and God forbid, one of the devil's soldiers. By your choice, how you deal with your sexuality can enable you to be either one of God's soldiers to glorify God with this holy gift of sexuality and by using it in the proper time and in the proper way within the boundaries of marriage, or Satan can use you to destroy this holy, pure, and beautiful gift that God gave to all of us.

5. Sexual Immorality

In Proverbs 7:6–27, we have an example of how Satan destroys this beautiful gift of sexuality.

> "For at the window of my house I looked through my lattice,
>
> And saw among the simple,
>
> I perceived among the youths,
>
> A young man devoid of understanding" (Prov 7:6,7).

"A young man devoid of understanding" means he is not trained in godly work—in godly understanding. He is devoid of understanding. The passage continues:

Passing along the street near her corner;
And he took the path to her house
In the twilight, in the evening,
In the black and dark night.
And there a woman met him,
With the attire of a harlot, and a crafty heart.
She was loud and rebellious,
Her feet would not stay at home.
At times she was outside, at times in the open square,
Lurking at every corner.
So she caught him and kissed him;
With an impudent face she said to him:
'I have peace offerings with me;
Today I have paid my vows.
So I came out to meet you,
Diligently to seek your face,
And I have found you' (Prov 7:8–15).

That is how Satan creates traps. Anyone who allows himself to cross the boundaries will end up falling into sin. You need to be very watchful. Do not cross boundaries. You need to protect your boundaries and the boundaries of others. Once you cross boundaries, you will fall into sin. This woman continued by saying,

"I have spread my bed with tapestry,
Colored coverings of Egyptian linen.
I have perfumed my bed
With myrrh, aloes, and cinnamon.
Come, let us take our fill of love until morning;
Let us delight ourselves with love.
For my husband is not at home;
He has gone on a long journey;
He has taken a bag of money with him,
And will come home on the appointed day.'
With her enticing speech she caused him to yield," (Prov 7:16–21).

The phrase, "Caused him to yield," means that at the beginning, he did not want to yield. However, gradually, because he crossed the boundary—he allowed himself to talk with her—she caused him to yield. This, in fact, goes both ways; it is not necessarily a woman enticing a man, but a man can also entice a woman.

"With her flattering lips she seduced him.

Immediately he went after her, as an ox goes to the slaughter, [he is killing himself]

Or as a fool to the correction of the stocks,

Till an arrow struck his liver.

As a bird hastens to the snare,

He did not know it would cost his life" (Prov 7:21–23). [Again, *it will cost you your life*].

"He did not know it would cost his life.
Now therefore, listen to me, my children;
Pay attention to the words of my mouth:
Do not let your heart turn aside to her ways,
Do not stray into her paths;
For she has cast down many wounded,
And all who were slain by her were strong men" (Prov 7:23–26).

Do not say, "I am strong." Humble yourself before God. The word "her" mentioned in this proverb is in reference to sin—the sin of sexual immorality. "Do not let your heart turn aside to her ways," means to not let your heart turn aside to the ways of sexual immorality. "Do not stray into her path," refers to the path of sexual immorality. "For she [sexual immorality] has cast down *many wounded*." Anyone who allows himself to practice sexual immorality will end up wounded. "She has cast down many wounded, and all who were slain by her were strong men." Those who never humbled themselves before God and trusted in their own power ended up slain, slaughtered by her—slaughtered by sexual immorality. "Her house [the house of sexual immorality] is the way to hell." Sexual immorality is the way to hell, the way "descending to the chambers of death" (Prov 7:27).

As I told you, Satan wants to ruin and destroy this beautiful gift, this holy gift that God gave us, the gift of sexuality. Be alert, be watchful, be strong, and keep praying. Ask God to strengthen you and empower you. Your purity is your strength. Living a godly life is your strength to overcome and be victorious in your life.

Part III

DEALING WITH DIFFICULT CASES

A | DEALING WITH DIFFICULT CASES

1. Identifying a Difficult Person
2. Having Hope
3. Understanding Difficult People
4. Diagnosing the Problem
5. Understanding the Underlying Issues
6. Making Evaluations
7. Focusing on the Process
8. Attempting Unsuccessful Solutions
9. Spiritualizing

Often, at the end of parenting lectures, parents comment and ask me, "Everything you said is good for parents whose children are infants and still being raised. What if our children have already grown up, and dealing with them is difficult, and we do not know how to handle them?" I respond by speaking to them about dealing with difficult cases. Dealing with difficult cases is not just about dealing with your children, but could also be about dealing with your spouse, boss, employee, Sunday school student, friend, or anyone else. This section should enable you to deal with difficult cases, in general, and you can apply it to your specific situation.

1. Identifying a Difficult Person

When we deal with difficult people, we usually experience certain negative feelings in our hearts, such as frustration, anger, fear, and anxiety. They may put you in a "no-win" situation, leading to feelings of frustration; or you may feel helpless and unable to help them because of their stubbornness. You may also feel isolated and disconnected from them, or concerned and afraid. When dealing with difficult people, you may feel confused, as if you do not even know what is right or wrong anymore. They may bring out the worst in you. For example, someone may make you very angry and you wonder, "Why do I get so angry when dealing with this person when I am not an angry person in the first place?"

If you experience any of the feelings described above, most probably you are dealing with a difficult person. However, there is another point to consider, which is that *you* may be the difficult person. How could you discern this? If you have problems in your marriage, at work, with your children, friends, priest, family members, and neighbors, most likely, *you* are the difficult person. You should not deny it, but accept and own it in order to start working on it. It is neither logical nor reasonable that *all* these people are wrong and you are the one who is right. You would also need to listen to feedback from some spiritual people, such as a spiritual father or a dear friend, and be willing to accept it if they tell you that you are indeed a difficult person. However, if there is a general consensus that the other person is difficult—for example, if your spouse causes problems at work, at church, with your children, and with friends—this spouse is probably the difficult person. Thus, the important question arises, "How should I deal with this person?"

Of course, there are some things that make dealing with difficult people harder than with others, such as if they have any underlying psychological issues or disorders. Morality problems, such as addiction, or ideological problems, such as atheism, would also make it difficult. In addition, family problems, such as abuse, exploitation, or violence are problematic and require extensive effort.

2. Having Hope

Before we address how to deal with difficult people in more detail, I would like to emphasize the importance of hope. You have to have hope that change is a possible reality, through the grace of God. If you do not have this hope, you will never learn how to deal with a difficult person. If you say, "My husband is a hopeless case. I have tried several times, and he has *never* changed and *will never* change," you have lost hope and will not be able to deal with him. We must have hope, not in the person himself, but in God who is able to change the person. Change is possible through God's grace.

There are examples of "hopeless cases" presented in the Holy Bible, such as St. Paul, whom God was able to change. St. Paul said about himself that he was a persecutor, a blasphemer, and an insolent man (1 Tim 1:13). God completely transformed him from a blasphemer and persecutor to a great apostle and saint.

In the Book of Job in the Holy Scripture, Job well said, "I know You can do all things, and nothing is impossible for You" (Job 42:2). God can do everything and nothing is impossible for Him. Again, I repeat, you need to have this hope in your heart if you want to know how to deal with a difficult person. Without it, you will not see any progress or improvement in your relationship with him or her.

3. Understanding Difficult People

a. Denial

The first point in dealing with difficult people is to try to understand them. Try to understand the reason behind why they are difficult. In reality, the main problem for difficult people is not that they are just difficult or that they put themselves in difficult situations, such as moral or psychological problems, but rather, the core issue is their denial. They refuse to admit having a problem or to assume responsibility for it. Therefore, they also refuse to work on it. If your son is an addict, the problem is not that he is an addict, but that he believes addiction is not a problem. When your son thinks addiction is acceptable because everybody does it and that he can quit whenever he wants, this mindset is the problem. He will not be able to quit. Denying that he has a problem and refusing to take it seriously and work on it *is* the problem. This is what causes problems to exist for a lengthy period of time. If he admits that he has a problem, it will be easy for him to solve it.

A parent may say, "My son has been like this for the last twenty years!" Why? Because he does not know that he has a problem. Why does he not know that he has a problem? It is because his problem does not cause him any discomfort, so he does not realize it nor tries to solve it. If he is getting along with his problem and is living a happy life, why would he change his life? It is a fact that any problem should cause some harm or discomfort. So, why does a difficult person not suffer any discomfort, hurt, or harm? The reason for this is that *someone else* is bearing the burden of his discomfort or hurt away from him. Most of the time, it is parents, friends, or family who do this out of their love. For example, there is an irresponsible son who drives carelessly but has gotten away with four tickets, because his parents always pay them off. This irresponsible behavior should have caused him some distress, but that discomfort was actually taken away from him by his parents by paying his tickets for him. Thus, why would he start being a careful driver? This love is not the right love, but a wrong type of love.

Another example is someone who has a problem with spending too much money and the more he spends, the more his parents give him. Why would he stop spending when someone else is supporting him and giving him everything he needs? Someone else is an angry person, and because of his anger, everyone fears him and does whatever he wants. Why would he stop being angry when this anger is actually working in his favor? He gets his way all the time because everybody fears him. Another example is someone who has wrong relationships and his siblings cover for him and do not tell his parents, again, out of love. Rather, they do this out of a misperception of love. Why would he change? He is getting away with his relationship.

Therefore, there is a divine law that is called, "the law of sowing and reaping." The Holy Bible says, "whatever a man sows, that he will also reap" (Gal 6:7). Thus, a person will reap from the same field in which he sowed. If I sow thorns, I should reap thorns. If I sow roses, I should reap roses. But if I sow thorns and I reap roses or someone else reaps the thorns for me, then, why should I change? Let us assume that when the father of the prodigal son heard that his son did not have any food and even wished to eat from the swine's food but nobody gave him, he started to have compassion on him and said, "This is my son whom I love. Here, I have plenty of leftover food. Let me send him some." If he had sent him some food, do you think the prodigal son would have returned? Never. Why *did* he return? Because he was so hungry and wished to eat from the swine's food but *no one gave him* anything. This is a key phrase in this parable: "no one gave him" (Lk 15:16). Because no one gave him, he started reaping the thorns that he had planted and that is when he came back himself, which was the first step in on his path to change. This was the turning point in his life. That is why there is something called, "tough love." Tough love is to withdraw your compassion from the person that you love in order for him to learn and reap the thorns that he planted. This will allow him to change.

Many times, we, as clergy, parents, spouses, friends, Sunday school teachers, or servants intervene to stop this divine law out of a misguided sense of compassion and love. When we do so, the person gets away with his problem, and therefore, does not change. This is the key point in understanding a difficult case.

b. Additional Factors

Additional reasons for people not realizing that they have a problem in their lives and not taking responsibility for it include lack of experience and knowledge. For example, youth who start using drugs think that drugs are not a big deal, thus, creating a major problem in their lives. Another reason is fear of self-confrontation or fear of change. We all dread facing ourselves and accepting our weaknesses and problems that need to be changed in order for growth to occur. This is why the beginning of true repentance is returning to oneself and followed by self-confrontation. We also fear change and the unknown. "What would my life be like? I have friends now and I am comfortable with them, but if I change, what would my life be like?" Therefore, one may just settle in his comfort zone and refuse to change or take responsibility for his personal problems.

Pride and selfishness are other reasons. These attributes cause people to reject criticism. They take it very personally, and become adversarial. A person who is proud thinks that everyone around him does not understand and that he is the only one who does. He is the only one who knows how to manage things. How would one give advice or talk to such a person?

Envy can also be a reason that many people do not own up to their problems. Envy is when a person always looks at what he does not have and not at what he has, and he is convinced that he will be happy if he gets those things that he is missing. This is why you find that he is always upset and compares himself with others. For example, if someone does not have a car, he is unhappy because he does not own a car. He believes that if he were to get a car, all of his problems would be solved. He remains upset; and because he is upset, this is reflected in his interactions with others. If he finally gets a car, he will look for something else that he does not have, which will upset him. Because he is always upset and complaining, it is difficult to deal with him. Alternatively, when a person counts his God-given blessings, this brings forth happiness to his heart. "There is no gift without increase except the one without thanksgiving" (Mar Isaac the Syrian). Thus, God will give him more and more.

Of course, if living in sin, evil and darkness would cause a person to not take responsibility for his problems. The Holy Bible says about those people that the darkness has blinded their eyes (1 Jn 2:11). The person who is walking in darkness will stumble because he does not know where he is going, since the darkness has blinded his eyes.

Physiological and mental illnesses, as well as psychological and personality disorders can also be reasons that some people do not assume responsibility for their own their problems. Moreover, another reason that one would not own up to his problem is if he is demon-possessed.

4. Diagnosing the Problem

When dealing with difficult people, we first need to understand that their main problem is their denial and not the problem itself. The second point is how to diagnose the problem(s). In order to deal with the problem, we need to diagnose it. When you diagnose a difficult person's problem, try to be specific. Do not simply say, "My son is so difficult. I cannot deal with him." Or "My son is troublesome; he has many problems in his life." That is very vague. Examples of being specific are, "My son does not have friends," or, "He is a nervous person and is always angry," or "He is irresponsible," or "He is having an affair." These are specific problems. You also need to count how many problems he has. For example, he smokes, he is angry, and he is irresponsible; so, this person has three problems.

After doing this, you need to diagnose the severity of the problem. Is it mild, moderate, severe, or extremely severe? When you are doing this, you need to be realistic. This is important because how you deal with the problem depends on its severity. Some people overreact to small problems. On the other hand, some problems, such as heroin addiction, are beyond your ability or the church's. Though we can pray about it, such problems need to be referred to a professional or specialist.

Some people may wonder what would happen if the person refused that referral. In this case, if you do not interrupt the law of sowing and harvesting, they will encounter a major crisis. Perhaps, they will get arrested. Now, this crisis will demand treatment. However, as mentioned previously, we, usually, interrupt the law of sowing and harvesting, and that is why the problem does not reach crisis level for them. Thus, they forego treatment. Therefore, you need to hold back your compassion and let the problem cause a crisis. When this happens, they will start treatment.

5. Understanding the Underlying Issues

All problems usually have underlying issues. You need to understand what the underlying issue is. For example, many young men start to smoke cigarettes because they want to prove to others that they have grown up and are men. In their minds, in order to be a man, one needs to smoke cigarettes. Maybe a person is selfish and that is why he does not have friends, or is irresponsible because he was spoiled earlier in his life. Maybe he is an angry person because he is a controller and wants to force his opinion on others. He uses anger in order to make everybody fear him and listen to his opinion. Someone could be having an affair or an inappropriate relationship because he is deprived of love. I am not justifying this, but trying to understand and explain the underlying issue that pushed a person to engage in this type of relationship.

When a sick person presents with multiple symptoms, such as fever, sore throat, or stomach pain, it is best to try to find one diagnosis for them all, instead of one disease per symptom. Similarly, if a person has more than one problem, it is better to find one underlying issue that causes all of these manifestations instead of trying to find an underlying issue for each problem. For example, maybe a person's selfishness and pride cause him to become angry, lonely (without friends), irresponsible, and to smoke cigarettes. One underlying issue can cause four problems. When you find one underlying issue behind all the problems, you will most likely be closer to finding the actual debility.

6. Making Evaluations

Afterward, you need to evaluate how much he realizes that he has a problem and how much he is willing to work on it. If he knows that he has a problem and takes responsibility for it, this is *much* easier than a person who denies that he has a problem and refuses to deal with it. It is important to differentiate between a person who *denies* having a problem and a person who *cannot* solve his problem. When we were serving youth in Egypt, they knew that they had problems, such as smoking, dating, or going to nightclubs, which are wrong. So, they would come to us and say, "I know that what I am doing is wrong, but I do not know how to overcome these issues in my life." However, when I came to America, I was shocked that many youth do not realize that these things are wrong and that these are problems in their lives. I needed to begin by bringing to their attention that these things—dancing, dating, going to nightclubs, drinking, doing drugs, etc., are wrong. That is why we differentiate between someone who knows that he has a problem but cannot overcome it, and a person who is in total denial and does not own his problem.

Taking responsibility for your problem means that you need to confess and admit that you have a problem and that you have a strong desire to deal with it. When you evaluate a problem, try to do so based on what you see and not on what you hear from that person. If he is in denial, he will try for hours to convince you that he does not have a problem. Some problematic people are very persuasive. His Holiness Pope Shenouda III of thrice-blessed memory said, "Believe your eyes more than you believe your ears." You also need to differentiate between, "I cannot" and "I do not want to" change. In confession, if someone tells me, "I do not want to change," he cannot be absolved. His confession is not acceptable. However, if he says, "I want to change but I do not know how" or "I cannot," this person can be absolved. Then, I would give him some spiritual exercises to help him overcome this problem in his life.

7. Focusing on the Process

Focus on the process more than on the content when diagnosing the problem. The content could be that he smokes cigarettes, does not have friends, or is having an affair. The process is how to deal with this problem and what his perception of it is. Does he see it as a problem or not. For example, in family problems, if there is a husband and wife who come to you because they have a conflict, you need to focus on how they deal with each other—that is the process—and not on the content itself. In reality, the content may differ from one situation to another, but the process is the same. If there is a controlling husband, the content will differ. He may try to control his wife by refusing that she works, or serves in church, or travels to visit her family. He may also try to exercise control by refusing her to have outings with her friends. These four problems are the content while the process is that he is a controlling person. Instead of trying to solve each one of these problems at a time, focus on the process so you can solve all these symptoms of the real problem, and the couple does not return with different issues or other complaints.

8. Attempting Unsuccessful Solutions

When dealing with difficult people, I often hear, "Your Grace, I have tried *every possible thing* and there is *no* change. There is no hope." Therefore, I would like to explore with you some of the unsuccessful attempts used to solve problems. If you recognize your unsuccessful attempts, you will avoid using them and will know how to properly deal with difficult people.

a. Interrupting the Law of Sowing and Reaping

The first unsuccessful attempt, as mentioned earlier, is interrupting the divine law of sowing and reaping. As parents, if the difficult person is your child, his discomfort may come from you taking away privileges. The punishment should be in proportion to the severity of the problem, because if it is less or more severe than the problem, it will not be successful. Discipline, taking away privileges or punishment, should always be in proportion to the mistake. In the Book of Proverbs, there are many verses about discipline and how it leads children in the right way. If you avoid discipline, there will be no change because they will get away with their faults.

When the Lord Jesus Christ said, "First remove the plank from your own eye, and then you will see clearly to remove the speck from your brother's eye" (Mt 7:5), the plank, here, can be interpreted as your attempt to interrupt the divine law. Before you remove the speck from your brother's eye, you first need to stop interrupting the divine law.

b. Doing More of the Same

The second unsuccessful attempt is "doing more of the same." If you tried something five times and it did not work, it does not make any sense to try it again. One time, I was going to a visitation with a priest, and both of us were, apparently, very tired. We were at an apartment building that had two doors. We tried opening, pushing, and pulling one of them repeatedly, but it did not work. We could not get inside, and both of us did not know what to do. Then, someone came, simply opened the second door, and walked in. The problem was that we had been trying to open the *wrong* door. If you are using reason with an unreasonable person, it will get you nowhere. Many parents lecture their children to convince them that something is wrong. Meanwhile, the child puts on headphones to listen to music and replies, "Okay, whatever you say." The more you lecture, the less successful you are. You need to try something else.

c. Separating Love and Discipline

The third unsuccessful attempt is to separate love from discipline. The Holy Bible says, "whom the Lord loves He chastens" (Heb 12:6). Similarly, there must be a combination of the two in order to raise healthy children. However, we cannot divide these roles between parents and have the father be the disciplinarian and the mother as the loving one because they will nullify each other. If the father is too strict and the mother is too kind, the child will become more connected to the mother, and together, they will form a "team" or an "alliance" against the father. This is dysfunctional. If you are trying to win your child by forming this triangulation, you are actually hurting your child. Both father and mother should be loving and strict at the same time, or else, it will not work.

Some mothers say, "His father is so strict; that is why I am so gentle with him." Some fathers say, "I see that his mother spoils him; that is why I am strict with him." In reality, if one parent is strict with his child regarding something specific, that same parent should be the one comforting him. For example, if the mother sees the father being very strict about something, she should intervene through the father, not directly with the son. She should tell the father privately that his discipline was beyond the severity of the problem and that he needs to be compassionate. It is better for the child to suffer from this discipline than from his mother's intervention of compassion. The hurt that the son will suffer from her intervention will be more than the hurt from the strictness of his father. In this case, the child could take advantage of the situation by always seeking his mother's sympathy since he knows his father is stern. Once one parent minimizes the authority of the other parent, this will hurt the child.

d. Nagging

The fourth unsuccessful attempt is nagging. Some people believe that nagging will solve the problem. Actually, the more you nag, the more you complicate things, and nagging would be a very easy problem-solver if the issue were that the other person simply needed reminders. Nagging does not occur with everyone. People, usually, nag someone who is avoidant, meaning that one tries to withdraw from a discussion or situation. The person, who nags, believes that the more he nags, the other person will yield. Actually, the more you pursue, the more the other will withdraw. Likewise, with an irresponsible person, the more you nag, the more irresponsible he will become. "Every day I tell my daughter to make her bed and she never does." Then, you need to think about doing something else because repeating it has not solved the problem. A husband once told me, "I remind my wife *every month* to pay the bills on time." Of course, nothing had changed for two years because she would forget and he would continue to remind her every month. I told him not to remind her and to let her pay the penalty. Only then, did she learn to pay the bills on time. Facing the consequences successfully changed her behavior, whereas the husband's nagging had changed nothing.

People do not, usually, nag an angry or defensive person because he will explode and they will have to stop. Someone else may become stubborn and perceive you as a controller because of the constant nagging. You would, then, enter into a vicious cycle: the more you nag, the more he will perceive you as a controller, and the more he will rebel against you, and the more he will not comply, etc.

e. Threatening without Following-up

The fifth unsuccessful attempt is threatening without following-up. For example, a father threatens his son that if he comes home after midnight, he would not be let in the house. The son arrives at 2:00 a.m., opens the door, and casually enters, and his father lets him in. The son would say to himself, "My dad yells without enforcing any rules; he just yells and does nothing." Why do we sometimes threaten without enforcement? It is because the parent knows in advance, that he will be unable to enforce what he is threatening to do. He already knows that he would never lock his son out at 2:00 a.m. and leave him to spend the night outside. So, he has to let him in to spend the night. As such, when you threaten to do something—rather, when you *warn* that you will do something, the warning must be realistic and enforceable. If you give a warning, you must carry it out; so, make sure it is fair and reasonable and enforces the right goal.

You could say to your son, "Look, my beloved, if you choose to do this, then, you have also decided to not go on the school trip; so, think and carefully choose what you wish to do." If he chooses to take the wrong path, of which you warned him, then, he will indeed not go on the field trip. If a child, for example, overuses his cell phone, his father may tell him, "Look, my beloved, if you continue to use your cell phone in this wrong way, I will not pay the bill for it. Choose what you would like to do." If the son chooses not to be careful, the father will not pay the bill. However, if the father sympathizes with his son and pays the bill anyway, the son will never change his behavior.

This is what God did with Adam. He said, "for when you eat of it you will surely die" (Gen 2:17). Adam ate from the tree, and was condemned to death. This is why God gave us choices, and told us, "See, I am setting before you the way of life and the way of death. I am not forcing you to take a certain path, but I advise you to choose life, so you can live. You choose. However, if you take the other path, then, it is death."[41]

---

41 Cf. Jer 21:8.

There is a difference between "threatening" and "warning." Threatening is a desperate expression of my failure to change the other person. That is why it is, usually, illogical. For example, saying something like, "If you do this, I will throw you out of the house!" This would be said to someone I do not know how to handle, so I get nervous and express my desperation in a futile manner. I am threatening an illogical consequence, knowing, in advance, that I would never throw him out. This is what makes the other person not take me seriously. He knows I get angry, and then, calm down, without doing anything that I said I would. This is wrong.

Warning, however, is explaining the expected result of the bad behavior. "This is the consequence of your own actions. Decide for yourself what you want to do." According to the Bible: "but of the tree of the knowledge of good and evil you shall not eat, for in the day that you eat of it you shall surely die" (Genesis 2:17). Herein, God explained the result to Adam, letting him think and decide for himself. God did not stop Adam from eating from the tree because He respects our free will. He did not obligate Adam to not eat from the tree, but He explained the results of eating from it. This is "warning."

f. Denying the Existence of a Problem

Sometimes when dealing with difficult cases, people deny the existence of a problem, as an attempt to deal with it. They become unrealistic, trying to avoid dealing with the difficult issue. For example, the priest may warn parents about their son's behavior, and the father's response is, "All children do the same." "All children do the same," means that there is no problem. Actually, the parents, here, do not know how to deal with their child, so they appease their own conscience, by saying, "All children do the same." The father might even say, "But he has many good qualities; who is perfect in this life?" This is a way to avoid and deny the existence of a problem, which actually needs to be addressed.

The opposite of avoidance and denial is exaggerating the problem. I may make a big deal out of a small problem. This is why I should examine whether or not my opinion and definition of the magnitude of the problem is realistic, and if I am understating or overstating the issue. I must consult faithful people who can help me see the issues realistically to determine the size of the problem in order to deal with it. Living in denial, saying, "There is no problem. All children do that. All boys go out with girls. Life changes. You have no knowledge of how the world is going now." This kind of talk only makes the problem grow without a solution.

9. Spiritualizing

The seventh unsuccessful attempt is what we call, "spiritualizing," which is different than spirituality. Spiritualization means seeking spiritual principles or spiritual methods to defend negative issues. There are two common ways of spiritualization: either preaching or passivity. Preaching means that I would continue to lecture the other person even though he completely refuses to hear the word of God. Nevertheless, I insist on preaching to him, mentioning the Bible and pertinent verses, while the young man is not concentrating and refusing to listen. God did not tell us to continue to preach to those who refuse to listen. He said, "But whatever city you enter, and they do not receive you, go out into its streets and say, 'The very dust of your city which clings to us we wipe off against you'" (Lk 10:10-11). The rich young man who came to the Lord Jesus Christ was told, "If you want to be perfect, go, sell what you have and give to the poor, and you will have treasure in heaven; and come, follow Me" (Mt 19:21). The young man went away sorrowful. The Lord did not call him back and say, "Okay, come, let us negotiate with each other. How about selling 75% not 100%? Or how about 50%? 25%?" Often, we try to negotiate in an attempt to convince the other. The Lord Jesus Christ did not do this. He began to let people bear the consequences of their own mistakes. In this way, He led people to repentance.

Naturally, if someone is responsive to preaching, continue. When the Lord Christ spoke with the Samaritan woman, she was responsive, so He continued to speak with her. However, do not continue with someone who is not responsive to preaching. With Simon the Pharisee, the Lord clarified his error for him; then, the subject was closed (Lk 7:39). Unless there is acceptance to preaching, it is more beneficial to live the commandment.

Passivity is when you say, "It is over. There is nothing more to do for my son. I shall pray. Just as St. Monica prayed for St. Augustine, and was told, 'the child of these tears shall never perish,'[42] I will pray; there is nothing else I can do." Of course, prayer does miracles. Prayer can move mountains, but prayer does not cancel my role in dealing with the problem. Otherwise, the Lord Jesus Christ would have said, "You did not catch any fish? Go, pray about it, and you will find the fish jumping into your boat." He did not say this.

---

42 The Confessions of Saint Augustine.

Dealing with Difficult Cases

I must do my role. To achieve any kind of success in life, in any field, there is both a divine element and a human element. They complete each other. The human element is what you are able to do. The divine element is what you are unable to do. God will never do the human part for you; what you are able to do, God shall never do for you. When you fulfill your part, God does the divine role, which you are unable to do. If a student complains of being unable to study Physics and decides to just pray about, will he succeed? No. Even if he prayed for twenty-four hours every day, he would not succeed. He must study, and then, pray; if he is unable to understand, God will give him comprehension, but he must do his human part. He must present the five loaves and two fish. How to feed five thousand men, other than women and children, was indeed a problem. If each man was accompanied by his wife and two children, we are talking about twenty thousand people. Had one of the disciples thought, "How could five loaves and two fish be sufficient? I would even be embarrassed to present them," God would never have fed the multitude. It was necessary for them to present their capabilities, no matter how small. This is the human part. Present it to God, who would intervene with the divine role, which you cannot do, in order to make the five loaves and two fish sufficient for approximately twenty thousand people. Take away the stone from the tomb—that is what I can do—and God will raise the dead.

As such, I must perform my role as long as there is something for me to do. If I do not do what I have to do, but be solely content with prayers, prayers alone shall never solve my problems. This is why when people say, "There is nothing I can do. I shall pray, and place his name on every altar," I call it being passive. It is lovely and necessary to pray. I am not saying prayer is wrong. Of course, prayer is required in everything. However, if someone uses prayer as a crutch without exerting every effort to fulfill his role in difficult circumstances, he has not done his job faithfully. While prayer is very important, it does not cancel your role.

In conclusion, we discussed how to know you are dealing with a difficult person, not losing hope, and understanding that the real problem is their denial of the problem. We discussed the importance of being specific when diagnosing the problem, as well as diagnosing the severity of the problem, finding one underlying issue that causes all the manifestations in a person's life, and focusing on the process not the content. Finally, we discussed seven unsuccessful attempts to improve behavior: interrupting the divine law of sowing and reaping, doing more of the same, separating love from discipline, nagging, threatening without following up, denying the existence of a problem, and spiritualizing.

Part IV

QUESTIONS and ANSWERS

Questions from Parents

1. **How can I be a good parent when, I, myself, was abused physically and emotionally as a child? I had a terrible childhood, and now, as a parent, I feel that I am spoiling my child (as a reaction, since I do not want my children to suffer through any of what I endured in my childhood).**

This is a very good question. In order to be a good parent, you must first take care of your needs. If you do not take care of your own needs, you cannot take care of your children. As an example to this, recall any time that you boarded an airplane. If there are any issues with the plane that cause the oxygen masks to deploy, you might be emotionally inclined to install the oxygen masks on your children first, before installing them on yourself. However, we are instructed to tend to ourselves first before attempting to help our children. The reason for this is that if you were to install the mask on your child first before installing it on yourself, and you faint due to the loss of oxygen, your child would not be able to help you. However, if you take care of yourself first, you would, then, be able to help your child. It is the same principle here; if I was wounded in my childhood because of my abusive parents, I need to take care of my wounds before I can successfully raise my children. The good news is that God is the true Physician of our souls and bodies. Therefore, we need to acknowledge our pain and wounds and ask God, through prayer, to heal us. He is capable of completely curing our wounds. Remember that Jesus Christ, Himself, is the Wounded Healer, since, by His wounds, we are healed (Cf. Is 53:5). In addition, we can seek professional help to cure damage from our childhood.

2. **Our children spend more than seven hours every day at school with their classmates. We often do not know whether to tell them not to befriend their classmates or to tell them to only befriend people from church, especially because children can become very confused if we give them mixed directions on who and not to befriend. How do we judge our children's friends and instruct them on how to choose their friends?**

The first rule is that we need to teach our children to be friends with godly children. You are assuming that all the friends from school are unrighteous (ungodly), and that all the friends from church are godly. Unfortunately, not all the children who come to church are godly (of course, this makes me sad, but it is a fact). Also, not all the children who go to school are ungodly; they may have different belief systems, but are still good people. Therefore, we need to teach our children how to choose the right people who will have the right influence on them. For very young children, we have to be more involved in the actual selection process since they still do not have the wisdom to make their own decisions.

Also, there are levels of friendship. There are some people who will be companions and some will be just acquaintances. They may just share classes or activities together. Therefore, I need to teach my children how to deal with everyone with respect but within boundaries. For other people, I will become much closer and these will be the "friends." These are people, whose homes I may visit, and they may visit me at my home. This person is allowed to influence me more than the acquaintance. That person must be selected to be godly, and will bring me closer to God and to my family. Keep in mind that unwisely chosen friends might negatively influence your relationship with your children because they may mock them and say things like, "You still listen to your parents?" This will result in them weakening your children's relationships with you. Therefore, we must teach our children how to develop boundaries that are suitable for their choices of friends and how to differentiate between godly and ungodly ones. We must teach them this starting at a young age.

One way to teach children how to choose friends is to take them grocery shopping, and give them simple lessons about making good selections. For example, we can take them to select fruits and show them that we are selecting the good fruits because they will not harm us and are not selecting rotten fruits since they can give us a stomachache. By doing this, we show them that we must make wise selections that will benefit us. At this point, we can tell them to apply the same logic to selecting friends. In general, raising our children involves giving them lessons from everyday tasks instead of lectures. We should do this while they are young so that the lessons remain with them when they grow up.

3. What happened to Eli the priest and his children that resulted in their terrible ending?

Eli the priest followed the permissive parenting style. The Holy Bible says, "his sons made themselves vile, and he did not restrain them" (1 Sam

3:13). He gave them a very light warning but never took any strict action against them. His permissive parenting style was the reason that his children became vile, and it, ultimately, led to their demise.

4. Unfortunately, I heard that one of the public schools put on a play about masturbation and homosexuality, and was encouraging such things. The play was for Grades 8 and 9. I was so scared. How can I deal with this in relation to my son, especially since my son is still young?

We need to be more active. When something like this happens, all conservative parents should unite and raise formal complaints against these teachings, since this is not why we send our children to school. If we take a strong stand, we will be able to make changes and have a positive influence. I remember that, on the topic of homosexuality, a year and a half ago, there was a law being discussed about same-sex marriage, and a vote on the subject was being held in California, Florida, and Arizona. At the time, H.E. Metropolitan Serapion and I wrote several articles called, "Churches", and encouraged people to vote. We also conducted a campaign in agreement with other churches to advise people to vote against the same-sex marriage law. Honestly, I thought the law would not pass in Arizona, since it is a conservative state, but would pass in California, since it has a large homosexual population, and may or may not pass in Florida. However, due to the large coordinated effort between all churches to fight this law, the law did not pass in any of the three states.

The point I am trying to make is that we have to play an active role in defending our principles and protecting our country and our children from these ideologies. I encourage you to take a brave stance and not to give up easily.

5. My husband lives in his own world, and I have to act as both the mother and father. This puts me under a lot of pressure and stress, especially when I am dealing with my children. I am scared of failure. I put in place a number of rules that my kids need to follow.

This is a big problem that develops when one of the parents is uninvolved. Children need the involvement of both the father and the mother. I advise you to do what you can to raise them in the fear of God. Try to keep the balance between love and control. Do not speak negatively to them about their father, and do not complain about him, so that the image of their father does not get distorted in the eyes of your children.

Try to gently talk to your husband about how you need his help. Some men, in general, have a problem with ego. If you were to talk forcefully to your husband and place blame on him, he probably would not listen to you because you are hurting his ego. Instead, tell him that you need his help, and phrase it in a way that makes him feel good about himself (for example, go ask him about advice in what to do in a particular situation). Get him involved.

Also, sometimes, mothers, solely assume all the responsibility of raising the children, and do not give the fathers a chance to be involved. Therefore, you can also try to slightly take the back seat, to give a chance for your husband to be involved. I remember once there was a deacon who was complaining that he does everything in the church, and that no one else does anything. My response to him was that he was not allowing anyone else to do anything. I told him that if he were to slightly take a back seat, other people would get more involved. Later, this deacon moved to another city, and the other people in the church started to serve and became more involved. Therefore, if you are doing all the work yourself, without ever giving the chance for other people to get involved, they will not. If you were to start sharing the responsibility with your husband, you will most likely get him more involved in the raising of your children together.

6. What do I do if my husband has a bad temper, is very busy, and has no time? I try to keep the house peaceful, but my husband is always easily angered and does not know how to take good care of the kids.

Anger is also a problem since it creates a tense atmosphere in the household. This is why St. James told us to be slow to anger. Anger is energy. It is like a car. If I want to slow a car, I need good timing and good breaks. Otherwise, the car will collide with the object in front of it. If I do not want to "collide" with the person in front of me due to my anger, I need the same two things: good timing and good breaks. To clarify this this point, we need to understand that anger is not a sudden feeling that happens out of nowhere. It is an energy that has been growing inside a person. The person who is trying to combat anger must first figure out what triggers it. This is the timing aspect. You must understand when it is that you become angry. At this point, you must start to "use your breaks." When you start to feel uptight, you need to start doing exercises that will slow your anger down to a stop. These differ from one person to another. It can be singing a hymn, saying, "Lord have mercy on me, a sinner," leaving the room and going somewhere else, or making the sign of the cross. Do not allow anger to control you, but control your anger before it overcomes you. Most people who suffer from anger will tell you that they normally lose the discussion when they are angry. I hope and pray that your husband will learn to be more calm and less angry.

> 7. **My son is seven years old. He grew up in an atmosphere that was full of love, but also had a lot of anger. As a result, the boy, now, has a very bad temper. Our home, today, is a lot calmer than it was before and all the issues that were causing anger in my son's first years have now been resolved. Is there hope that we can cure his bad temper? Is there an age after which it is impossible to cure a problem like a bad temper?**

Of course, there is hope to cure your son from his bad temper. There is no age after which there is no hope. Even if a man is sixty years old, there is still hope that he can manage his anger and cure his bad temper. All of God's commandments can be achieved through the power of the Holy Spirit and God's grace.

From your side, do not enable his anger. We enable his anger by giving him what he wants when he is acting out in anger. It is easier to just give him what he wants, but, by doing so, we are teaching him that anger yields his desired outcome. He will realize that anger works, so he will use it again and again to get what he wants, and he will continue to escalate it each time. However, if you start to teach him that every time he acts out in anger, he will not get what he wants, but will only get it when he calms down and asks politely, you will not be enabling him. Keep in mind that when he does not get what he wants immediately when he is angry, he will escalate the anger and try to push the limits even more. In any event, you need to have a firm stance and to insist on not giving him what he wants no matter how angry he gets. Gradually, he will start to realize that anger is not working for him and that asking politely works better. Therefore, he will learn to control his anger.

Your child also needs to be surrounded by a spiritual, loving, and caring atmosphere. Bad tempers, usually, result from a sense of insecurity. It is a defense mechanism. The more insecure the child is, the worse his temper becomes. Conversely, the more calm and peaceful the household atmosphere is and the more his sense of security, love, and importance is, the less he will feel the need to resort to anger.

> 8. **Suppose a child lies, what would be the discipline or steps you would take? Or if the child is daydreaming in church—they are standing but not praying; they are just there but their mind is somewhere else. How do you discipline for something like that?**

As I said, there are many steps we need to take. For example, if he is distracted during the Divine Liturgy, I need to educate him about this and give him some tools on how to overcome and deal with distractions. Then, maybe, you can use positive reinforcement and tell him, "If you manage to concentrate on the prayers, you will earn so and so" (something he wants). Maybe, if the child really loves to serve as a deacon, you can tell him, "If you are going to be distracted, you will not serve as a deacon for the next two weeks.". However, if it is the other way around, the child does not like to serve as a deacon and the parents push him to do it, it would not be an appropriate form of discipline. The child would feel like it is a privilege not to serve. If he likes reading, perhaps ask him to do research about prayer and to write some reflections and meditations about how to pray without ceasing. I remember when I was taking the youth's confessions before becoming a bishop, and one of my sons in confession was struggling with sexual immortality. I asked him to do research about purity in the Bible and I guided him with some references. He did wonderful research and this was a transformation point in his life because he learned, on his own, about how this could be destructive to his life. There are many ideas. Parents should be creative in how to choose what is best for their children in this specific area.

> 9. **Sometimes, we get a bit confused between disciplining and consistency. For example, we give a punishment, but then, when we think about it, we feel that this punishment was harsher than it should have been. Sometimes, we get into a**

debate: should we be consistent with what we said we would do or should we lessen the punishment?

First, I have to be very careful before deciding on the discipline. To the best of my ability, I have to choose discipline proportional to the age and the behavior. Of course, I will manage to do this correctly if I do not choose the discipline while I am angry. Usually, choosing severe punishment proceeds from anger. However, if I discover later that it was out of proportion or excessive, I should go to my son and tell him that when he did such and such, I was angry, and that was why I told him that this would be his punishment or discipline. However, it is more than he deserves, which is why I re-examined myself and decided to reduce the punishment to so and so. Here, you are teaching your son a lesson in honesty and a lesson in taking responsibility, in showing him that even when parents make a wrong decision, they are brave enough to confess this even to their child, to tell him that they made a wrong decision, and that they made this decision out of anger. Here, you are teaching him by example, and at the same time, you are consistent. When you show him that you reduced the discipline because you discovered that you did something wrong, this is not inconsistency. Through this method, you teach your son honesty, consistency, and responsibility.

10. My children are ten and six and I am not sure if attending church is sometimes too excessive, and fear that they would feel this way when they grow up. Maybe they would think that going to church and keeping up with everything that is going on with church deprives them from other activities or things they would like to do.

You always have to make sure that when your child attends all these activities, he does so out of love and not out of pressure or fear. Even if he does not enjoy the activity, at least he is convinced that it is the proper thing to do. Many times, a child may not enjoy all the activities in which he participates, but is convinced that they are in his best interest. If your child starts complaining about things like this, you need to address it with him; do not just ignore him without talking to him about it. Because if you do not talk to him about it, he will comply until he grows up, then, he will say, "I am not going to go with you anymore." I always teach the story of Moses to this kind of child. In Hebrews, Chapter 11, St. Paul says that when Moses became of age, he chose *not* to enjoy the pleasure of sin in Egypt, but to suffer shame with the people of God (Heb 11:24–26). Most of our children do the opposite. When they are young, they obey to suffer with the people of God, but when they become of age (teenagers or young adults), they choose to enjoy the *pleasure of sin in the land of Egypt* (meaning—outside of Church). By giving them the example of Moses, starting from around age eight to ten, reading this verse to them or even writing it and having them put it in their rooms so they see it constantly and keep it in their hearts can help them when they grow up to make the choice of remaining with the people of God and not to drift away with outsiders.

11. This is a continuation to the question about spiritual discipline. I see that my son is serving as a deacon and I feel like he is distracted, but when I talk to him, he tells me, "No, I am listening." However, he does not sing the hymns, even when he has them memorized, and he does not want to look in the "Kholagy,"[43] even though we have it with us. Sometimes, I feel like I do not want to pressure him too much, to the extent that I overpressure.

Do not pressure him, but talk to him about it. If he says, "I am not distracted, but I do not want to sing," tell him, "Okay. Let us read Isaiah, Chapter 6, about the Seraphim angels. If the Seraphim were not singing, imagine we would go to heaven and not hear any singing because the Seraphim are tired and do not want to sing. What kind of heaven is that?" Explain it to him, or have him research the Midnight Praises and Church hymns and praises. Trust me, the method of doing research, in regard to the children, is very useful. I remember the first research I did when I was in 7th grade. My Father Confessor told me to do it. He said, "You are a deacon. I want you to research the priestly attire." He also gave me books, and I started studying them and writing about them. Therefore, teach your children. This is a chance to teach him about Church hymns and praises and how to contribute and be an active participant, not just an observer. Teach him that he is not going to church to watch a play or a skit, and that everybody is a participant. He can also research the liturgy and what the word "liturgy" means, that it is the work of the people. When he discovers

---

43 Liturgy Book (Arabic word origin)

this and more, he will realize that if he is not participating or singing, he is excluding himself. There is a question here, however: Are the parents themselves observers or participants? If the child finds that his father is silent and does not participate, especially if he is a deacon, but does not dress, then he would think, "Why would I have to sing if my father does not?" These are all things we need to take into consideration.

12. If the child refuses to go home with his parents, and wants to stay at church with his friends until a late time, what shall we do? Will the child believe us if we tell him we will leave him there? Would this also work vice versa, when going from the house to the church?

The advice for dealing with children, in general, is to not get into a power struggle with them. Avoid saying, "Do not do this," and then, the child goes and does it, and thereby, breaks your word. When he breaks your word, then, that is it—he has gotten used to defying you. Rather, give your children options, and explain to them the consequences of each decision, and then, leave them to decide. This is for older children. Regarding young children, I cannot give them choices. They are young and need to learn to say, "Yes," with obedience and submission, and learn about the blessings incurred by this.

When God was dealing with Adam and Eve, He could have sent someone to Eve—for example, one of the angels or one of the Seraphim or Cherubim—once the devil started talking to her, to stop her from eating from the tree, but He did not do this. Sometimes, we do this when we see our children about to do something wrong, we force them not to do it, but this creates a kind of rebellion. God gave Adam and Eve options and explained the consequences. He told Adam, "If you eat from that particular tree, you shall surely die."[44] He explained the situation, the decision, and the consequences. And He gave him freedom to make the choice, but He did not enter into a power struggle with him. We must also not get into a power struggle with our children. "Do this!" and he does not do it and breaks your word—then it is over. Rather, tell him, "If you do this, this is what will happen, and if you do that, then, that is what will happen." Do not give them options you will not use. For example, if you tell him, "We

---

44 Cf. Gen 2:17).

will leave you at church or at home," but, in reality, you will not leave him, so the child will not believe this statement. He knows his parents will not go and leave him. Children tend to test their parents. He would refuse to leave with them, and see that they are still there and did not leave him. Therefore, he will know that this statement has no effect. Furthermore, before saying, "No," try to think about the reason the child is not listening. Figure out the reason behind the behavior before you refuse. Maybe the child does not have a chance to go out and this is a chance for him to spend time with his friends. Maybe he truly needs more friends. Perhaps, if you tell him that next Saturday you will take him out and have a nice time together, when you offer him a solution, this may encourage him to go home with you. But, of course, the solution you give him should be a solution you will actually do, not just something said for the time being.

13. Should parents treat sons and daughters the same or differently?

They should treat them the same and different. How is that? Boys and girls are equal in honor and equal in dignity. That is why parents should not differentiate or distinguish between boys and girls based on their gender. Regarding honor, dignity, love, respect, and control, both boys and girls should be treated the same. However, they should be treated differently in order to prepare the boy to be a man and to prepare the girl to be a lady. Maybe some activities are more suitable for boys and less for the girls, and vice versa. I should treat both genders differently regarding how to prepare them to be successful, responsible men and women. Raising a man is different than raising a woman; raising a boy is different than raising a girl. So in this aspect they should be treated differently. But when it comes to love, honor, dignity, respect, and control they should be treated in the same way.

14. Should parents allow their children to go out before marriage?

They will have opportunities to meet many people when they are adults and ready for marriage. I do not know if this question means to "date" or just to "hang out." In general, there has to be some control and rules and everyone should respect the rules of the house. Learning how to respect the rules of the home helps children to be more mature. In life, there are rules. Nature has rules. When they go to work, they will find a lot of rules.

Freedom is not the absence of rules. A lack of ability to respect and follow rules is irresponsibility and will cause a person many troubles in life.

15. Should parents allow their children to move out before marriage?

There is not a single answer for all situations. Every situation is different. If it will help this person to detach from his parents—for example, if a person is twenty-nine or thirty years old but still very attached to his parents in an unhealthy way—maybe, as a church, we encourage this young man to move out. If this son is wise and mature and ready to move out, but there are some financial concerns, we may recommend that he stays with his parents and helps with supporting the family financially. Maybe the parents are old or ill and need the physical or emotional support of their son or daughter. In these circumstances, the presence of the son or daughter, even if they are 30 or 35, may provide support for the parents. Every situation should be treated differently and what is best for in one situation maybe different than what is best for another family.

16. Our son is eight years old and there is rebellion. Yes, there are rules and structure in the home, and also love. If we deal with his rebellion with love, he takes advantage of it and takes control. What is the solution?

There is not enough information to understand all the dynamics in this situation. The reason for the rebellion may be that the parents' understanding of love is different. What does this mean? Perhaps, the father thinks that because he works and provides a good life for the family and puts his child in a good school to educate him, that this is love. Yet, it is possible that the child needs love to be expressed in an emotional way, and maybe this does not exist; thus, this is why there is rebellion. Perhaps there is love and firmness, as they said, but also comparison, and this could be the reason. Maybe the reason for the rebellion is that the child wants attention from the parents. It may be the nature of the child to be active and a bit mischievous; some children are naturally like this. Some children are hyperactive (I do not want to call it "disorder"), which requires professional consideration. Perhaps the child experienced some kind of abuse outside of the home. There are many reasons for a child to be rebellious. We need to learn the reason—we would need to have a case history—and the parents would also need to review their method with the child. The question says, "We tried to solve the problem with love"—does that mean that love is not always there and is just used as a solution? Love should always be there, not just as a temporary fix to a problem. From the way the question is written, it is likely that love exists in the heart of the parents as a feeling that they are doing everything for their children, but there is a kind of control in the house. There needs to be a balance between love and firmness, and love needs to be expressed. Again, do not enter into a power struggle with your children. Give them choices and explain the consequences of each choice.

17. Is the Coptic Orthodox Church against parents hitting their children to discipline or punish them?

The Bible and the teachings of the Church are against corporal punishment. Maybe a small, light tap on the hand is okay, but hitting is unacceptable. It causes a lot of rebellion and anger in the heart of the child. Hitting and severe beating are not acceptable at all, and it hurts and damages their self-image. When a child is hit, it leaves a mark in his heart and in his psyche that may stay for a very, very long time. This is unacceptable!

18. If the parents together do not reach one opinion on something, how can they adjust the wrong advice given to the children by one of them?

After you discuss your differences, give time for both of you to process the discussion. Sometimes, when we discuss an issue, we want to come to an agreement immediately. We want the other person to agree with us right now, without giving time to process the information or the discussion itself. If you did not reach an agreement, maybe you can say, "We will leave it alone for one or two days, and then, we will talk about it." Maybe after these two days, when you think and rethink about what you discussed, you can reach an agreement. If not, then, you need to consult, perhaps, with your spiritual father or a trustworthy person in the family who both of you respect and whose opinions you value. If you cannot reach an agreement together, you should agree to consult with a third person—that is wise and trustworthy, like your spiritual father—but you should agree that when you go to him and explain the situation, at the end, both of you will follow whatever he says.

QUESTIONS and ANSWERS

19. My children are hyper and they drive me nuts, to the point where sometimes I lose control and I shout, and sometimes I hit. I forbid them from watching TV, from using the computer, or from playing games. I know that maybe I do not know how to raise my children right, but I wish that God would calm them down and make them truly His children. Can God correct the mistakes that I made toward my children and make them good children in the future?

A mother once asked me to pray for her because she had three sons who were driving her crazy. I tried to encourage her, and I told her, "Your sons are angels!" She said, "Yes, angels that 'cry out continuously, without ceasing…'"

You need to learn to control your temper, because shouting and screaming and getting worked up are all expressions of anger. Hitting them and forbidding them from watching TV—all of this will make them more rebellious with you. Every morning, ask God to give you grace and calmness to be able to deal with your children. Have patience. Try to let things go. Do not interfere in every little thing. "If you do not see blood, do not get involved." Of course, this expression is a little bit extreme, but there is some acceptable troublemaking. Do not use punishment with your children to release your anger. Try to keep them busy; usually the fighting and the troublemaking are because they have nothing to do. Try to think and keep them occupied with something positive; if they are active, this is good. You could also have them get involved in sports. They would come home tired. Try to involve them in a lot of activities. The more you keep children busy, the less trouble they will cause. Of course, it is clear that you love your children a lot. God can definitely fix the mistakes we make because they are His children before they are ours. God is caring for their salvation and their eternity. God willing, they will be a source of joy, as St. John the Baptist was a source of joy for his mother and father.

Questions from Youth

20. Why do parents always say we are doing something bad when we are having a conversation with a boy? (Question from a girl)

If you have a one-on-one relationship—if you are speaking with only one boy and you are calling each other all the time, speaking to each other all the time, and wasting each other's time—this means you have started to cross a boundary. Do you remember when I told you that once you cross a boundary, gradually you would end up doing something wrong? This is crossing a boundary. You need to be careful not to cross that boundary. I want all the boys to be your friends, not to focus on one person. Watch your emotions. If you start to develop emotions toward somebody, do not deceive yourself. Do not say to yourself, "It is a pure love. We are not do anything wrong." You know that Satan is not stupid. He will not tell you to do something wrong from the first time. He will drag you step by step. When your parents tell you that this is something bad, it is because they are concerned. They are afraid that you will develop emotional affection toward this boy. As I previously mentioned, more than 99% of these relationships break up, and the damage of ending a dating relationship is not less than the damage of divorce (in terms of the emotional dimension). Many people are broken because they ended a relationship. Do not be wise in your own eyes; listen to your parents' advice.

21. What are the boundaries of physical sexuality?

Before marriage, there are no kinds of physical touches or emotional attachment. Emotional attachments and physical attachments before marriage are wrong.

22. Is it bad if you marry someone older than you?

It depends on how many years, and whether you are male or female. Usually, the male should be older than the female. In some exceptions, we allow the girl to be older, but this is an exception. In most situations, the norm is that the boy will be older than the girl (anywhere from three to six years is acceptable).

23. Is nagging a boy who is a friend okay?

This question has two points, one about nagging and one about a boyfriend. In general, nagging is not good. It irritates the other person. When a girl nags a boy, this is not good and can be misinterpreted. Be careful and be wise.

24. How do you know that it is the time for marriage and getting into a relationship?

The right time for marriage is when you are spiritually, intellectually, educationally, financially, and socially mature.

25. What if a boy tells a girl that he loves her so much and he is going to marry her when he grows up because he really loves her? Is that still bad?

While you are growing, your feelings toward people will change. Some people whom you think you love very much right now, these are just feelings of having a "crush," because you are attracted to these people. A "crush" is actually an attraction, and as I mentioned, being attracted to someone is normal. But, here, you are attracted to just the person; it can be just a physical attraction. When you grow, you will change. You cannot decide now whom you will marry after ten years. As I said, you are immature now. You are growing during the period of adolescence. Your perception of many things will change over the years. If you act on this crush (recall we spoke about how it is normal to be attracted, but how it is handled will affect the person), it can lead to sin or not lead to sin, so we need to be wise.

26. Not all relationships end badly. Some people benefit from the experience. They teach you what you have done wrong. Relationships are not a bad thing for teenagers.

They say that the foolish person learns from his own mistakes, while the wise person learns from the mistakes of others. This question reminds me of the saying: "It is not bad to put your hand in fire, to know it burns. So, you will learn something." Yes, you will learn that fire burns, but at the end, you will not have a hand. So yes, you learn from your mistakes, but you may lose your integrity or your peace or your joy over this.

I did not say that relationships are a bad thing for teenagers. I encourage you to have relationships with all the boys and all the girls. Relationships are healthy. Our souls are relational souls. We grow in relationships. However, one-on-one relationships involving emotions at an early age are *destructive*. Whether you like it or not, it is destructive. You can argue about it, but it is destructive.

27. Since God gave us the gift of sexuality, why does it lead to sin in so many ways?

We cannot blame the gift. Rather, we should blame our reckless behavior with the gift. For example, if you drive your car in a reckless way, there will be many negative effects. I cannot blame the car, but I can blame the way I drive the car. In the same way, sexuality is a holy gift to help us grow, praise God, glorify God, and love one another. If we use this gift recklessly, then yes, it will lead to many sins.

As I said, Satan wants to ruin and destroy this gift and he is using you as a tool. It is your choice to be on God's side or on Satan's side.

28. What is the point of having sexuality when it has so many negative effects?

Actually, it has so many positive effects, if we use it correctly. If we use it incorrectly, I cannot blame sexuality. However, I can blame my abuse of this gift.

29. What do you do if you have a gay friend?

It depends on what you mean by this question. This question can mean two different things: It can mean that your friend is gay and you are asking how you should deal with this person; or it can mean that you both have the tendency, or mindset of homosexuality.

If your friend is gay and he is a non-believer, then, just consider this as an acquaintance. St. Paul teaches us in 1 Corinthians 5, that it is not our responsibility to judge people who are outside (1 Cor 5:12–13). If the student at your school is gay, then deal with him as an acquaintance in school and that is it. Do not get into a discussion about it.

If he is a believer, then, we have a responsibility, because if we love him, we should not allow him to go in the wrong direction. We need to bring him to the right direction. Maybe at your young age, you cannot do this. Therefore, keep praying for him. If everybody knows about it, bring it to the priest's attention. If it is confidential information, you need to handle this wisely, and encourage him to speak to the priest about it to get help.

www.ingramcontent.com/pod-product-compliance
Lightning Source LLC
Chambersburg PA
CBHW022114080426
42734CB00006B/119